Croquet Lawn
Warren Spinney
The Warren Field
Old Tea House
Riviera Corner
Hogbush Hall
Avenue House and Grounds Ampthill Bedfordshire 1919-1964
E.A.S.H.

SIR ALBERT RICHARDSON — THE PROFESSOR

Sir Albert Richardson
THE PROFESSOR

Simon Houfe

White Crescent Press Limited
Luton

Printed and Published by White Crescent Press Ltd, Luton

ISBN 0 900804 26 2

Contents

	List of Illustrations	7
	Foreword	9
1	A Background of Buildings	11
2	Country Neighbour	37
3	Bedfordshire Sketchbook	58
4	An Afternoon with Thomas Hardy	77
5	A Lifetime of Collecting	91
6	The Chimes of Eaton Socon	111
7	Royal Occasions	124
8	Cambridge	140
9	Travels with a Grandfather	162
10	'Nylons, Pylons and Skylons'	180
11	Presidential Honours	193
12	Pregnant Penguins	216
	Index	237

Illustrations

between pages 128 and 129

Plate 1   At work in his painting room; about 1960.

Plate 2   Aged three, a *carte de visite* photograph of 1883.
Aged twenty-one, a pencil portrait by Charles Gascoigne.
As a young man in Verity's office, about 1903.

Plate 3   A decorated envelope written to Elizabeth Byers.
Elizabeth Richardson, a pencil sketch by Hanslip Fletcher, about 1912.
As an officer in the RFC. An ink study by Hanslip Fletcher, about 1918.

Plate 4   Avenue House, Ampthill, in 1919.
The drawing-room of Cavendish House, St Albans.

Plate 5   The drawing-room of Avenue House, Ampthill in about 1921.
The drawing-room of Avenue House nearly forty years later.

Plate 6   An illustrated letter to his wife.
A carved corbel in St Mary's church, Eaton Socon.

Plate 7   Caricature of Richardson by Sir Edwin Lutyens.
Houghton House, Ampthill in 1925.

Plate 8   Her Majesty Queen Mary leaving Avenue House on 28 May 1934.
Elizabeth Richardson in the grounds of Avenue House, about 1936.
Richardson sketching with friends at Annecy, 1936.

Plate 9   'The Professor' in costume playing the pianoforte at Avenue House.
In costume rehearsing a play.

Plate 10   At Southill Park, Bedfordshire, about 1938.
Richardson's Rolls Royce *en vacances*.

Plate 11   His greatest antique 'find' the missing bust of Lord Somers by Le Marchand.
Her Majesty The Queen at the Royal Academy with Richardson and Sir Henry Rushbury in March 1955.

Plate 12   A characteristic watercolour of Dinan, France.

Plate 13   At the opening of an art exhibition in 1957.
'The Professor' relaxing at Hagbush Hall in about 1958.

Plate 14   Sorting through his collection of drawings at Avenue House.
At the opening of the *Courier Exhibition*, January 1956.

Plate 15   The installation of 'the pregnant penguin' outside Avenue House in 1957.
With his friend Ernest Marples.

Plate 16   Strolling into his garden with shooting-stick and trilby hat.
With his favourite dog 'Sherry' in the grounds at Avenue House in 1962.

Illustrations at the head and foot of Chapters are taken from various sketchbooks. The end papers were specially drawn for the book by Eric Houfe.

Foreword

At a private dinner at the Royal Academy in 1956, Sir Albert Richardson, its then President, was engaged in a conversation on artistic taste with Sir Winston Churchill. The former premier's comments had been monosyllabic but suddenly he leaned over to his companion and growled 'My dear Richardson, it *all* ended in 1800!'

The remark struck an immediate response in my grandfather's unashamedly Georgian breast and was often repeated to friends, visitors and students. For him it was true that much that he most admired had ended in 1800, craftsmanship in the face of industry, pure classical architecture in the whirlpool of styles, a rural England in retreat from a metropolitan England. Born out of his time, my grandfather was nevertheless not so concerned at putting the clock back as in building on the sure foundations of a century that he understood and trusted. Its principles and precepts were ones that he liked to employ in his own life and the genial and unbuttoned attitude that he brought into a grey twentieth century, stimulated and encouraged those around him.

These chapters on my grandfather are culled from the memories of my mother and myself and can be taken not so much as a portrait as an impression. Some of the material was gathered together in about 1968 with the intention of writing an architectural monograph on the Professor, showing his place as an Edwardian designer and teacher. This I hope will be done one day, but the present book is a personal view of the man, flamboyant, sometimes maddening, usually endearing, as he appeared to his family circle, neighbours and friends. If each chapter is looked upon as a different page from one of his own sketch-books, then slowly, the enigmatic and almost mercurial figure of the Complete Georgian himself, will emerge, in his centennial year.

S.H.
August 1980

CHAPTER ONE

A background of buildings

On a very foggy and damp November day in the early eighteen-nineties, a pair of walkers set out from Hampstead to make their way across London on foot. They were father and son; the father, well wrapped up, portly and bearded with a Roman nose and bushy eye-brows, the son, small and nimble in breeches and stockings but with quick, darting, inquisitive eyes. They made their way down the sloping streets of Frognal towards Swiss Cottage and Regents Park, the fog sometimes swallowing them up, sometimes peeling back to reveal the great masses of a plane tree or the terracotta cliffs of hidden houses. They passed knots of people on street corners, figures peering into lighted shops and followed the shapes of hurrying hansoms and butchers' vans as they passed out of the halo of one gas lamp into the faint glimmer of another. It was Queen Victoria's London that they were traversing, the London of the horse, the London of a million wheels and bright harnesses, of elegant equipages and great drays, rattling buses and trundling barrows. It was the London at the hub of an Empire, smokey and smelly perhaps, dignified and purposeful certainly, its docks full of masts and tall funnels, its houses filled with unbelievable wealth or indescribable poverty. It was the city of Doré, almost of Rowlandson, and the father, a romantic and a dreamer, an historian born out of his time, saw this and tried as they walked to impart its wonder to the ten year old at his side.

Anyone observing them as they approached the busier streets, where the fog was less penetrating, the crowds more active, would have noticed how often the father stopped in his tracks to point out to the little boy a clock-tower or a steeple as it loomed through the greyness. Scarcely a street was passed without some building, a tall Italianate bank, a cramped medieval church, a square Georgian town house or a group of lawyers' chambers, being pointed out to the little boy in woollen stockings, whose feet began to ache long before they had reached Bloomsbury. The bearded man was enraptured with all he had to tell on his own account, almost as delighted with it as if he had been talking to himself, yet he was encouraged, for the child was bright and stimulating in his responses, always wanting more despite his weariness.

The father talked of Charles Lamb and Samuel Johnson, of the alleys and courts of Dickens, of Samuel Pepys and Hogarth, Fielding and Defoe and Fanny Burney. After the trim squares and crescents they passed the bustle of Covent Garden and the symmetry of Somerset House to reach the muffled presence of the river, lying under its blanket of fog. The start of their journey had been in those neat suburban streets of North London, resembling more than anything else the murky land-scapes of Atkinson Grimshaw; now by the riverside they were in the half-discernible atmospheric world of Whistler, forms, lights and colours, fused together as arbitrarily but as drama-tically as the millions of lives blended together on its banks.

For seventy years the small boy remembered the excitement of this pilgrimage; first of all the privilege of going with his father, then the stories which made the streets and the houses live for him, then the glowing braziers of chestnut sellers, the strolling musicians, the knife-grinder whose barrow was over-turned by a carriage, fleeting childish impressions, but most of all he remembered the buildings. To him they seemed to hold a grandeur and a timelessness that nobody could measure, they represented everything that his father was telling him and more, the grey sides of the city churches, the bulk of St Paul's, the masses and the silhouettes of offices and clubs, the gigantic span of the bridges, all of them striving after beauty, power and structure in a way in which he longed to be a part. Almost at once he wanted to be at home again, drawing out on large pieces of paper all the things he had seen, capturing the images of city and street and perhaps inventing a few new ones of his own.

The bearded Victorian gentleman with a taste for history was my great-grandfather Albert Edmund Richardson of Hampstead, late of Islington, the small boy was my grandfather Albert Edward Richardson, to become in later life architect, writer, teacher and President of the Royal Academy. Despite his great love of the city, my great-grandfather was not truly a Londoner, but the son of a Border man who had been Freeman of the Borough of Berwick-upon-Tweed. His father had come south in the 1840s and Albert Edmund had been born in London, but it was the traditions of the Border Country that lived on in his memory, making him an incurable romantic, even in the drab streets of North London. A dreamy, bookish man, weak in relationships, poor at judging character, he had become a printer and then drifted in and out of various small businesses, all of which had been less than successful. He had married in 1879, a forceful Londoner, Mary Augusta, the daughter of Thomas Richardson, but no relation, they had four children of whom my grandfather was the eldest, born in 1880. Mary Augusta Richardson's powerful personality ruled in the Richardson household, *she* made every decision that was necessary, *she* organised the children and governed her husband's business. Traits of irritability, impatience and a desire to be busy were the most marked of her characteristics, traits that she passed on to her eldest boy in large quantities. But it was the same dominating obstinacy in her nature that drove the contemplative Albert Edmund out of the house on his lonely walks and which, five years later, was to drive my grandfather away from the family circle.

My grandfather attended the gaunt Boys' British School in Hampstead until the age of fifteen and had private tuition at home when the family felt that it could afford it. He was an average child at school, average that is in everything except drawing and design in which he was outstanding. A fellow pupil of the eighteen-nineties told me how the other boys would gather round to see Albert Richardson drawing a flower or performing another trick, that of drawing an almost perfect circle on a blank sheet of paper, by eye. There was never any doubt from this age that he wanted to be associated with buildings and that the ambition of his life was to work as an architect. A love of the past, which came naturally enough to him through his father, was encouraged by visits to a pair of ancient great-aunts in Clerkenwell. These ladies had been born in the reign of George III, still wore their ringlets and their dim house was all furnished with the mahogany and rosewood that their parents had bought new. Of equal importance to the perceptive child were the visits to their bachelor brother Edward Massingham Worboys, who could recall cornfields coming nearly into the city and was as well read as the elder Richardson in the lore and stories of London's streets and alleys. The ten-year-old boy admired in his uncle's hall a tall rosewood longcase clock with silver chimes that had been bought new in 1830. On the strength of this, my grandfather became his heir and received the clock and a library of books at his death, starting him off as both antiquary and collector.

A little after his fifteenth birthday, my grandfather was articled to an architect, not a great figure, but the nearest person that Albert Edmund knew to a real architect, Victor Page of the Gray's Inn Road. This gentleman had a very small practice in the suburbs altering houses and banks. The next two years were happy ones, he was installed in his chosen career, feeling his way forward in the profession, enjoying the new fields which his natural aptitude for drawing were opening up to him. Friendships with fellow pupils brought him into contact with the rage then filling the minds of London's youth – cycling.

He had been given an early safety bicycle by his father when a child and the glamour of the machine, its design, modifications and comparatively high speeds fascinated him. He tried all sorts of bicycle as newly patented ones were offered to the public, the Townend solid tyred safety bicycle, the Crypto with its forty-eight inch front wheel and the spring-frame cycle. He very soon joined himself to a number of cycling clubs, particularly the North London Cycling Club, some of whose members belonged to the more famous North Road Club. The memberships consisted chiefly of city clerks, undergraduates and a sprinkling of professional gentlemen like doctors and lawyers, among whom an architectural student was welcomed. My grandfather was not a gregarious man even at seventeen and liked bicycling because it brought out individuality and could be a solitary pursuit. The competitive side of the North London lay principally in endurance tests and reliability trials rather than in open races and he was eager to break time records in the solitude of the open road.

In spite of their social standing, the racing cyclists of the 'nineties were actively disliked by at least three sections of the community, the police, the local gentry and the van drivers. The police, ever vigilant to trap the early motorist, were also on the alert to catch racing cyclists exceeding the speed limit. Often, as in the case of some of my grandfather's record runs, the average speed was well over eighteen miles an hour, which was considered scandalously fast! Sometimes he acted as scout for the bigger races and on at least one occasion had a great success to his credit. Cycling along, he had spotted the police setting up a check on the North Road at the bottom of Ridge Hill on the way to Barnet. He pedalled furiously back to Colney Heath and was just in time to divert the whole of the road race through Shenley. 'The police were left at Ridge Hill crouching behind farm gates all night!', he chuckled sixty years later, 'all without the sight of a single bicycle!'

From the Dukeries southwards the racing cyclists were looked upon with the 'utmost scorn' by the local magistrates and gentry who described them as 'road lice'. As my grandfather used to explain of his Victorian England – 'it was very difficult in those days to convince one set of gentlemen that another set of gentlemen existed!'

The van drivers were even worse; they merely resented being passed on the road by these craned figures with rapidly twirling legs and my grandfather took in good part their oaths and abuse and the smart crack of the horsewhip across the small of his back! Among his new acquaintances in the cycling world were Frederick Bidlake, the architect, Frank Shoreland, and Schofield, a well-known rider of his day. His closest friend on two wheels was J. Percy Clarkson who lived near his own home.

During his late teens he pursued this sport vigorously, just how vigorously is shown by a long distance journey from

London to York and then from York to Edinburgh, undertaken
in the astonishing time of three days in August 1897. My grandfather referred to it as a 'training run' but the excitement and
romance of it come over strongly in an account he has left
of it.

'I left London as the Big Ben struck twelve, passed under
Highgate Archway and rode seventy miles through the night
to Norman Cross where I breakfasted six hours later. Then I
went on to York, where there was just time to sketch the south
door of the Minster before I continued northwards over
Carter Bar and into Edinburgh that way. I met a gentleman
who was cycling, on the road beyond Newcastle, in the characteristic very tight green jacket and tight green breeches of the
day. He asked me if I was going over Carter Bar and when I
said I was, he asked me if he might accompany me. This he did,
and told me all about Chevy Chase and the legends of the
landscape through which we passed'.

My grandfather only had five shillings in his pocket for the
journey to Edinburgh and could barely afford the two shillings
and sixpence for one night's lodging before returning home-
ward. 'I managed on the money', he reminisced, 'and got home
to within sixty miles of London with sixpence left'. On the
return run, his chain broke on a desolate piece of moorland in
North Yorkshire. By the time that he had made it good, his
hands were completely covered with grease and he looked round
vainly for something on which to clean them. Miles of scrub
met his eyes with nothing at all except a white goat tethered at
some distance; so he went over and wiped his hands on that
before continuing his way!

The cycle rides did not distract but rather added to his first
love – architecture. The bicycle gave him freedom and independence and as in the case of the London to Edinburgh trip
there was always the opportunity to snatch a few minutes for a
drawing. He was continually packing little cloth-covered
sketch-books concealed on the journeys in a hip pocket, with
meticulous pencil drawings of fonts, arches, finials, Gothic
tracery and lettering. It was all a passion and an adventure that
he could no longer share with his family, not even with his
father. They somehow recognised his special talents and left

him alone, as his sister said years later 'We just knew that he would leave us all far behind him'.

The sketch-books were mainly filled with medieval buildings at this time because my grandfather had made an important step in 1898, moving from the suburban office of Page to the commodious rooms of the ecclesiastical architect Evelyn Helicar. It was a step both aesthetically and geographically in the right direction, because Helicar's office at 11 Serjeant's Inn was not only an ample William and Mary building but situated close to the major Georgian monuments of the City. Every morning he went to the drawing-board up a superbly joined staircase of 1720 and every lunch hour he was out, sketch-book in hand, roaming around the precincts of St Pauls, the Temple or Lincoln's Inn. Talking of those days of his youth when he was fired with the inspiration for a great revival of English classic architecture, listeners would get the impression that all his contemporaries were as dedicated and as enthusiastic as he was. But many of his friends were a good deal lazier and at least one told me that 'Richardson was regarded as a bit of a swot!'

The scale drawing of buildings was a very important part of an architect's training at the time, it was essential that he should be familiar with all past styles and be able to draw them out in fine pen line for examinations, competitions, as well as for his own benefit. My grandfather's extraordinary knowledge of London churches and public buildings was certainly learned in this way, the hard way, early rising, a lot of work with a tape measure, a stout note-book and a good eye. One day, determined to get a close view of some stonework in the Temple, he had gone over to the gateway at dawn and clambered up the front of the façade with nothing heavier than a rule and a stub of pencil. He was just completing the work, when a window was raised to reveal an elderly lawyer's head encased in a night cap and holding a blunderbuss.

'Get down at once!' shouted the old man.

My grandfather hanging suspended between string course and cornice found the weapon being poked right at him.

'No!' he shouted back defiantly, looking straight down the barrel, 'Not until I have measured this splendid cartouche!'

The practical side of the architect's apprenticeship was

supplemented by the evening classes that he attended at the Birkbeck College. These were courses in Building Construction and Design and included Life Drawing and Drawing in Light and Shade, the typical syntax of a Victorian art room. He made many friends at the Birkbeck, but a particular one was Hanslip Fletcher, a ponderous, lantern-jawed young man, two years his senior and intent on making a career as a black-and-white artist. Fletcher, the son of an impecunious lawyer, who had once acted for William Morris, had the same love and sympathy for old buildings as my grandfather and became his companion on hundreds of sketching expeditions. Once, in 1898, they had gone together to draw and measure the old timber-framed houses of Wych and Holywell Streets near the site now occupied by Aldwych. My grandfather buried his nose in the bookstalls that flourished in this district, while the industrious Fletcher drew a 'portrait' of an old lady's cat! He was rewarded for it with the amazing sum of five shillings and both poverty-stricken students were able to go off to a nearby chop house and have the biggest meal that they had enjoyed in months.

The picture of my grandfather simply as a single-minded, swotting architect, burning the midnight oil, could be a misleading one. As in his relationship with Fletcher there was an easy-going camaraderie as well as a wit and sense of fun complementing his more serious side. At twenty he was of medium height with a rather oval face and straight black hair brushed across his head. The most noticeable features of his face were still his eyes, hooded under bushy brows, his full lips already having a sort of Augustan curl to them, the long nose appearing most sensitive when in profile. His friend Gascoigne's sketch of him in 1901 shows a thinker and a dreamer, but one who is very conscious of the ridiculous in the world around him.

If the Birkbeck students were up to mischief, it was usually my grandfather, popular, lively and a natural leader, who was there to egg them on and devise the more outlandish pranks. In 1900, a party of a dozen or so of the Birkbeck students, including both Fletcher and Richardson, went to see Sir Herbert Beerbohm Tree's famous production of 'Oliver Twist' at Her Majesty's Theatre. Perhaps as an implied criticism of Tree's lavish and rather melodramatic performances, my grandfather had mischievously persuaded his friends to smuggle in their coats, large and grotesque papier-mâché animal heads. At a pre-arranged signal from my grandfather these were to be donned!

After Bill Sykes' savage murder of Nancy in the second act, the curtains fell on a hushed and darkened house. When the gaslights slowly rose for the interval, the pent-up audience was amazed to see a long line of monsters sitting in their midst, goats, asses, cats and elephants, all in the ludicrous colours of the pantomime horse. The effect was electric, several ladies screamed and then there was a general cry of 'Turn them out!' When they refused to move they were belaboured with sticks and umbrellas and were finally ejected into the street by a party of bouncers drafted in for the purpose. Only then was calm restored within and my grandfather who had evidently enjoyed the rowdy Georgian aspect of the situation, noticed Tree himself, looking on with satisfaction as his friends and himself were thrown down the steps!

Nor did the evening of revelry end there. They paraded round the streets in their animal heads, pouncing on passers-by with loud whoops and terrorising horses and dogs! They were eventually scattered by the police and chased away in ones and twos into side streets. The octogenarian Richardson vividly recalled his crouching behind a dustbin in an area, while a policeman waited for him on a nearby corner!

In 1902 there was another architectural move, this time to the office of one of London's most famous ecclesiastical architects, Leonard Aloysius Stokes. Stokes had built churches up and down the country, made additions to colleges at Cambridge and Oxford and built two monasteries. A devout Roman Catholic he was more remembered by my grandfather for his rages than his buildings. The regime at Great Smith Street, Westminster, in the shadow of the Abbey was authoritarian and stern. The assistants worked from 9 am to 6 pm with the great architect keeping a watch on them from his room and swearing at the top of his voice when things went wrong. One day, after a great bout of oaths, clearly audible to the cowering staff, the whole ceiling of his office collapsed, leaving him unscathed but shaken amid the heavy plaster! Stokes immediately fell on his knees to give thanks for a merciful escape and then distributed cheques to all the assistants and sent them home. 'Next day', commented my grandfather, 'he was back again, even worse than before'. To get some peace away from their temperamental and difficult master, the draughtsmen retreated to the men's lavatory to read. Stokes then descended on them, battering on the door and shouting 'Come out damn you – I know you're only reading the *Daily Mail* in there!'

My grandfather always acknowledged how much he had learned from Stokes, but the autocratic architect of Great Smith Street was too unpredictable to endure for long. At the end of 1903 he moved back across the park to become the designer to the firm of Frank T. Verity at 7 Sackville Street, a responsible job in an important firm for a young man of only twenty-three.

Verity's architecture was totally different from Stokes, it was Parisian and grandiose and neo-classic, it worked itself out in squares and crescents and vistas and appealed to the fast set in Edward VII's London. Verity himself was bearded, Francophile and extravagant, a complete contrast to the almost ascetically Arts and Crafts Stokes, a bonviveur, a connoisseur of wine, women, travel and the theatre. The classical style of his designs were the lynch-pin as far as my grandfather was concerned and re-awakened his interest in the eighteenth century. He admired Verity's life-style for the tremendous prestige it gave to architecture and he emulated it, putting into it his own brand of eccentricity and showmanship!

There was a further reason for the change to Sackville Street, a financial one, for my grandfather had become a married man. In the summer of 1903 he had married a young Irish girl, Elizabeth Byers, two years younger than himself. He had first met my grandmother at the house of his cycling friend Percy Clarkson and had been meeting and corresponding with her for some months. She was twenty, had been born at Newry in County Down, where her father farmed and after his death had been sent to England to be educated. She was small and slender and elegant with a classical face and a great pile of golden-red hair over lively laughing eyes. My grandfather fell completely under her spell and she was totally captivated by the presence and dynamism of the young architect. For her, all things and everything that he touched were endued with a kind of sparkle and mystery, far from being the least of his critics, she never criticised him at all, resigning all matters outside domestic life to the strange and wonderful being with whom she lived. He had a magical way of enchanting people through his pencil and had no hesitation in applying the same technique with Elizabeth Byers. All the love letters written to her with the ardour of a visionary who believed great things for English architecture, were encased in the most delicately painted envelopes. For her delight, scenes of cathedrals, scenes of inns, Georgian streets, ships and towers, sometimes incorporating the stamp in the design, were put on the envelope and dropped through her door. The whole spectrum of the architecture that he loved was literally posted to her and laid at her feet! The same kind of love and concern for her approval in little things characterised the setting up of their first house in Hampstead, at Denning Road. She liked the appearance of old furniture and Morris fabrics, he designed a piano for her and true to the Arts and Crafts tradition had settles and cupboards made by the local craftsmen.

The work for Frank Verity was a good deal easier than that for Stokes, he had free rein with some notable London buildings, particularly the blocks of mansion flats that the firm was erecting in the West End. He made excursions to Paris with Verity and became fully acquainted with French styles and planning, at home, he worked on the building of the Scala Theatre and other theatres in which Verity had a large practice.

One of his early tasks for Verity in 1904 was to go to Buckingham Palace to survey the work being undertaken by Verity in the Ballroom for King Edward VII. He clearly recalled making his way through piles of discarded furniture that had belonged to Queen Victoria and which the King was anxious to throw out. The tables were crowded with wax models of Highlanders, cows, sheep and pet dogs, the toys of the Queen's old age, which King Edward was ridding himself of as the last vestiges of an autocratic mama. Finding himself alone in the Throne Room, he sat down on the throne, took his tape measure in one hand, his rule in the other, and ruled England architecturally for a minute and a half! Almost at once the Lord Chamberlain came in and my grandfather had to spring on to the floor and pretend to be measuring the dais!

Another outlet for his powerful ideas and equally compulsive sketching was as a teacher. In his days as a student at the Birkbeck he had been enrolled as an additional teacher on the history of architecture and on his own admission had remained 'one page ahead of the class'. He was now looking for other opportunities to propagate his theories of classical architecture, planning and architectural education and found the Regent Street Polytechnic a good platform. Three years of work for Verity proved enough, architects are independent beings, and in 1906 a disagreement with his libertine employer resulted in his taking a lectureship in design at Regent Street.

This was the ideal psychological moment to break all ties and set up in practice on his own. He searched for a suitable office and found the only one he could afford over an oil shop in Red Lion Street. Unable to pay for a brass plate on the door, he laboriously drew out his name and occupation 'A. E. RICHARDSON Architect' in flowing ink on a piece of card in the currently popular Jacobean style of lettering. Every morning when he arrived, the card had been torn away and removed, its careful replacement and refixing to the door providing his only occupation for many weeks! He was soon joined at Red Lion Street by another friend from Mr Verity's office, Charles Lovett Gill, a dapper and precise parson's son from Devonshire with important connections in the commercial world. The two of them became the firm of Richardson and Gill and they had expanded sufficiently in 1908 to move into a Georgian office on the first floor of 46 Great Russell Street, its windows overlooking the neo-classic grandeur of the British Museum. Richardson's dynamism, ebullience and ability to design, were exactly matched to Charles Gill's business sense, practicality and expertise on the building site, such a partnership was bound to succeed.

For some years my grandfather had been collecting material for a book on London town houses, the sort of compact and elegant residences that made up the squares and streets but which nobody had hitherto noticed. This was his first attempt at authorship, although he had already contributed essays to evening papers on London's bridges and monuments. Sketch-books were packed with information, photographs were specially taken and the book came out under the Batsford impress in 1911 with Gill as joint author. It was only right that the first copy should be sent to his father who had opened his eyes to the beauty of London's architecture; the ailing man was delighted with it, but it was the only book of his son's that he was ever to see, he died tragically early in 1913.

An added incentive to study and enthuse about the Georgian period was my grandfather's continual collecting of books, pictures and furniture. By 1909, when my mother, Kathleen, was born, the tiny Hampstead house was overflowing and my grandparents decided to move with their baby daughter into the country. They chose the northern side of London because its countryside was associated with my grandfather's boyhood and they chose St Albans because it was full of superb eighteenth-century houses.

Cavendish House in the London Road happened to be on a lease with an option to purchase and they took it because of its attractive flint façade set with Gothick sash windows. There was a huge monkey-puzzle in the front garden and an orchard filled with fruit trees at the rear, across the roof-tops rose the grand and hatless tower of the Abbey, giving the whole place the feel of a Barchester or a Casterbridge. For once my grand-father was able to spread himself, his books and drawing things were in one room, my grandmother had the sitting-room to herself and there was the luxury of having both a maid and a gardener. Best of all, they now had the opportunity to entertain their London friends who would cycle down the North Road for the famous Cavendish House breakfasts.

Seven or eight of his cronies, including Hanslip Fletcher, Emile Verpellieux the artist, A. P. Nicholson the *Times* correspondent, Bernard Sullivan a diplomat, Herbert Freeman his lawyer and Cedric Whitaker, would set off at six in the morning and free-wheel into St Albans for breakfast at eight o'clock. Steaming porridge and cream was served on giant Staffordshire plates while my grandmother prepared the next eighteenth-century course of kidneys and bacon for the hungry bicyclists. There would be talk about buildings, talk about books, talk about paintings, before they all took off on a sketching and writing expedition, perhaps to a nearby church or ending up at Sir Edward Salisbury's home at Limbrick Hall near Harpenden. Sometimes an affair of the heart was involved! Once my grandfather had to stand guard at the foot of a Hertfordshire tower while Fletcher proposed to a girl on the top of it!

Another feature of the early days at St Albans were the Trafalgar Day dinners. On the evening of 21 October, his friends would arrive at Cavendish House from London, most of the cycling friends and in addition F. L. Emanuel the artist and James Bone of the *Manchester Guardian*. The dining-table was laid out with porcelain and silver appropriate to the date of 1805 and down its centre were placed little flotillas of model ships, representing the English and French forces. Busts of Nelson and Napoleon stood either end of the spread and prisoner-of-war models in ivory and bone decorated the place settings. The health of George III and Queen Charlotte was drunk, the British Navy was toasted and then my grandfather read accounts of the battle and the Admiral's death before the rest of the evening was spent in singing sea shanties.

From Cavendish House my grandfather started to mount a series of tours to all the main cities of Great Britain, the towns and ports of the West, the country centres of East Anglia, but also the main burghs of Scotland and as far afield as Dublin, Cork and Galway. This was the preparation for his first solo attempt as a writer, *Monumental Classic Architecture in Great Britain and Ireland during the XVIIIth and XIXth centuries*. The crusty head of the firm of Batsfords, Herbert Batsford, had asked him to do it after the success of *London Houses*, but the busy office in London and the calls on his time as a lecturer, postponed publication from year to year.

These tours in search of monumental architecture landed him in some picaresque adventures, particularly during his gleanings among the Irish buildings. His interest in classical town halls, banks, universities, markets and corn exchanges had led him on to consider early railway architecture and he was an early admirer of termini like Kings Cross, Euston and Newcastle stations. All these appeared in the book, but he also wanted to include the lesser known Dublin stations.

One morning in 1910 while staying with his Dublin friend R. M. Butler, my grandfather found himself in front of the sombre grey pile of Broadstone station with its neo-Egyptian doorway and lofty entrance hall. He was intrigued by the grandeur of the place and went to the booking clerk's window.

'Good morning, can you tell me the name of the architect of this magnificent station?'

'I can't tell you that', said the clerk, 'but if you step up the stairs and see the Board of Directors, they'll be sure to tell you, they're having a meeting this very minute!'

Thus, with agreeable Irish informality, my grandfather found himself first on the stairs and then inside the Board Room at Broadstone Station. Inside a dozen elderly be-whiskered men were seated round a huge mahogany table, all looking very solemn; they looked up expectantly as my grandfather entered and he knew exactly how to handle them.

'Excuse me gentlemen', he began, beaming and radiating the Richardson charm, 'I have been admiring your magnificent railway station, it is as fine an example of the Greek revival as I have ever seen – just look at that fireplace!'

Twelve old bearded heads swivelled round in their chairs and stared at their own fireplace as if they had never seen it before.

'Can you tell me who designed this grand building?' pursued my grandfather.

The bearded heads conferred together amid a burble of low voices.

'Sure now it *is* a beautiful station', said the Chairman at last, 'but I couldn't tell you who did design it, but if you would be stepping down to Trinity College to see Dr Mahaffy, he would be telling you who it was!'

'Are there any other stations further down the line like this?' my grandfather tentatively enquired.

'Why to be sure there are!' said the Chairman, he then put his head together with those of his fellow directors again. After a moment he said 'Mr O'Halloran will make out a special pass for you to travel and see all the buildings'. Turning to his neighbour he added 'Make out a pass for the architect gentleman to go down to Mullingar, Athlone, Athenry and Galway, put the directors' coach at his disposal and all the station-masters must be informed!'

A visit to Dr Mahaffy revealed that the architect was John Mulvaney and next day my grandfather arranged to travel westwards with his special pass. The directors' coach, all fringes, button upholstery and gleaming brass was waiting for him and he steamed out of Broadstone on the most luxurious piece of architectural research that he had ever undertaken. At every station the station-master was waiting for him with doffed cap to give what information he could about the architecture of the town. At several stops he arranged to have the chief buildings photographed and printed, ready for him on his return journey that night!

At Mullingar he confronted the station-master with the usual question.

'Do you know what I mean by Doric columns?'

'Indeed I do sir', replied the station-master, cooperative but a little perplexed.

'Well are there any buildings in the town with Doric columns?', continued my grandfather describing with his stick as he did so an invisible picture of a portico and steps.

The station-master looked strangely at the wild-eyed and excited enthusiast.

'Are you sure you'd not be meaning the lunatic asylum?' he said cautiously!

In Bath he had an even more amazing encounter. Walking around Milsom Street and looking at the shop-fronts, he was approached by a very old gentleman.

'That is the way to design a shop-front', said the stranger to him, 'you apply it – don't cut it in like the other architects to-day'.

He had introduced himself as Goodridge the younger of Bath, the son of Henry Goodridge, architect of the Lansdown Tower. Over sherry and biscuits in the old architect's house my grandfather had been carried back into the distant past. This old man had known William Beckford and had frequently led his horse and followed him about on Lansdown Hill. Grandfather listened hungrily to the anecdotes of a hundred years before that by chance had linked his own life with those of the author of *Vathek* for a single afternoon!'

My grandfather's ambitions for his new book rose every time that he met Batsford; the book should be bigger, better, more carefully designed, more profusely illustrated, than any other book of the decade. Batsford harried him mercilessly and my grandfather danced rings round the publisher's carefully laid plans. One minute he was in Edinburgh, another in Plymouth and another in Bristol, but the final draft was never submitted and Batsford sent frantic telegrams to try and find him. With a characteristic flourish the mischievous Richardson arranged for the book to appear on 23 April 1914, Saint George's Day and Shakespeare's Birthday. It was a vast work, it cost five guineas and was dedicated to the Prince of Wales. He celebrated by entertaining his artist friends to an excellent lunch in the Hall of Mirrors at the Vienna Café; Mr Batsford was not present.

The two years prior to the Great War were ones of tremendous energy and excitement for the young Richardson and this made the grey years that followed seem all the more wasteful. The great series of lectures on the Neo-Classical Style that had been delivered at the Carpenters' Company in 1913 had made the lecturer's name, older architects and severe critics, had downed tools in the early evening to go and hear him. It was not so much the scholarship, though that was sufficient, as the sheer exuberance of the man. He took his audience through all the architects from Inigo Jones and Wren to Cockerell and Barry and included the American giants of his own day. Stocky for his thirty-four years, wildly gesticulating, black hair ruffled, bushy eye-brows quivering, he resembled a black raven in striped trousers and a cutaway coat! The lectures had heralded the book but so too they had heralded the move to more spacious premises at 41 Russell Square to accommodate a fashionable London practice.

The office in a dignified town house of the 1780s afforded exactly the sort of background my grandfather required for his designing, magnificent marble chimney-pieces, fine cornices, elegant double doors, the perfect setting for Regency furniture. Never very careful he became joyously extravagant, fitting the new house up with mirrors, Empire clocks and Hepplewhite chairs until Charles Gill was forced to protest.

'Very nice,' he commented wryly, 'but will the firm stand it?'

One American friend described his reception at Russell Square as like visiting Pierpont Morgan, even the partner's office table was wreathed in history.

While attending a client in the West one day, Gill and my grandfather were given a light lunch in the housekeeper's room and the inquisitive Richardson's fingers began to investigate under the table-cloth. Beneath linen and baize was a delightful pillar dining-table of 1790 in perfect condition and of unusual form.

'I say Gill! Look at this!' he whispered.

They made an offer for the piece there and then and my grandfather discovered that it had come from the Devonport Dockyard and was probably made for a ship of the line. From this he ascertained by association that it was Lord Nelson's table and it was duly installed at Russell Square.

'We must do things properly!' was his cry, as expenses mounted up, 'especially as we now have generals queuing up for our services!'

This was a slight exaggeration to pacify Gill, there was only one general on the stairs and his sister, an elderly peeress who liked the firm's buildings. General Sir Bruce Hamilton was an old soldier of an almost Georgian outlook and cut who had commissioned my grandfather to build him a country house at Ascot. It was the first sizeable country house with which he was involved as sole architect and he designed it in the sympathetic proportions of the American Colonial style with great attention to woodwork and windows. He also had the entirely new experience of designing the extensive gardens for his client, walks and parterres, rose bowers and croquet lawns, dotted about with small garden buildings.

The General warmed to all his ideas despite a rather peppery attitude to life, my grandfather recalled one example of the old man's eccentricity while the plans were under way.

They were all seated round the dining-table, discussing the new house when Sir Bruce's chauffeur approached his master in a great state of agitation.

'Excuse me Sir Bruce,' he began nervously, 'I thought I ought to tell you that the stable is full of rats!'

'Is it?' said the gaunt old General, wheeling round on him, 'then 'tack 'em before they form!'

The year 1912 had seen the completion of the largest of the firm's civic projects, the New Theatre at Quay Street, Manchester, later the Manchester Opera House. This was the size and the scale on which my grandfather liked to build and he took great pains over its refined classical detail both inside and out, the interior plasterwork and gilding being of a studied chasteness and dignity. The company who were financing the project were not very sound and although the theatre was completed in good time, the architect's fees were not forthcoming. My grandfather had therefore taken the law into his own hands and actually sat in the box-office on the opening night of *Kismet*, collecting the gate-money from the public until his business was settled! With such buildings behind him, a string of grand city offices promised from the firm of Herbert Reeves and Co and his reputation growing as a lecturer, writer and after-dinner speaker, the First War came as a terrible and painful blow. The contracts gradually fell away and one country house, the largest yet, in Lincolnshire, was abandoned at the foundations.

In his middle thirties, not particularly fit or used to the rigours of life, it was difficult to know what sort of part he might play in the war. Hanslip Fletcher had enlisted with the Artists' Rifles but was over age for combatant units, fortunately the General came to his architect's aid. Sir Bruce Hamilton felt that my grandfather could be most usefully employed in some way with the Royal Flying Corps and in 1916, the Complete Georgian exchanged his more easy fitting wigs and cloaks for the uniform of a 2nd lieutenant in His Majesty's Service.

As mentioned before, my grandfather had a chameleon-like capacity for adapting to all and every situation, the Royal Flying Corps would seem the least likely ground for such an individualist to flourish, but with extraordinary skill he made the service work for him during the next three years. As an officer with some professional knowledge of structure and engineering he was sent first to the School of Military Aeronautics at Reading to qualify in basic mechanics and aerodynamics. He did not find the work very congenial, but threw himself into the practical side of it at once, burying himself in books about aero engines, wind flows and altitudes. His irrepressible spirits never let him down of course, if there was something to draw. He began to transfer every aeroplane discussed in the classes into a stocky black note-book, B.E. 2c's, Bristol's and Sopwiths, Armstrong Whitworths, De Havilland's and Vickers Scouts were all crammed on to its pages in inky silhouette with now and then a lively little flash of watercolour. Larger scale technical drawings followed, engines, bodies, wing formation, shown in graphic structural detail with sections and notes, grasped with an almost Renaissance intensity. Many of these splendid designs found their way to the Science Museum at South Kensington.

In odd moments away from Reading, my grandfather was still involved in a few civilian activities, most notably in the newly founded Civic Arts Association. This was a body founded to promote good design in civic monuments and particularly in war memorials which it was feared might sprout up in awful tastelessness as soon as the hostilities were over. He was still acting as contributor to *The Architect's Journal* and managed to snatch a day here and there at Cavendish House.

On 13 August 1917 he was posted from Reading to Farnborough and began work in charge of a salvage operation, receiving damaged aircraft from the coast by rail and transferring them to workshops. He was uncertain what Farnborough would entail and during his first leave from there, which happened to coincide with one of Fletcher's, the two of them determined to improve their fitness through a days marching. They left Cavendish House early, caught the train to Bedford and then proposed to march back to St Albans on the high road. The plan was doomed to failure; no sooner had my grandfather begun the march than he began looking at buildings, his steps dragged and he trailed to a halt. Eight miles from Bedford they arrived at the small market town of Ampthill, filled with Georgian houses and almost aromatic with the past. My grandfather looked at the church and the almshouses, for he was not familiar with Bedfordshire, not having visited it since a holiday at Bolnhurst in 1907. In Church Street he admired a large red brick house that looked somewhat neglected and on enquiry was told that the place was 'tenanted'. 'I'll have that after the war' he remarked confidentially to his friend.

His stay at Farnborough was briefer than expected, a rumour that he was to be posted to Mesopotamia proved false and instead he was transferred to another part of the Salvage Section of the RFC at Millbank Dock, Southampton, this remained his base for the duration of the war. As soon as he had settled in, my grandfather began to make himself comfortable. He found a nice billet in a Regency house where Elizabeth and Kathleen could come and stay with him, but better still he began to transform his office and its surroundings at the dockside. He was feverish to build. It was not long before he found a man who was a bricklayer in civilian life and with his help and that of the REs he began tearing down all the old quarters and erecting new. There was no great problem in finding materials with so many old pieces of aeroplane lying around and he and his men ventured farther afield to 'improve the effect' as he put it. This improvement included the arrival of a lorry filled with most of the external woodwork of a demolished Georgian house. My grandfather roused himself to a fever of excitement while a magnificent panelled entrance door was erected at the end of his office, a portico and flanking corinthian columns were added to it and a wrought-iron balcony joined them above. The 'effect was splendid, exactly like the west front of a baroque church!' This was not all, however, he began on the interior when the exterior was completed and collected enough old furniture to make the officers' quarters like a small museum. He toured the antique shops of Southampton with his motor-cycle driver, sitting bolt upright in the sidecar and ordering oak settles, wall clocks, warming pans and country tables from wherever he could find them. The result after weeks of preparation looked like a stage set from the *Beggar's Opera* rather than the dockside power house of a country at war!

My grandfather was undeterred by adverse comments but there was at least one occasion when he had to think very quickly. The unit had a surprise visit from the Embarkation Commandant General, Sir Alfred Balfour, a seasoned soldier with no time for trivialities. He stopped short in his tracks at the sight of the office, billowing flags from Georgian balconies and smart sentries did not disguise its somewhat unusual appearance.

'Good God man!' shouted the General turning to my grandfather after surveying the brass knockers, columns and Regency door scraper, 'what the devil's the meaning of all this rubbish!'

My grandfather remained impassive.

'The builders sir! Damned fools!' he remarked cooly!

His own contributions to the war effort were essentially practical, even through the haze of clay-pipe smoke and the ticking of eighteenth-century clocks he could summon up enormous feats of ingenuity. On his arrival, his first task had been to organise the despatch of large bombing aircraft to the Continent, which it was hoped might attack Berlin. Neither the RFC or the Navy had supplied suitable tackle to get the aircraft despatched, Richardson was called upon to improvise. He set his mind to work to design a gantry thirty feet high which would have to be complete in twenty-four hours for the departing ship. With typical bravado and a certain eighteenth-century panache he set about 'liberating' the necessary materials from the unsuspecting tradesmen of Southampton. He marched twenty of the toughest looking personnel down to a neighbouring timber yard and interviewed the quaking merchant.

'I want two long beams, 32 feet at least and other timbers!' he barked at the man, 'we can't pay for them, but there's a war on and I demand them in the king's name!' He got them very speedily.

Having achieved this he procured a steel beam from an old ship as a crowning piece and then found he would need raking stays to complete the structure, but there were no bolts to fix them. Again he marched the same contingent into the town and called on the ironmongers with sufficient money for a handful of bolts. While he talked and paid for the few they could afford, the men filled their pockets with bolts before marching back to Millbank Dock. Even then his troubles were not ended; the first lorry that arrived at the gantry sank up to its axles in mud and a floor had to be constructed. My grandfather dressed in dark clothes went with a party of men to the railway station and took as many old sleepers as they could find to bury under the gantry. This surface was still not sufficient and gravel was surreptitiously moved from the Southampton-London roadside to form a hard ground.

'How shall we get it flat?' queried a young aircraftman.

My grandfather thought for a moment as a childhood ambition seemed to dawn on him.

'The city steam-roller', he crowed, 'the very thing!'

In this way the City of Southampton steam-roller was quickly 'borrowed' under armed escort and with my grandfather aloft, the final touches to the gantry were completed! All the aircraft were despatched in good time and my grandfather returned to his vigil of books and pipes and candles in his elegant office.

There were times when he could get away from the service life and enjoy the scenery of the nearby New Forest. He made cycling tours into the outlying villages, visited Romsey, Lynd-hurst and Brockenhurst and enjoyed sketching afternoons with Fletcher. In the city itself he was beginning to jot down notes about the old buildings and the historic sites he passed day by day, these were the basis for a pamphlet entitled 'Southampton' published after the war. Nor was he lacking in an audience for all this new-found information or in an outlet for his impromptu lectures!

By some stroke of fate at the War Office, my grandfather had been put in charge of some two hundred women in the RFC who were employed in the repair shops. Every morning he took them on a march through the main streets of Southampton, a march that started at the dock gates in strict military discipline but which developed a style of its own as they progressed. Soon the orders were given more and more summarily and the whole troop halted in front of every Georgian building they came to! They were asked to compare the spires of Holyrood and St Michael's and told to observe stucco and brickwork.

'Eyes right!' shouted the excited figure in the rear, 'notice the neo-classical beauty of Guillaume's granaries and Hack's Yacht Club!'

A little further on it was 'Eyes left! Look at the rubicund features of *The Dolphin* where Jane Austen stayed!'

The girls seemed to enjoy these morning route marches with

their eccentric officer, more senior officers turned a blind eye to his bizarre methods.

Another idea occurred to him during his strolls along the quayside and through the workshops where the carcasses of aeroplanes were being stripped down and re-built. There was sufficient good wood, most aeroplanes being constructed of it at that time, to make good craft ornaments out of the remainders. He soon got several of the men to work on this, smooth round propeller shafts hollowed out made the most attractive clock cases, a little Adam vase turned in the metalwork shop really completed it! A piece of tail intersection from a Sopwith, carefully jointed was almost as successful as a watch-stand and two of them mounted on podiums made a pair of pyramids for the drawing-room mantelpiece! A small industry began at Southampton which the newly named Royal Air Force was powerless to stop, small neo-classic ornaments, architect designed, gradually infiltrated the shops and homes of the area, proudly displayed on counters or arranged on the pianos and plant-stands of semi-detached houses. My grandfather chortled at his success in bringing one of his pet schemes to effect, that was introducing good design into the sitting-rooms of the country.

This was his last venture at the workshops before the armistice and he recorded that day in the little Pepysian diary that he had begun to write during the war.

'Up betimes and with Fletcher to Millbank, took parade and marched girls through the streets. Worked all the morning. At 12 o'clock a tremendous commotion, hooting of syrens from the fleet of liners in the docks, whistles, cheering and flags run up, could not restrain the emotion of the personnel of this establishment. Rumour has it that the armistice with the enemy has been signed to our great benefit. Paraded the girls and told them to take the news of our great victory calmly'.

There was one last scene in which the Richardson touch was self-evident before he finally left Millbank. The following day he paraded the whole establishment at the quayside at 5 o'clock in the evening, the November night already dark, a host of lanterns lit all around. Dressed in a cloak and a wig he read them the terms of the peace and followed this by a ringing declamation of his favourite poem 'The Burial of Sir John

Moore', perhaps the weirdest conclusion to an army life that there has ever been!

A month later he was back at Cavendish House, St Albans, trying to pick up the threads of his old life. It was not easy, many things had changed, the architectural practice had lapsed and he himself had become disenchanted with his home, now perilously close to an expanding London. To his great delight in March, the Advisory Committee of University College, London recommended him for the chair of the Bartlett School of Architecture in succession to Professor F. M. Simpson. This offer had come almost entirely from his reputation as a writer and polemicist and particularly as the result of his Carpenters' Company lectures in 1913. He was appointed in the spring amid the feeling that the right young dynamic man of thirty-nine had got the job. At almost the same time he was appointed editor of *The Architects Journal*, a small paper with a reputation, an ideal outlet for his ideas and writings in the next few years.

Circumstances seemed to be smiling on him and he and Elizabeth found themselves with six months in hand to find a new house before his first academic year began. Together they toured villages in Buckinghamshire and Hertfordshire looking for houses that met their requirements, but my grandfather still secretly hankered after the house he had spotted in Ampthill some years earlier. It seemed unlikely that it would be available, but they decided to visit the town and entrained with their bicycles at St Albans for the twenty-mile trip into Bedfordshire. They cycled up into the town from Ampthill station and found the house in Church Street, shuttered, forlorn and neglected but apparently up for sale! My grandfather scarcely able to conceal his excitement, found the agent, and insisted there and then on a complete tour of the property. His whoops of delight echoed through the empty rooms each time he came across a period fireplace, a moulding that pleased him or a beautiful but long unpolished finger-plate. My grandmother followed at a discreet distance, judging the whole enterprise more sternly and peering into gloomy closets with a slight foreboding.

Travelling back on the train my grandfather asked her what she thought of it.

'Think of all those curtains,' she replied innocently.

By June the Avenue House estate was bought by them for
£2,000 and by the end of that month they were planning to
leave St Albans.

CHAPTER TWO

Country neighbour

Three early motorised pantechnicons had laboriously brought over the whole contents of the St Albans house to Ampthill in late June 1919. From his lodgings at the *White Hart*, which had not yet metamorphosed from smelly inn to smart hotel and still reeked of bitter and horses, my grandfather excitedly directed the operations of the removals' men. My grandmother who had been wringing her hands at the vast quantity of furniture, paintings and porcelain that her husband had collected, was very soon wringing her hands at the sparseness with which they decorated the new rooms at Avenue House! Regency sofas and tables of gleaming mahogany that had seemed perfect in the comfortable setting of Cavendish House were swallowed up in the open spaces of John Morris's Georgian residence. The older part of the house, dating from the 1780s, was smaller inside and the dining-table and dining chairs looked magnificent in the new interior; but the 1819 wing at the east end of the house, had bigger rooms and higher ceilings and the drawing-room seemed like a major problem in curtaining alone. My grandmother busily organised, Ethel Butcher her St Albans maid was put in charge of the twenty-two rooms and local staff were recruited.

The untouched character of Avenue House made it all the more absorbing for a writer and historian of my grandfather's temperament and passions. The country-town house was for him the apogee of Georgian style and civilisation, even more so than the manor or the great estate. In these places were combined the merchant and the man of taste, the traditions of country craftsmanship and the refinements of classical art which had given the Regency its elegance and its robustness. It was in this sort of 'middling' house that the poet William Cowper had written, the novelist Sterne lived and Dr Johnson most convincingly talked. The Morris family of Ampthill brewers were not ashamed of their connection with the town when they built their house flat on the pavement of Church Street in the 1780s. Two rows of seven windows overlooked the street and apart from the handsome portico and flight of steps, nothing but a range of railings divided it from the doings of the town. The very scale of the house and its proximity to the cottages about it, had ensured that whoever lived there took a very active part in what was going on!

The Morris's had created a delightful family home, spacious and well-proportioned and elegant, bright with sparkling light on sunny days, murky with grey shadows on dark ones, as all Georgian houses seem to be. But much more, they had created a house which was a microcosm in itself of Regency living, their customs, their needs and their manners were evident to the practised eye in every corner, almost in every cupboard, and it was that sort of eye that my grandfather possessed. The house with its dresser-lined kitchens, stone-sinked sculleries, flagged floors, large cellars and box-like reception rooms, was as close to the smaller houses of Jane Austen or Maria Edgeworth as anyone was ever likely to find.

The early death of John Morris II, brewer and townsman in 1827 had left the house exactly as he first wanted it. A family bankruptcy in 1858 had prevented any alterations at that ominous period for provincial building – the High Victorian – and spinster granddaughters had kept the flag flying until 1906 without touching a fireplace or a brass knob anywhere. By this extraordinary good fortune, Avenue House had remained asleep and unsullied in its mellow skin of red brick since the Regency and it only needed a genius with an understanding heart to kiss it back to life with his magical touch.

Ten years had separated the sale of Miss Sophie and Miss Maud Morris's treasures in 1906 from my grandfather's first glimpse of the house in 1916. All the original contents from clocks to spoons, from brass to bed linen had been disposed of during four days in the April of that year, a completely intact Georgian household. That lost opportunity must have seemed tantalisingly close to my grandfather when he was arranging his rooms that first year. His predecessors had made some alterations but never lived much at the house, preferring a home in Devonshire, subsequently it had been tenanted. At the close of the Great War there were rumblings that the house might become offices and the garden a memorial to the dead or even a garage! So that ironically, in a lifetime of architectural rescues, it might be said that his own house was the greatest rescue of all!

Viewed from the north, the house was T-shaped, the left and right arms of the T being the 1819 and 1780 wings, its stem the offices and secondary bedrooms of the latter period. On one side of this stem was a handsome cobbled courtyard enclosed by bailiff's house and coach house, on the other a slip of garden leading to a terrace. The Morris's had remained Quaker businessmen, but had built the house on the corner of quite an extensive estate, which with their grounds and farms, gave them some claim to being country gentlemen. The land had not originally run with the house but had been acquired from the successors of Sir Simon Urlin in about 1800. It was for him that this large hillside pleasure garden had been enclosed in the 1730s, bounded by a brick wall and with an embanked avenue leading to a gazebo at the very crest of the hill. This avenue of wych, cornish and common elm was the main feature of the garden and had given the house its name from at least 1870.

The grounds were approached through a wooden screen at the end of the courtyard, first came the pretty walled rose garden with its Portland stone sundial surrounded by treillage, encircling trees and clinging espaliers of pear and apple. This was in a terrible state of neglect, weeds grew everywhere and what had once been a lawn was sprouting potatoes, vestiges of economies during the war. Winding paths led from this sheltered spot into the older garden, terraced walks at various levels passed large greenhouses, bending yews and rows of lime trees, before the end of the avenue was reached with its vista of the 1725 wooden temple at the end.

Beyond and to the right of the temple was the Warren Field, part of the estate, where the Miss Morris's broughams, dog-carts and bathchairs had been auctioned thirteen years earlier. The brick wall between this and the garden followed the sloping contours of the land, cutting off an overhanging spinney of oaks and disappearing behind great Edwardian clumps of rhododendron. Although a perimeter gravel walk circled the whole five acres of garden, the best views out were from the avenue. Looking eastwards, my grandfather had a clear and unspoiled sight of green Bedfordshire fields, unusually undulating for this part of England. Turning back from the same height, towards the south and west, he was met by a thick screening of chestnut and elm, but not sufficiently thick to obscure through the trunks and foliage the little clock cupola at the centre of the town, the projecting sides of tall houses, sloping tiled roofs and the gentle march of dormers and chimneys. The garden like the house was still, restful and thought provoking, somehow preoccupied with its own memories.

What was true of Avenue House was also true of Ampthill itself; a small compact market town straddling the crossroads in the very middle of Bedfordshire, it had seen its greatest prosperity in the Georgian period and its four streets were lined with the signs of it; ample inns, bow-fronted shops and houses ranging from the neatly artisan to the nearly palatial, everywhere red brick with stone dressings or white-painted woodwork under airy fanlights. To the west of the town was Ampthill Great Park where the Dowager Lady Ampthill lived, to the east the Ampthill House estate, where Sir Anthony Wingfield presided over the bison and llamas of his private zoo. Hardly any cars penetrated this remoteness except the Duke of Bedford's landaulette visiting his cousins at the Park or the hire cars of Mr Albert Grimmer, inventor and aeronaut, who had the only garage in the town. When my grandfather took his sketch-book up into the walled garden behind his house, there was nothing to disturb him but the sounds of LMS trains a mile distant and the pervasive smell of hops drifting over the rooftops from the brewery. If he took his drawing materials further out into the countryside, he found a landscape untouched by anything but the repetitious lines of telegraph poles on the snaking Bedford road, the only movement being the plough-horses above Houghton House that he added to his portfolio.

The closely-knit community of a country town might not have taken easily to a less eccentric, less flamboyant stranger than my grandfather proved to be. But his genial personality and unbridled enthusiasm, coupled with the fact that he was both 'professor' and 'artist' for which allowances had to be made, soon won him support. Unashamedly curious about his surroundings, full of a childlike delight in visual experiences, his neighbours found it difficult to ignore this excited figure who positively skipped along their pavements, drawing attention to things they had always lived with, but never seen.

'Your windows are 1805 and very fine!', he told one amazed shopkeeper, 'change them at your peril!'

Another shop interior at Mr Stanniforth's, the cobbler's, so fascinated him that he made a watercolour of it. Before many months were out he had inveigled himself into those Cranford-like parlours behind the sash windows and was adding their chimney-pieces, carvings and even inhabitants to his bulging sketch-books.

One woman, when a little girl, recollected the way in which a frenzied figure had burst into her parents' kitchen, hair flying, eyes raking every corner and with a drawing pad tucked under its arm. Catching sight of the dresser, the visitor had fallen on one knee and begun to stroke it enthusiastically 'You beauty, you beauty!' he intoned. 'Of course we all thought he was barmy' she commented of this memory.

Fits of excitement over a dormer window or a pilaster followed by shouts of 'By George, its good, by George!' and then a whistle, came to be regarded as commonplace. Wild gestures over ironwork in the older buildings, feverish draughtsmanship and frenzied sucking at the pipe began to be seen as normal. 'Its alright, it's only the professor!' they consoled themselves and 'the professor' he remained to most of the population.

One day, a year or two after his arrival, they awoke to find themselves featured in an article with illustrations in *The Architectural Review*. My grandfather had entitled the article (it ran in parts) 'The Charm of the Country Town' and in it he showed the small houses as well as the big houses, the estate cottages as well as the private mansions, all linked by the history of the place and by his undisguised joy in buildings as he wrote about them.

'It is in the nature of hill-towns', he wrote in the first of these articles, 'to withstand the spoliation of progress, even as history records their successful defence in times of siege. In this is to be seen the true secret of the preservation of Ammetulle, Anthill or Antehill, the sentinel town of the landscape of the home midlands. No place in this island of its dimensions and population enjoys airs more healthful or views more enchanting'. Even the most suspicious of his neighbours could hardly fail to be captivated by such disarming words, recognising if unwillingly, that they had a real champion of the place in their midst, even if a champion by adoption.

A little way down Church Street from Avenue House was the combined store of Messrs Bates & Parmiter. A double shop-front contained two doors on the splay, that to the left occupied by Mr Parmiter in the hardware side of the business, that to the right, Mr Bates in the grocery line. My grandfather struck up acquaintance with Mr Parmiter soon after his arrival and found much to fascinate him in the cavernous interior. William Parmiter, thin, pink in the face and with thick spectacles set over blubbery lips, waited patiently for orders behind gigantic Victorian scales. He must have been one of the gentlest men ever to serve behind a counter, scarcely talking above a whisper, turning mechanically to dusky pigeon-holes and dark corners, rummaging through trays of archaic screws and bolts to find the required article. Above him were suspended mysterious packages and obsolete containers hung from the roof, still with their brown paper wrappings upon them.

Some months after his arrival, my grandfather was in William Parmiter's establishment and passing the time of day. His eyes getting used to the dim shop suddenly noticed an interesting shape in a distant corner.

'What's that Parmiter?' he exclaimed, 'that thing lying over there'.

Parmiter obediently went into the recesses of the shop and brought back in that strange diffident way of his, a fine straw-coloured besom broom.

'I think it's rather old stock, Professor', said that gentle voice.

It certainly was, my grandfather realised that it had been bought new for stock in about 1830, being the sort of implement seen in *Pyne's Rustic Sketches* or the interiors of Rowlandson and Cruikshank. The 1830 price ticket was still there too and he bought it for his collection at the 1830 price of threepence three farthings!

Further conversations with Mr Parmiter revealed more history. Buried in his shop my grandfather found sets of pattens, iron-framed shoes that the poor people had used for walking the muddy streets of the town from the 1820s to the 1880s. He bought sets of adult and child's ones and these joined the array of domestic utensils and wooden objects that were on display at Avenue House. William Parmiter was not an Ampthill man himself but had memories through his grandfather of Bedfordshire in the early 1800s. This man had walked from Hitchin to Ampthill and back in a day to buy wood from Lord Holland's agent at Ampthill Great Park. My grandfather delighted to capture fragments of history for himself and his writings and he was never tired of hearing William Parmiter tell how he had once met G. F. Watts, the painter. As a young man in trade near Guildford, William Parmiter had had to deliver an order to the Watts at Compton, and Mrs Watts steering the young man in to the great artist's studio had told him 'You may speak to him, but you mustn't *touch* him!' as if Watts was some strange wild animal.

Visits to Parmiter's were frequent and my grandfather was returning daily with fresh curiosities under his arm, jelly moulds in old copper and brass, butter pats, sugar nippers and obsolete stewing and brewing vessels. A final stop to this flow only came when my grandmother's patience finally ran out.

'Mrs Richardson came in to me one morning', Mr Parmiter told me years later, 'and politely explained that the house was getting full of *my* old rubbish and asked me what I intended to do about it! She forbade me to sell any more to the Professor whom she said could not be trusted!'

Soon after their arrival, their neighbour, Miss Newman, called to see that 'they were quite all right'. That was actually what she had said, but the object of the visit was to discover who they were, what were their politics and whether they attended the church, she was accordingly christened 'Miss Find-Out'. Her favourable reports and the enthusiastic reception of my grandfather's *Architectural Review* articles, created a stream of callers. A flurry of visiting cards swiftly arrived at Avenue House from Ethel, Lady St John, Emily, Lady Ampthill, the Wingfields, the Pye-Smiths, the Eagles and other local families. My grandparents returned these visits, she placid, pretty and serene, he excitable, restless, brimming over with talk, measuring their mouldings as he ate their teas, exclaiming over their portraits.

Chief among these new acquaintances was Emily, Dowager Lady Ampthill who had lived at the Park House since her widowhood in 1880 and brought up all her children there. She was a daughter of Lord Clarendon and had married the very gifted Lord Odo Russell who after a number of key diplomatic appointments was created Lord Ampthill. She had been with him at Rome when he was handling the tricky negotiations after the First Vatican Council and at Berlin when he became British ambassador there. Her periods as ambassadress and hostess had made her regal, formal and slightly frightening, even her family were in awe of her and she cut a considerable figure in the neighbourhood.

Tea at the Park was a gruelling experience even for my grandfather, his natural verbosity a little tempered by Lady Ampthill's compelling presence, hawk-like aristocratic visage and straight back. The rooms of the vast Queen Anne house were cluttered with Victoriana, little tables, screens, heavily padded armchairs and smotheringly heavy curtains at the windows. Every shelf and ledge was crowded with endless photographs of the Russell family and the walls were hung with innumerable portraits of German princelings and princesses that Lady Ampthill had met at Potsdam. At the beginning of the First World War all these paintings were patriotically removed and only one, of the Kaiser, remained in its place in her private sitting-room. A strong swimmer in her youth, Lady Ampthill had saved the Kaiser from drowning during a boating accident on the Spree and she never tired of mentioning this. But she had a ready answer when challenged about the Kaiser's continued presence on her walls.

'I shall keep the portrait there', she answered unrepentantly, 'and if the German troops arrive, I shall bargain with them over it for the lives of the people of Ampthill!'

Invitations always came by letter in Lady Ampthill's flowing script and answers were called for. A short drive to the Park, brought my grandparents to the magnificent north front altered by Sir William Chambers and then up the graceful flight of steps to the door, opened by Ladyman, the butler. My grandfather loved the fuss, and the dowager, although well on into her seventies, continued to enjoy the attention due to her and the aura surrounding her as Queen Victoria's last Lady of the Bedchamber.

She was always to be found in the great drawing-room at the Park, erect in her chair, tightly laced in black and with the most enormous jet brooch pinned to her front proclaiming in gold letters ODO. 'It actually means 'Oh do!' whispered my grandfather to a nervous guest mischievously! She was usually flanked by her two unmarried daughters, standing, the Hon Constance Russell and the Hon Romola Russell. The first was fat and round and the second tall, thin and beaky, more similar in appearance to the mother. Both the Miss Russells lived in mortal dread of their mother and scarcely uttered a word when she was present. On one of his first visits my grandfather had referred Lady Ampthill to some article he had read in *The Times*.

'Constance' barked her mother, 'find me *The Times*'.

Constance Russell went off in search of the newspaper only to return pink and agitated saying that she could not find it. Lady Ampthill demanded a further search be made but the daughter returned yet again without it.

'Then go to your room!' commanded Lady Ampthill, in perfect control but obviously unspeakably irritated.

To my grandfather's amazement, this adult woman, nearer fifty than forty had murmured 'Yes mamma' and left the room, not to show her face again before the visitors left.

On another occasion the grandparents had taken with them my grandfather's old artist friend Hanslip Fletcher. Fletcher was nervous and also very deaf, a combination that strained Lady Ampthill's patience to its limits. After shouting across the tea tray at Fletcher who was some way off, and getting no results, she made one last effort.

'Come closer Mr Fletcher!' she ordered.

Fletcher heard this and leaping up, tea-cup in hand, dragged a huge satin poof across the carpet and sat down on it right under the dowager's left elbow. Lady Ampthill was horrified.

'But not SO CLOSE!' She cried with raised eyebrows and poor Fletcher had to pick up his poof and retreat once more.

A less taxing neighbour was to be found at the other end of the town. Sir Anthony Wingfield owned the Ampthill House estate which lay south-east of the church among fine trees and parkland. His handsome Regency house with stone portico was yet another creation of the Morris family of Avenue House, a junior branch had built it to the designs of H. E. Kendall in about 1830. The Wingfields had improved the formal gardens and terraces with their clipped yew hedges, planted round the ornamental lake and started an arboretum, but they had enlarged the house in the 1890s, doubling its size and turning it into an unmanageable monster.

Sir Anthony, who was knighted in 1936, was a great grand-son of Viscount Powerscourt and had come to Ampthill House with his mother Mrs George Wingfield, at the age of three in 1859. He had grown up among the fields of Ampthill in the 'sixties and 'seventies and after attending Harrow and Christ Church, Oxford, returned to Ampthill House to manage his property and pursue the interests of pedigree cattle and zoology. He was about sixty when my grandfather got to know him and as he survived until the great age of ninety-seven, he was a link that spanned nearly a century, joining the pre-railway age of the 1850s to the welfare state of the 1940s, an amazing achieve-ment. His memory remained fairly crisp in extreme old age and sometimes in conversation with my grandfather he would say of some vanished Victorian 'Yes, my dear Richardson, I knew her well', adding in parenthesis, 'about a hundred years ago!'

Strangely enough Sir Anthony did not alter very much be-tween late middle age and extreme old age when I remember him calling on my grandfather. He was very tall and stout with a military bearing, accentuated by his sharp nose and moustache and ramrod back. In truth he was a figure of almost Punchian proportions as might have been seen through the eyes of Du Maurier, Belcher and their like. Sir Anthony's considerable girth and frontage was encased in grey or black suits, the bulging waistcoats suspending watch-chains and fobs, the ensemble completed by a bowler hat on Sundays or a grey cap on less formal occasions. Thus accoutred 'Old Pop' as my grandfather affectionately called him, sailed through the streets of Ampthill, inspecting his property, calling on his tenants, or gently prodding a bonfire that he kept stoked near the Maulden Road, not a person to be trifled with!

Rigidly schooled in a society that new its duty and its privileges, he was a tireless county man on the bench and in the prisons, subscribed to any good cause and began a men's bible study in the town, building them a meeting room on the edge of his park. Nevertheless he was not a man to tolerate insubordination and was quite feudal in his attitudes. Walking across the park one day with a friend, he heard some shooting and cries coming from a distant wood. Somewhat disturbed by this he despatched a servant to uncover the mystery. The keeper returned shortly afterwards to say that a group of farmers had been allowed in to shoot pigeons.

'Thank God for that!' exclaimed Sir Anthony with surprising vigour, 'I thought the mob had risen!'

Totally Victorian in posture and attitude, Sir Anthony belonged as much to the era of Palmerston in his house, as my grandfather further down the road, belonged to the era of Pitt.

Sir Anthony was not, however, without his own brand of flamboyance. Before the First War he had entertained lavishly at Ampthill House, filled its numerous rooms with house-guests and kept a sizeable retinue of servants. In addition to this there was his private zoo to the east of the house, where ostriches strolled beyond the ha-ha and llamas cropped the grass. A large staff of keepers was employed for these creatures, many of which were trained to be ridden; my grandfather frequently looked outside his study window in Church Street to see a keeper riding past on a llama to deliver the Ampthill House letters to the post office in the Square! A member of the Zoological Society, Wingfield was instrumental in founding the Whipsnade Zoo and became its first President, many of his own animals being transferred to the Dunstable Downs to found it. My grandfather was asked to design the first keeper's house there and produced an attractive weather-boarded structure, later burnt down. Another side of Sir Anthony's showmanship had emerged when he was High Sheriff for Bedfordshire in 1903. A tremendous traditionalist, he had discovered that the greatest number of horses allowed a commoner visiting Buckingham Palace was five. He accordingly harnessed five to his carriage for an official visit to the new King. The gesture had its desired effect, nothing like it had been done since the eighteenth century and many of the staff went on to the roofs to witness his audacity!

By the time my grandfather became a frequent visitor to Ampthill House, the great entertainments and garden parties for the Spanish and German royals were a thing of the past, but the old gentleman still lived in great splendour. A large staff was presided over by Cooper, Sir Anthony's butler, who afterwards wrote his reminiscences, and the kitchen was ruled by the former chef to the Polish embassy. A curious sidelight of Wingfield's involvement with the prison service was that ex-prisoners were recruited and dragooned into becoming footmen for him. Many an old lag from Bedford Prison found himself in livery with powdered hair and white gloves, moving noiselessly round the corridors of Ampthill House! Every Sunday evening for twenty years my grandfather was bidden to dinner with Sir Anthony. Every Saturday an invitation to 'a little food' came in writing and was accepted in writing, open-ended invitations not being in the rule book. My grandfather was expected to carry with him all the male guests at Avenue House, no ladies being required on these occasions. The young painter Denis Flanders was staying there in 1938 and found himself whisked into this evening from another century.

'I remember a wide sweeping drive, and a large, plain box of a house looming up. And this is about when my most vivid impressions began. A hoot on the horn as we slowed down opposite the porch (I believe this was a practice of the Professor's to announce his arrival!) and a footman appeared beneath the lamplight between the pillars of the portico. Through the hall and down a long passage, lighted by a seemingly endless row of torchéres, with several more footmen, each indicating us to move forward, down to the end and into a small den, where our host, seated upon the red-leather of a fender seat before a roaring fire, greeted us.

'My recollection of the dining-room is of a vast apartment, with an elaborate ceiling hung with plaster pendants in the gothique manner. The only light was at the far end, where an oil lamp stood on the circular dining-table. I was now almost in a trance, so unreal seemed our surroundings. Each cover had three glasses and each of us three guests, as well as our host had a footman to himself. I ate everything and drank everything – not knowing how to say "No"! Professor Richardson warmed by the food, the wine and the feeling that this was the proper condition and state in which to live, talked in an even more animated manner than usual. His deep fruity voice became even richer. He excelled himself. The talk ranged widely, then settled on the world-wide crisis that had just culminated in Munich. "Do you know why they were digging the trenches in Hyde Park," he cried, "they were *not* intended as air-raid shelters, as we were told. They were to BURY THE DEAD IN". This so horrified me that I remember little of the rest of the evening. Only that we got back at midnight to find Mrs Richardson still up (very quiet she seemed by contrast with her husband) and had to listen to the Professor complaining bitterly about a new Irish maid, whom he had just discovered had chipped one of a set of valuable painted chairs acquired.'

There were musical evenings too, when Sir Anthony's niece might entertain on the piano at Ampthill House or the 1800 pianoforte at Avenue House would be accompaniment for my grandfather's singing. This provided him with an excuse to don eighteenth-century costume, silk frock-coat, silk stockings, wig and buckled shoes and suddenly surprise his guests in the candle-lit drawing-room. When in good voice, he could warble his way quite happily through any number of Dibdin's sea songs and knew most of the refrains from Gay's *Beggar's Opera*, always a great favourite with him.

Guests did not escape these costume parties, the ladies were

supplied with original gowns and patches, the men with
waistcoats and breeches and given passages to read from Defoe
or Swift. His enthusiasm for this was never satisfied and as each
newly-attired friend re-entered the room, he would take a
candle to them, stepping back in admiration and exclaiming
'Wonderful – a Lely' or 'My dear lady – pure Gainsborough!'
When exhausted by his own talk, he would slip on to the piano-
stool and produce excellent if simple sounds from the instrument. The evening often ended with a churchwarden pipe
smoking session, everybody but he feeling frightfully sick as
a result of it!

The wearing of costume, the assumption of roles whether
Pepys or Fielding or one of the great architects, was not confined to the house. When Fletcher was staying he spurred my
grandfather on.

'We both delighted in dressing up', he wrote years later,
'sometimes Fletcher would don 18th-century costume, including
the three cornered hat and would walk in my garden. Then he
would venture in the village streets and curiously enough, when
we both appeared, little comment was made. I do not mean
that we were in the character of bona fide actors, but rather as
two men enjoying putting the clock back. We felt that by dressing up we could invoke the genius of the past.'

Soon after their arrival, my grandfather acquired a sedan-
chair which he claimed had been made for the Fitzroy family
in about 1740. This was soon pressed into the service of his
charades for it was complete in every detail and had all its
original poles and straps. Friends of the family were suitably
attired and with my grandfather sitting inside, the whole party
went on visits. When there was an evening at Sir Anthony's my
mother went inside the sedan-chair 'so as not to get her feet wet'
and my grandfather strode out in front with a glowing lantern.

The journey from the doorway of Avenue House along the
street to the church and then sharp right into Sir Anthony's
grounds took about six minutes, but it was a journey packed
with incident. On one occasion my grandfather's lantern
caught fire opposite the church, flames leapt up round his
wrists and he was forced to fling the burning cage into the
gutter. Without thinking, the two porters dropped the sedan-

chair in the middle of the high road and ran to the rescue. For a minute or so my mother was left a helpless prisoner on the roadway, unable to move and at the mercy of any passing car!

The local constabulary which had heard of these 'goings on' was determined to put an end to them. One Saturday when my grandfather was late for dinner and hurrying on his bizarre little procession over the crest of the hill, a policeman stepped from the shadows.

'I beg your pardon sir' he began with a slight salute, 'but are *you* responsible for this?' He pointed at the sedan-chair with its suffocating occupant.

'I am officer', replied my grandfather lantern in hand.

'Then are you aware sir that it has no rear light?'

My grandfather's eyes hardened as if ready for a fight but softened again as a thought occurred to him.

'But officer' he said in his most engaging tone, 'we're carrying a parcel!'

This Georgian logic was so elegant and so convincing to the constable that the procession was able to continue to Ampthill House unmolested.

The ebb-tide of the Victorian age had left any number of pieces of interesting driftwood along the four streets of Ampthill. In Church Street and Dunstable Street they mostly consisted of spinster ladies living in twos or threes, forbidding females who had seen the great Queen's first Jubilee in the bloom of youth and had scarcely stirred since from their neat houses. There were the three Miss Bartons, the three Miss Wingfields, the two Miss Eagles, the two Miss Pye-Smiths, not to mention 'Miss Find-Out' and the unfortunately named Miss Fitts. Lady Ampthill once told my grandfather that she cured her insomnia by counting the old spinsters of Ampthill jumping through a gap in the hedge!

My grandfather got to know them all, enlivening their sheltered existences with his boundless enthusiasm and repartee. Christmas Eve became a special time for visiting them. After lunch he would put on his eighteenth-century clothes, place a wig and tricorn hat on his head, and wrapping his cloak round him, begin his calls. First there were the Miss Bartons at the Old Gates who would usher him into their cluttered drawing-room and give him a little madeira; next door there was a little sherry at the Miss Eagles and finally at Dynevor House, Miss Wingfield was waiting with a glass of cherry brandy. Sometimes he took with him his 1848 barrel organ and whirling its handle round produced for the ladies its one and only tune 'The Sailors Hornpipe', singularly inappropriate for both Christmas Eve and land-locked Bedfordshire.

But perhaps his favourite old lady was not an Ampthill lady at all, but lived two miles away in Maulden. Miss Louisa Moore of Maulden Cottage was not only much older than any of the others, but she had a much deeper sense of history. Well past ninety when he first met her, she carried all the customs of the Regency with her into the twentieth century, the hot water urn standing on the tea table, thin slices of chocolate served between bread and butter, tea made appetising to the weary with a new-laid egg beaten up in it. The curtains were drawn at dusk, wine and cake were served together while Miss Moore reminisced about travelling to London on top of the Bedford Times coach and attending at Flitwick Manor, a meeting to protest at the coming of the railways. Her great mahogany four-post bedstead with its chintz hangings and the superb ivory model of a man o'war in the same room, had belonged to her father when he served under Lord Nelson. The week of her death my grandfather committed his feelings to paper –

'It is in the spirit of reverie that pen is put to paper to record events related at firsthand. There is something affecting in memories of scenes that can never be revisited. How well I recall the Drawing Room on the first floor where guests were received. The writing desk with the invitations for bazaars and fêtes, the neat piles of letters answered, the miniature candle-stick and the sealing wax ready for use. The room had remained unchanged since her parents time. It was always in the neatest order, the sofa by the fire, the worktable with its miscellaneous assortment of articles. Then there were the parcels and presents arranged for children's birthdays and the package of clothing for a deserving case. The mantelpiece held specimens of old china attendant upon a gilt clock protected by a crystal shade. The bell-pulls, by which she summoned her faithful retainer, were of needlework. Conspicuous among her books were the bible and church service. Such things at the time half-noted cannot be erased from the memory. A few days since I passed by my friend's house, there was a sprinkling of snow on the ground, the blinds were drawn, yet another house was closed to me'.

He was not only making friends with the bookish and the educated in Ampthill but with ordinary people whose ancestry was part of the fibre of the town's history. There was Francis Handscomb, the undertaker, whose ancestors had provided the towns of Ampthill and Woburn with clocks, a silver pocket-watch with the name of Ebenezer Handscomb upon it, hung on a stand in my grandfather's bedroom. Even more characteristic than the clockmaker-undertaker was the trade of the carrier and my grandfather's dealings with these gentle souls reads almost like a page from Thomas Hardy. The two Ampthill carriers were Rudkin who plied his cart three times weekly to Bedford and Gayler who worked the shorter road from Ampthill to Clophill.

Young Rudkin had a cart that was fifty years old pulled by a piebald grey of sorts which had been in and out of Bedford for seventeen years. Young Rudkin usually travelled alone on carrying days but sometimes when the weather was good old Rudkin, aged eighty, joined the cart, accompanying his sixty-year-old son 'to keep the lad in check'. My grandfather soon discovered that the old man was uncommunicative on all subjects except the Peninsular War, on that alone he would talk for hours.

On carrying days old Rudkin plodded round the most likely customers but always made a bee-line for Avenue House where he was sure of an answer and gossip. Rat-ta-ta-tat and the maid fetched my grandfather.

'Good morning sir – have you found out anything more about Corunna?'

'Not much Rudkin', replied my grandfather, himself hopeful of details.

'It was a great battle sir – a great battle', Rudkin would go on, 'my father was a soldier of the line under Sir John Moore, he was a hard general but he got the men on to the ships right in the teeth of the French too!' Here Rudkin would drop his wheeze into a whisper – 'It wasn't the French who shot him as the history books tell sir, *he was shot in the back by his own men!*'

'Not by your father, I trust, Rudkin!'

'No sir, although my father had the name of the man who did it, slap from a sergeant with whom he was friendly – anything for Bedford sir – No! Thank you, sir'.

The encounter with the other carrier Gayler, was more dramatic. Gayler was a diminutive little albino, his white hair protruding from under a battered straw hat and his pink eyes almost obscured by great goggle-like spectacles. My grandfather always hailed him in the street, but one day found him in a very sorry condition, he was walking dejectedly along, head down and as my grandfather approached he saw he was weeping.

'Good gracious Gayler', he said, putting his hand on the man's shoulder, 'what's the matter with you?'

'I've lost a friend' spluttered the disconsolate Gayler, 'my horse is dead!' And he held up the well-worn harness he was carrying for inspection.

'We can't have you like this Gayler,' he added reassuringly, then he had an idea, 'Come round to Avenue House courtyard at three o'clock this afternoon!'

Gayler nodded his assent and then marched away in stunned silence still clutching his pathetic harness. As soon as Gayler was out of sight my grandfather began work. He walked up to Ampthill House and called on Wingfield, explaining that Gayler's horse was dead, 'Somehow he must be kept on the road' he told his friend. Wingfield jingled the coins in his pocket and said that he would start the fund for a new horse with a contribution of five guineas.

Next grandfather called on all the shopkeepers, raising a pound here and a pound there for 'Gayler's horse'. He went to each of the old ladies in turn and they all dipped into their purses for small change in order to keep 'poor Gayler on the road' and provide him with a horse. By the end of the morning he had accumulated the princely sum of fourteen guineas and the only home left unvisited was the Park House. After lunch he called on Lady Ampthill and the Miss Russell's, succeeding in getting a further two guineas and bringing the total to a very respectable figure of sixteen.

He then took the money round to the back of the *Crown and*

Sceptre public house, where he knew an old fellow called Aspen 'did a little bit in horses'.

'Good morning', said my grandfather in a jaunty way when he caught sight of Aspen in a yard full of lugubrious looking animals, 'I want to buy a horse for about sixteen guineas, what have you got?' He wished to appear business-like with Aspen in order to get a bargain although he was a complete greenhorn in such matters.

Aspen looked grandfather up and down and pointed out a large and particularly soulful looking animal in one corner of the yard. 'He's old and a bit spavined,' said Aspen, 'but he can pull and he's very cheap at the price!'

'Ah' said my grandfather, 'a bit spavined, yes, a bit spavined.' He had no idea whether this remark referred to the beast's tail, legs, underbelly or ears, but he gave the whole horse a knowing general appraisal.

'I'll take him', said my grandfather and the big soulful brute was led by him out of the *Crown and Sceptre*, through the Market Place and into the courtyard of Avenue House where it was tethered to one of the Georgian wall-rings.

At three o'clock, the wicket gate slowly opened and the crest-fallen little figure of Gayler advanced up the yard. My grandfather was waiting for him with the horse at his side and briefly explained what had happened.

'There you are Gayler!' he said, 'Take your horse away with you!'

'Ohhh' sobbed Gayler, completely overcome and looking as if he was about to hug my grandfather, 'I never knew I was loved!'

'Loved man, good heavens, take your horse away with you!'

Gayler led the horse off through the big gates and my grandfather thought this was the end of the story, but it was not. Ten minutes later Gayler was creeping back through the wicket-gate blubbering once more.

'Whatever shall I do now, the harness won't fit!' he moaned.

My grandfather paid there and then for a new set of harness for the spavined horse; every penny was worth it for he had kept an old friend in trade and the publicly-subscribed carrier's horse plied the Clophill road for several more years until its master's death.

The enthusiasm and excitement of the move and the fresh smells of the new garden and new countryside quickly transmitted themselves from my grandfather to his little daughter. He was the most unprofessorial of professors, the ideal companion for a little girl not yet in her teens and full of curiosity. Together they could explore the new domain, ramble through the spinneys surrounding it, discover old sheds in hidden corners, climb up to the rooms over the coach-house, work the rheumatic pumps that lay hidden in odd places round the garden. One of these was a great iron wheel supported on a Gothic frame which the Morris's had called 'the garden engine'. After rapid revolutions with the handle, a low gurgling could be heard from the well forty feet below and, by degrees, the sounds and reverberations increasing, ice-cold water spewed out into a nearby tank in bursts and dribbles. My grandfather's unbridled delight in all around him, created a world of fantasy for her, as it was to create a similar world for me thirty years later. There was the job of christening the different parts of the new landscape, the tumbledown shed with half timbering became 'Shakespeare's England', a contemplative path under the lime trees was called 'Scholars Walk' and the sun-trap in the north-east angle of the property, where my grandmother took her day bed in sweltering Julys, 'Riviera Corner'.

No enquiry about whether bears inhabited the ice-house would be met with a bland adult dismissal, but with the reply that three immense ones lived there and guarded the statues! A similar teasing question about how my grandmother had travelled over from Ireland to marry him received the same mysterious reply. 'She flew over on a broomstick and captured me!' he said, adding quaintly, 'I still have the broomstick!' My mother's prying hands were even more active than his, she climbed all the trees, investigated their hollows, had a house built in the oldest and most strategically placed one. Her hands also strayed into the apron pocket of Mrs Sugars, the laundress, to find tucked away there, the entire family supply of steak for a week prior to its removal through the back gate!

But perhaps more important than his settling down as a

neighbour or a family man, he was settling down as an artist. As a Londoner who had little experience of country living, he still craved for the society of other architects and artists and highly valued the discipline of studies and his teaching. His friends continued to visit him in their droves, satisfying his need for company. His weekday duties as professor in London gave the stimulation to write and draw. He was free to learn about his new home in the best way through pen and brush; in the town he assimilated the street scenes, the old houses, the busy figures at the market. Delicate black ink was mixed with translucent watercolour to catch the crowded door of the *Old Queen's Head* with its figures more eighteenth than twentieth century. Above all the landscape fascinated him and as he explored it, donning tweeds and plus fours to do so, the metamorphosis from townsman to countryman seemed nearly complete.

CHAPTER THREE

Bedfordshire Sketch-book

As I have already said, the owner of Avenue House has one foot in the town and one foot in the country, the trees and hill-side gardens are a veritable *rus in urbe*, but the sashes and railings are as firmly planted in the street. In one direction my grandfather could walk out, sketch-book in hand, and enjoy the hedgerows; in the other he could become embroiled in the controversies and quarrels of a town of two thousand people. Never a man to leave a stone unturned for long, he was soon involved in a storm of local politics. The fierce debate was over what memorial should be erected to commemorate the town's dead in the Great War.

Wingfield, as Chairman of the Memorial Committee had naturally consulted his friend. My grandfather had served on the Civic Arts Association during the war, had designed a number of monuments and was no stranger to the subject. The Civic Arts Association had tried to improve public taste, over-whelmingly preferred classic to gothic or latent *art nouveau* and in line with this he had designed a number of single memorials. Fired by the recently published designs for a cenotaph by Edwin Lutyens, he was determined to do his own version of this at Ampthill, more Greek in character, less exhibitionist in design. Whether or not this first design was intended for a site near the church, the rector, Archdeacon Syme, rejected it in the strongest possible terms and called it 'a pagan monument!' This was the first of many rebuffs that my grandfather had from the parish church over a period of more than forty years, he remained as architect to the fabric, but took himself and his family along the hill to worship at Millbrook, a pleasant walk through lanes and fields of about a mile.

The churchyard was given a more modest gothic cross, which might have appeared anywhere; the opposition, Wingfield and the Professor at their head, pursued their ideas elsewhere. The disagreement at least gave my grandfather the opportunity to select a far better and more dramatic site on the Alameda, to the west of the town. This broad walk of lime trees had been laid out for Lady Holland in the 1820s and given to the town as an avenue for exercise in the style of the Spanish ramblas. It had not been greatly used and needed a focal point, for its handsome trees simply petered out in a sandy moor. The end of the avenue with the hill rising behind it was the ideal site for a great Portland stone obelisk and my grandfather was busily producing designs for it from the end of 1920. He also grasped the opportunity of giving the Alameda a formal entrance, the original gates and piers having been removed. The screen facing the town was to consist of two main and two subsidiary piers, capped in stone and joined by handsome iron railings and gates, giving a triumphal entry to the limes and the town memorial.

This cenotaph was being completed in the early months of 1921 and was a considerable *tour de force*. The octagonal monument rose gracefully from its glade, the flat surfaces covered with the names of soldiers and sailors carved by Farmer & Brindley of London. The memorial was one of the very few works to be 'signed' by my grandfather, the names 'Richardson & Gill' being chiselled on the plinth.

It was very typical of my grandfather to suddenly feel that the gateway 'lacked that extra something' about ten days before the opening ceremony! He considered what was needed. Should there be more carving to the capital? A touch of gilding to the black railings? A grouping of temporary trophies, flags, and royal arms? He hit upon the idea that the centre piers needed grand vases and needed them very quickly! During that week he flew round the London antique shops and finally lighted on a pair of urns at Pratts in the Brompton Road. They were good neo-classical ones in the artificial stone patented by Mrs Coade in the late eighteenth century and dated 1795; the price was

£20. Wires sped between my grandfather at Russell Square and the Clerk to the Council at Ampthill and the Coade urns were finally secured for the town.

But there was still no time to be lost if this sudden inspiration was to be completed, the builder was authorised to send a lorry to Brompton Road and the urns were fixed in place only hours before HRH the Princess Beatrice arrived, superintended by a jubilant Professor.

The whole ceremony on 21 May was orchestrated perfectly by Wingfield, beginning with luncheon for the Princess at Ampthill House. My grandfather, by virtue of his reputation as a good conversationalist, was on the Princess's left, and expected to be a witty and entertaining companion. He found lunch very hard going, however. The Princess, youngest of Queen Victoria's daughters, had been so long immured at her mother's elbow that she had totally lost any independance of thought. A dialogue consisted of asking ma'am a question and having it returned to one like a ping-pong volley, everything the same but the words being in a different order. He valiantly rattled out some likely names and some likely places, always hopeful that it might stir some response through the royal ear. Finally, he mentioned that he had recently designed a scheme for Hughtown in the Isles of Scilly.

At last there was a dim gleam in the royal eye and the visible signs of some very distant memories being turned over.

'Are not the Isles of Scilly pretty?' came the response.

'Yes ma'am', he replied, catching at a straw. But the conversation ended there and the Princess relapsed into silence for the remainder of the meal.

'She was quite impossible to deal with!' He commented later, admitting defeat for the first time in his life. 'She had a brain like a chicken!'

Among the other mementoes of the unveiling were some postcards of the memorial drawn in rapid penwork by my grandfather and issued to the public for a penny. This was not surprising for his new life in the countryside had increased his zest for drawing and had really created his desire to be a water-colourist. Before the war, his sketches had been largely of buildings, generally in pen and ink and rarely made as finished pictures. Now the whole field of landscape watercolour was opening up to him although buildings, a farmhouse perhaps, a church or a group of barns, was the focal point, the countryside itself was the stimulus.

Following on the practice of his favourite eighteenth-century watercolourists, Rowlandson, Towne, Farrington, Cozens and Dayes, he was using a reed pen and sepia ink to draw the structure of his pictures and then painting over them in broad but subdued washes. There was a richness in the pen lines and a subtlety in the colours of these early years at Ampthill, that make these sketches among the best of his whole life. With friends such as Hanslip Fletcher, he searched out the old forges, windmills, lock-gates, water-wheels and unspoilt tracts of farmland, capturing them on paper before they became immersed in suburbia or decayed by neglect. Sometimes he hired a punt at Bedford and worked his way gently along the Ouse, pausing to make sketches of the willows and the views at Fenlake, or taking a boat out at Harrold or Olney for the same purpose. My grandmother was always at his side, smiling benignly from under a huge sunhat, steadying the paint-box while he dipped his brush, replenishing the water whenever he needed it.

As Fletcher drew the old London buildings with a sense of urgency, minutes almost before the demolition men arrived, so my grandfather immortalised his area in pen and brush conscious of its impending disappearance. Many of the drawings have a sort of wistfulness about them which underlies their sparkle and their charm; nowhere is this more apparent than in the long series of capriccios or 'fantasies' that he undertook in the late 1920s and early 1930s. The capriccio, a sort of dream picture in which buildings are transposed from different places and set together, imaginary landscapes surround them and historical characters inhabit them, was a very eighteenth-century form of pictorial amusement. My grandfather's huge 'fantasies' were partly inspired by the etchings of Piranesi, partly influenced by the drawings of the American, Bertram Grosvenor Goodhue, but mostly came from his own fecund imagination. As a lecturer at University College he was famed for the ease with which he created great architectural conceptions on the blackboard, the students applauding the feat and the college beadle timing him! Practice of this sort made perfect in the design of his fantasies.

The fantasies were very large for pen drawings, usually about 19 by 30 inches and they took up to fifteen hours painstaking work to complete. A theme having been decided upon, studies were made, garnered from various sketch-books, presses were ransacked and a large drawing-board set up on a table in one of the downstairs rooms of Avenue House. The designs were generally done on card, the pencil structure worked in, the ink lines following, building crowding in on building until the whole space was covered in busy wriggling lines. Then he cleaned his drawing with bread in the traditional way and started to apply the colour and add more detail. The whole process looked effortless as he crouched bird-like over his board, but in fact it cost him a great deal and he sometimes left his work in the small hours completely exhausted. When one remembers that the whole exercise was carried out at night in candlelight or at best, lamplight, the achievement seems more amazing. My grandmother sat up beside him whatever she felt like, reading, sewing, handing over endless cups of coffee to ensure that those restless fingers were kept moving.

The drawings themselves might be on almost any subject, the names he gave them were alluring enough 'The Tower of Babel', 'The Turn of The Tide – a fantasy of the Sixteenth Century', 'Medieval Twilight', 'The Road to Norwich', 'Feast of the Guilds', 'Old St Paul's', 'Spanish Fantasy'. Some of the most delightful and whimsical are the four fantasies inspired by Sir Edward German's *Merrie England* although brought up to date. These are 'Spring 1821', 'Summer 1851', 'Autumn 1885' and 'Winter 1900', nineteenth-century reveries where, in a wealth of detail, the artist put down his epitaphs on the Victorian age. In 'Summer 1851' the whole picture is tinged with a bluish colour and contained in one of the immense aisles of the Crystal Palace, crowds admire the latest inventions, worship a steam engine while overhead birds in top-hats fly past! In 'Winter 1900' the cold aspect of the City is shown in pen and black ink, the scene is opposite the Royal Exchange, the streets crowded with carriages and horse buses; vendors jostle one another and a policeman makes an arrest against the blare of a pavement band, overhead are the gathering clouds of war.

Perhaps the most poignant for my grandfather and certainly the one he most referred to was 'The Approach of Modernity – A Prophecy', drawn in 1931. In it he showed a vast and hostile city, filled with skyscrapers, warehouses, radio masts and concrete, ruled over by furies, and gradually engulfing a tranquil countryside. Motorways and bridges begin to penetrate the stillness, bulbous buses are shown hurtling by, hideous funfairs have sprung up and queues of trippers wait outside lavatories. To the right of the picture, vandals have begun the slaughter of handsome forest trees and the horse-team retreats, led away by a ploughman. The Scots pines in this picture were taken from a row in the Avenue House garden and many of the other details from life.

Any sketching expedition, either with friends or with my grandmother was usually highly successful, at least half a dozen drawings being made each time. I can recall only one occasion in twenty years when my grandfather had to tear up a drawing and this was through cold and hurry. Not everyone appreciated the way he just settled himself down anywhere and began to draw. One trip from Ampthill included a visit to the charming North Buckinghamshire town of Winslow and my grandfather decided at once to draw the majestic Winslow Hall, standing in the town centre and attributed to Wren. After walking up and down with his camp stool for some time, he finally took up a position opposite the entrance to the Hall and began. He had not proceeded very far when the door of the Hall shot open and a disagreeable man stormed out and began to shout at him; it was Mr McCorquadale, the owner.

'What the hell do you mean by drawing my house without my permission, how dare you presume on me in this manner, who the hell do you think you are?'

'My dear Mr McCorquadale,' said my grandfather with a bland accommodating expression, 'I am sorry to have troubled you, but I have always understood that beauty was free!' He then snapped his portfolio shut and added 'But I shall still draw your house FROM MEMORY ROUND THE CORNER!'

McCorquadale scowled and retired to his house. My grandfather was as good as his word. With his remarkable photographic memory he disappeared round the corner and drew the whole of the Hall from his remembrance of it. Then, he returned to the gateway with it and walked up and down like a sandwich-board man, displaying it for the benefit of the furious McCorquadale!

A favourite walk of my grandfather and his dog was from Avenue House, by way of the church and Holly Walk, to the crest of the hill overlooking the Vale of Bedford. Pipe in mouth, sketch-book under arm, he would saunter along the top towards the King's Wood, looking down to the flat expanses of middle Bedfordshire, where the sun occasionally picked out the façade of Wootton House or the detached church and tower of Marston five miles away. The scarp slopes were dotted with trees, often elm or oak but mostly the indigenous Scots pines that grow so well there, leaning and twisting into weird shapes under the battering of the wind. My grandfather began to collect their silhouettes in his sketch-books, page after page of tree shapes, rotund, tapering or stunted, some meticulously formed with the sepia pen, others flicked in with a brush. He was also making studies of tree boles in the same area, and although many that he sketched must have vanished under the axe, their near relations survive to echo these flowing drawings. His love of trees was life-long, perhaps partly the love of the creator who can see at once what shapes, textures and strengths can come out of them, but also the sheer love of their massive scale, wonderful groupings and gentle movement. He must have sketched some of the trees of the ridge a hundred times but always returned for that further drawing to 'understand them' better. 'In order to draw a tree you have to become a tree' was his usual remark, and while standing there, pen in hand, mesmerised, sturdy, there was an undeniable similarity between portrayer and portrayed. He also liked to comment that many of the trees he was showing were over four hundred years old and had been rejected by Samuel Pepys as unfit for naval use!

Most of his walks took him past the ruins of Houghton House, a great rectangle of crumbling brick and stone, hidden below the ridge and folded round with farmland and the stumpy remains of a great park. It was not easy to get a close view of this forlorn relic, the immediate area of the ruin was heavily fenced off, bulls prowled around the neighbouring fields and thick undergrowth covered the walls. Even a cursory glance showed my grandfather that the house was of early seventeenth-century date and of the highest quality; ivy had grown all over the stonework, trees were choking the empty windows, but the importance of Houghton was obvious. Vague recollections of seeing similar designs and reading contemporary accounts, drove him back into deeper research on the house.

Houghton had been built in 1616 for Mary, Countess of Pembroke, a notable blue-stocking and hostess at the Court of James I. She was the sister of Sir Philip Sidney who had dedicated his *Arcadia* to her and she had entertained the King at her new home above Ampthill, in the last years of his reign. But it was not the history so much as the architectural novelty of Houghton which fascinated my grandfather, for even with the dense undergrowth and falling masonry, he recognized that it was a key building in the development of the country house. Mary Pembroke had evidently employed a court architect for her house, its plan was daringly modern, the medieval great hall was abandoned in favour of a central hall behind the entrance, moderate-sized reception rooms leading off it. Most exciting of all, Houghton had three grand frontispieces on the south, west and north fronts, all in carved and dressed stone, all in the height of the fashionable classicism of the 1630s, a few years after Lady Pembroke's death. This could have been the work of either Inigo Jones or John Thorpe, the finest façade being that to the west, unique in England at the time, ascribed by my grandfather as a direct transcription of Palladio's Convent of the Carita, Venice. Defying stinging nettles, thistles, and the occasional tumbling brick, my grandfather drew the place from every angle, undertook a complete survey and tried to stir up local feeling.

Its more recent history had not been happy. Unoccupied by its owner Lord Ailesbury for much of his life, it was tenanted in the eighteenth century and finally dismantled except for the outer walls by the Duke of Bedford in 1794. It had been admired by Horace Walpole, painted by David Cox, but year by year had sunk into greater and greater desolation and obscurity. It was a suitable spot for Victorian picnics, visitors could root among the walls for wild flowers and startle jackdaws and owls from the gloom within, it was a favourite resort for Edwardian lovers who scratched their names and hearts in the crumbling stone. It was deplorable to think that most of this great building, the central tower of its entrance, the corner turrets and the balustrades, the mullioned windows and the internal plaster-work, survived until the 1890s. Townsmen could remember it intact and photographs showed every piece of pointing and every piece of stonework as clear as the day it was put up, only a generation before. The National Trust visited Houghton in 1895, but after this it rapidly decayed and nothing was done.

My grandfather's academic reverie about Houghton was rudely interrupted in 1923. It was announced in the press that the ruins, which had always been a considerable bugbear to the nearby farmer, were to be demolished. Worse still, the colonnade and other features were to be sold to Americans to cover the cost of clearing the site! The sketch-books were put aside, the gentle researches were abandoned for a campaign in real earnest to save Houghton. It proved to be my grandfather's baptism of fire in the developing movement for preservation, it was to be a long struggle and last eight years. To his amazement he found that there was nothing but the most vestigial legislation to protect ancient monuments, the National Trust had few resources at this time, the Royal Fine Arts Commission was only formed in 1924 and only the Society For The Protection of Ancient Buildings had any teeth whatever. The powerlessness of those that knew and cared, whipped my grandfather's feelings into a fury and from this time forward he was tireless in explaining the need for pressure groups in town and country to batter away at a detached government and an indifferent populace. Out of Houghton House were forged some long and lasting friendships as well as important contacts with existing societies; twelve years later he was to be instrumental in the founding of the Georgian Group, nearly forty years later in supporting the Victorian Society, the polemics of preservation were to occupy him increasingly for the remainder of his life.

The campaign to save Houghton began in earnest; my grandfather contacted influential friends in the architectural world and locally began a fund with the same sort of enthusiasm that had won Gayler his horse. Houghton was a very important building to architects but apart from its romantic appearance probably lacked significance for the general public. But it had one extraneous connection with a famous figure that was bound to give it considerable prominence. Since the publication of the Rev A. J. Foster's *Bunyan's Country* in 1901, it had been associated with the 'House Beautiful' of *The Pilgrim's Progress*. Bunyan's travels must certainly have taken him past it, he is supposed to have mended pots there and it is at least likely that he used familiar landscape in his book. Foster's conjectures became a very pleasant legend and it was exactly the story that my grandfather needed. The Bunyan connection provided a national point of interest and he was ready to write to *The Times* and announce that he was opening a subscription to buy Houghton.

He received tremendous support from all over the country from Lord Harlech and Lord Ullswater, from the explorer Sir Francis Younghusband and the writer and biographer Annette M. B. Meakin. The fund began to rise slowly and with the addition of a generous sum from S. H. Whitbread, the Lord-Lieutenant and his old friend Anthony Wingfield, it seemed that there was a real possibility of buying the third of an acre on which the mansion stood. Whitbread, Wingfield and Lord Harlech had each contributed £50, but important additional help had come from the members of the Bedford Arts Club. After months of activity, my grandfather was finally able to go to the farmer with an offer of £300 for the site, reasonable at the time for the small fraction of his land concerned. The farmer instantly refused this and all negotiations and hopes were halted.

Sir Francis Younghusband who was compiling a book on one of the families that had owned Houghton, wrote to my grandfather consolingly – 'If only I could finish these old collections of Letters, a few allusions to both houses might revive interest in the beautiful ruins. I know how much it all owes to you'. A gloom descended on my grandfather at Avenue House, but he was not easily beaten and stored up his energy and his facts for another attempt.

For four years nothing happened, the masonry continued to crumble and original features of great interest collapsed into shoulder high bushes, while the farmer remained intractable. My grandparents kept a watchful eye on the place, visited it from time to time and employed a photographer to record it. One day they took Alfred Gotch, the historian and author of *Growth of the English House*, round the ruins; he confirmed that it was unique and must be saved at any cost.

In 1928 they launched a second campaign to preserve Houghton, this was to coincide with the tercentenary of Bunyan's birth, wide publicity was given to the plight of the house in twenty newspapers, the net contribution of all this effort being a donation of £5! 'We are afraid that the opportunity to purchase the remains of the historical mansion will lapse if we do not get a powerful authority . . . to take it over,' my grandfather wrote to the National Trust in July 1928, 'that would be a thousand pities'.

That year Wingfield had an exhibition of Bunyan relics at Ampthill House in order to raise money for Houghton, David Cox's watercolour of it was shown along with many other mementoes of the Pembroke and Ailesbury families. This brought the fund up to £500 by the December of 1930 and my grandfather with the Bedford Arts Club were able to make an offer acceptable to the farmer.

The ruins were now in their hands and he and some enthusiasts began to make good the more critical places, removing ivy and undergrowth until a permanent owner could be found. The problem was to place it under permanant safe-keeping and undeterred by a refusal two years earlier, he again wrote to the National Trust with the support of both Sir Laurence Weaver and Alfred Bossom. Lord Ullswater replied to him in February 1931 –

'I happened today to attend a meeting of the National Trust Council, when the question of Houghton ruins came up. The Council's architect recently examined the ruins and reported that there had been such decay since 1895 when he had previously seen them that it would take from £1,500 to £2,000 to put them in safe and permanent repair. Some of the Council were in favour of taking over the ruins as they stood and letting them gradually fall down; but the majority thought that a Trust could not do this, as their duty is to retain any property in their hands and that they would be much blamed if the ruins fell down. Anyhow they decided against taking them over, but suggested very like the Office of Works would do so. The Office of Works have taken over ruins in different parts of the country and maintain them, charging a small fee to the public for admission.'

Ullswater's comments were sensible and my grandfather's toil was rewarded later in the same year when, with the aid of Sir Charles Pears, Houghton was at last taken over by the Office of Works, completely surveyed, the interiors cleared and the brickwork and masonry made weatherproof.

Even then my grandfather was not finished with Farmer Stops 'That beast on the hill!' Some way to the east of the ruins were the magnificent tithe barns that had served the Houghton estate for three hundred years, their timber frames filled with small Tudor bricks, a graceful contrast to the jagged teeth of the ruins opposite. As a group on that open hillside, they were superb, but they were dilapidated and the original tile roofs had been replaced by unsightly corrugated iron. The interiors however were like cathedrals and the woodwork of brace, beam and trusses was in perfect order. The barns were naturally not included in the deal with the Office of Works and as soon as that was completed, Farmer Stops decided to have them down! My grandfather again rushed into the fray and made all sorts of proposals which were ignored. One of these had a touch of originality. The tithe barn was to be surveyed, numbered timber by timber, and after demolition, re-erected as a church hall for St Stephen's, St Albans, where he was then carrying out work for the Rev Cavalier. This scheme failed too and the barns were pulled down without further attempts to save them.

The visitors continued to flow down to Ampthill for Georgian weekends at Avenue House; they were often taken up to Houghton to see the refurbished shell of the house 'Look at the devices of the Pembroke family between the metope and the triglyphs of the frieze,' cried my grandfather, 'Wild beasts exactly like the people who tried to stop me saving the place!'

Guests were mostly those architects, artists and writers, who shared grandfather's love of the Georgian age, any who did not, were quickly converted to it by even the briefest stay under his roof. Brendan Bracken, the fiery red-haired journalist, who later became a distinguished politician and cabinet minister was one of the regular occupiers of the four-post bedsteads. On one occasion, when turning up unexpectedly with Sir Edwin Lutyens' son Robert, he found nobody at home and realised that he was out of money! A very flustered maid fetched the elderly chaperone who was looking after my mother, then a little girl of thirteen. The chaperone took one look at Bracken's red hair and decided that neither of the young men should be lent any money and certainly not admitted! Bracken pleaded with her, told her that he was the editor of *English Life* 'the most up and coming newspaper', that his companion's father had designed the Cenotaph in Whitehall, all to no avail! The chaperone having been suspicious of his appearance was even more suspicious of his well-known charm, so the two of them had to sit on the Avenue House doorstep till eleven o'clock at night, when the grandparents returned!

Robert Lutyens' comment on this escapade was rather typical. Many years later on hearing that a friend of his had struck up an acquaintance with the Richardsons, he looked thoughtful.

'Have you ever stayed at Avenue House?' He queried.

'No' replied the other.

'Then don't!' came the reply, 'the mattresses are stuffed with Georgian wigs!'

The discomfort at Avenue House, no electricity, little gas, but liberal candles and lamps, was overlaid by the sheer excitement of staying there. The eighteenth-century frolics were only one side of the Professor's exuberance, the little pranks perpetually played on guests were another. In the collection he had a most remarkable series of painted wooden dummy-boards, cut-out figures with which the seventeenth and eighteenth-century gentlemen of quality had 'peopled' their rooms. Most of them were about six feet tall, very realistic and included a maidservant, a pipe smoker, a man with a monkey, a hooded female and a pair of children. There were also a spaniel, a lion and some soldiers but these were less obtrusive. My grandfather had a mysterious way of spiriting these figures about the house, so that they were suddenly on landings, round corners and in rooms that were not well-lighted at the best of times. The effect on guests was predictable, their surprise usually being followed by a delighted chortle from behind a nearby door! Nor was my grandfather above hiding in wardrobes in full Georgian costume, only to spring forth when the guest had extinguished his last candle! Denis Flanders' treatment in 1938 was typical of the *bonhomie* extended to most late-rising friends and family by his irrepressible sense of fun.

'I was awakened by a loud bang upon my bedroom door', he recalled, 'which opened to admit a helmet thrust forward on the end of a spear held by the Professor himself. "Up" he said, "Glorious day – lots to do!" '

The stream of friends continued year by year, A. C. Powys, the brother of John Cowper Powys was always staying, so were Sir Walter Peacock and Lord 'Jack' Stanmore, a specially close friend. Sacheverell Sitwell came over with a party of Georgians, the whole of the Art Workers Guild spent the day at Avenue House and parties of students from University College were generously entertained. One newcomer whom my grandfather immediately took to was a young poet and writer who came down from the *Architectural Review* to see the house, accompanied by his young wife. His name was John Betjeman and he was whisked through the rooms in a Georgian haze, returning to London to put his feelings into words. 'I hope I shall see you again soon,' he wrote, 'You have written the two bibles of my life; *Monumental Classic Architecture of the 18th and 19th Centuries*, and *Regional Architecture in the West of England*. If I were king, I would give you a peerage.'

His commitments in London were very heavy and Avenue House formed a welcome respite to them. He took the train from Ampthill or Luton nearly every weekday morning, dividing his time between the Bartlett School at University College with four lectures a week and the architectural practice at 41 Russell Square. Even the train journeys were periods of ceaseless work and research, a cursory glance at the newspaper being followed by renewed activity with sketch-books and lecture notes and lists of slides, his enthusiasm sometimes breaking out in discussions with fellow passengers! Some surprising chance friendships were procured in this way, the most spectacular being the Hodgsons.

One evening at St Pancras station, my grandfather had found a railway compartment to himself and was enjoying the prospect of displaying a whole series of new photographs of Avenue House all round the empty seats. A minute before the train was due to leave, the door swung open and much to his irritation, a wiry man with spectacles entered the compartment and sat down opposite him. My grandfather glared and then quite undeterred began to arrange his photographs all over the remaining seats and right up to the place where the stranger was sitting. After running to and fro and crowing to himself over the photographs, my grandfather turned to his companion with a triumphant snort.

'Do you realise', he said defiantly, 'that I live in the most beautiful house in Bedfordshire!'

'Nonsense', said the stranger, putting down his paper, 'I do!'

Such a reply was bound to amuse grandfather, first with astonishment and then with interest. His travelling companion was John Hodgson, an engineer and intellectual, who lived with his wife at Eggington House near Leighton Buzzard and was as forthright in his own views as the Professor. Eggington was tall and Queen Anne, three storeys of white sash windows looked out on to a carriage sweep and lavender-filled gardens, it deserved the high praise that John Hodgson had bestowed on it. The Hodgsons became firm friends and the visits between Ampthill and Eggington were frequent, both houses being bookish and conversational in a rather bucolic neighbourhood. John Hodgson was an engineer at Kent's of Luton, his wife Joan was a former suffragette and the granddaughter of a Scottish marquess. They were both extreme Fabians and had reached a remarkable level of emancipation for the 1920s, husband and wife each owning a three-wheeler Scott Sociable of equal horse-power! Short, slight and good-looking, Joan Hodgson had enormous presence and was the only woman from whom my grandfather would ever tolerate flat contradictions. 'His wife may be able to listen to him as if he is the sun, the moon and the stars,' she commented one day, 'but I am not!'

The Hodgsons came over with their three children to Ampthill and my grandparents returned the visits, occasionally by coach. Joan Hodgson later described this vehicle as 'what the Professor liked to describe as a coach'. It was in fact a rather broken-down brougham which he had somehow or other unearthed from the back of the *White Hart* hotel and persuaded Manton, the elderly hotel coachman to drive. After a perilous journey of more than two hours, the Hodgsons would come out on the steps to greet the cloaked and wigged party as they burst into the drive, propelled by a scraggy horse and the sounds of Hanslip Fletcher trying to blow a horn! The eldest Hodgson daughter found time at Ampthill to write her name on a piece of bare wall and my grandfather behaved absolutely characteristically when he found 'Quack Quack' in huge letters among the Serres and Rowlandsons. He turned the little girl over his knee and gave her a good spanking while her parents looked approvingly on!

One day in 1930 a telephone message came from Joan Hodgson asking if she might bring over a guest to Avenue House for the day, she did not add that she had thought of the idea because she was at the end of her tether! Mrs Hodgson's long pre-war devotion to women's suffrage meant that she had kept up a continual if not close connection with the Pankhurst family, particularly with Sylvia Pankhurst. The most radical of the Pankhursts, Sylvia had exchanged womens rights for communism after 1919, she secretly visited Lenin in 1920 and in the same year was inciting the army and navy to rebel against capitalism. But her individuality, drive and generosity were too great for doctrinaire members and she was expelled from the party, returning once more to the political wilderness. This was soon followed by some time in the *social* wilderness, because Sylvia, aged forty-five, decided to have a baby; this was not as a result of a great passion, but of her inalienable rights as a woman. The child was born in 1927 amid a great deal of controversy, attacking newspaper articles and hostile critics. For three years she weathered the storm, but when her little son developed an illness in 1930, she herself collapsed, the long years of hunger-striking and fighting having taken their toll.

Obviously the distraught mother and child had to be given

refuge away from publicity and it was John Hodgson's offer of shelter that brought them both to Eggington. Almost as soon as the pair had arrived in Bedfordshire, it was discovered that the little boy needed an operation for tonsilitis and it was arranged that he should have the surgery locally. Sylvia became absolutely hysterical when she had to be parted from her child and the Hodgsons had the greatest difficulty to keep her calm during the days until he was returned. They were also putting up with a barrage of questions from their children 'Why hasn't Sylvia got a husband?' 'Why hasn't Richard got a father?' Questions that were not easy to answer and were complicated when the father turned up at Eggington and proved to have a different name from Sylvia! Joan Hodgson wracked her brains for ways of occupying Sylvia's mind, at last she thought of my grandfather and a day out at Avenue House!

The visit was proposed to my grandparents. My grandmother was not very happy about it, she did not share any of Sylvia's causes, was the least feminist of women herself and was doubtful of the day's success. My grandfather was completely different, he responded immediately, insisted that they should come at once and determined to give them a wonderful visit. As was very often the case, my grandmother was overruled and they were asked to come in time for lunch and spend the whole afternoon and evening at Ampthill.

Sylvia came over from Eggington in a three-wheeler and was shown everything in the house by my grandfather. She looked at pictures and clocks, sat in the sedan-chair, examined the lock of Nelson's hair, heard my grandfather read, saw him sketch and looked at his latest books. During lunch, while he talked and she listened, the little boy played and piped under the dining-table, following with his fingers the patterns of the rich Persian carpet. Then there was a walk in the garden, grandfather showing her the Avenue and the Temple, pointing out the distant walled garden of 'the House Beautiful', the ice-house, the well and the brewery roofs. With enormous compassion and skill he steered this shattered woman with the horsy face and projecting teeth, through a whole afternoon of hope. He shared his hopes in art and architecture, his unquenchable love of the country, his unrivalled knowledge of its buildings, his infectious joy in all that he did. When the party finally met in the cobbled courtyard before the return to Eggington, there was something approaching a smile on that wan grey face.

His expanding interests within the county led to many other contacts, some with small but absorbing design work at the end of them. His commitments included a long service on the Grand Jury, the governorships of various schools and a long-standing membership of the Harpur Trust, Bedford's leading charity. He had also become friendly with Herbrand, 11th Duke of Bedford and had advised on improvements and restorations at Woburn.

The Duke was a strange mixture of the autocratic and the amenable, on some occasions when he was with my grandfather he could be as nervous as one of his own deer, at other times as obstinate as a mule. One afternoon when he had been bidden to tea at the Abbey and had made his way through corridor after corridor, he was greeted in the Duke's room with a barking of small dogs and a slightly agitated looking Duke Herbrand. The Duchess he was given to understand had been flying that afternoon, but had not yet landed her light plane on the air-strip. The Duke looked at his watch, then at the window, then at the footman who was laying tea for three. When the news was brought that Duchess Mary had returned, the Duke, still agitated, motioned my grandfather to sit down and in doing so collided with the flimsy tea table. A naturally clumsy man, he was unable to steady himself and brought down the whole contents on to the carpet. Cucumber sandwiches, small cakes and savouries were strewn over the room, and worst of all, a ton of lump sugar cascaded out of the top-heavy basket and rolled under the French furniture. The Duke looked at my grandfather in real consternation.

'Quick Richardson!' he said, 'for heaven's sake help me get it up before the Duchess arrives!'

Both men then went down on their knees, the Duke scooping up hand-fulls of cucumber and pastry, my grandfather ranging round the corners of the room, peering under the armchairs for the fugitive sugar. The last few lumps were being retrieved when the door flew open and the Duchess came in! Greeting her across the room, were a pair of well-padded behinds, one wedged under a French table and probably recognisable as Duke

Herbrand's, the other grovelling by the fireplace, his architectural adviser. The Duke turned round in absolute terror to face her!

The Duke retained a sort of skittishness when the Duchess wasn't present. On one visit when my grandfather was taken to see some special paintings on an upper floor, he was amazed to see Duke Herbrand drop to his knees at the foot of the main staircase and ascend it on all fours like a giant tweedy dog.

'I like it!' he commented over his shoulder to his astonished friend.

Although he lived in great awe of his wife, the Duke could be excessively obstinate and truculent as a client. After Duchess Mary's death, he consulted my grandfather over the placing of a stained-glass window in her memory at Woburn church. Her great love of wildlife was to be commemorated in wide panels of birds and flowers, all of the Duke's choice and all in rather bright colours. The ducal choice was not at all suitable for the church, a great French Gothic pile by the Victorian architect Henry Clutton. Worst of all the inclusion of this glass meant the altering of the window on the south side, destroying the unity of the interior. My grandfather, so tactful with clients, tried to get this changed, first the glass and then the window.

'It would be so much better my dear Duke, if the glass were brought into line with the architecture,' he protested, or again, 'If the windows are kept uniform it will be better for the architecture!'

'Why do you keep talking about the *architecture*', the Duke snapped back, 'I am not interested in the architecture, the window will be so beautiful that nobody will notice any *architecture*!'

My grandfather submitted; even among friends the job of the architect is not easy!

CHAPTER FOUR

An afternoon with Thomas Hardy

For some years previous to coming to Avenue House, my grandfather had been architect to the Duchy of Cornwall's West of England estates. It was an appointment that greatly pleased him for he felt a great affinity with the West Country, loved its rolling hills, dramatic coastlines and highly individual small cities and towns. The Duchy properties were very extensive so that he had been involved with new buildings as far apart as West Dorset and the tip of Cornwall, Hampshire and the villages skirting Bristol. Sir Walter Peacock, the able and benign Secretary to the Duchy had given him a pretty free hand and he had designed farmsteads, farm buildings, model dwellings, cottages and offices for the estate. For a Londoner with a score of office blocks to his credit, the simple forms of farmhouses and cottage rows were something of a new departure. On each succeeding visit he learnt more about the building methods of the far west, began to respond to stone and slate, notice the storm porches, gambrel roofs and hugging dry stone walls of those windswept farming lands. His own essays in this style were delightfully straightforward, solid farmhouses at Stoke Climsland and Whiteford, pretty rows of cottages at Princetown on Dartmoor, all the time storing up facts about the local techniques and continuing to use them wherever possible.

Designs of a similar nature were occupying him at home, in the years after his arrival in Ampthill he became involved in extending or restoring many of the smaller manor houses and in building some new homes. He had first of all designed and built the Homelands farmhouse for Mrs Ridgeway, in the Warren Field overlooking the Avenue House garden, using a frontage and plan of such subtlety and good manners that weathering has made it indistinguishable from a genuine house of 1810! There had followed alterations at Flitwick Manor, Harlington Manor, Milton Ernest and The Hale at Wendover for Sir Bruce Hamilton. These were the small *jeux d'esprit* of a very big and active practice, but they gave him an opportunity and excuse to use traditional methods. The stacks of sketch-books and notebooks which were added to in Cornwall and Devonshire or on the other building sites, found their way on to the loaded shelves at Ampthill. In the long evenings with the oil-lamp alight beside him, my grandfather compressed their contents into the more manageable form of books and articles.

Three books came out rapidly one after the other soon after his arrival at Ampthill. The first was the result of all the labours in Cornwall and the West, *Regional Architecture in the West of England*, compiled with his London partner C. L. Gill and illustrated by many of his own sketches. Every class of building was included, mansions and markets, shops and prisons, inns and gateways, all born out of his love for the subject and an infectious enjoyment of it that came through the pages. When it appeared in 1924 he inscribed a copy to my grandmother as follows 'To my dear Wife From The Author who sticks his head into books. A tribute to faithful aiding and abetting'.

The next book was a subject prompted by his country house work, almost by the move to Avenue House itself. This was *The Smaller English House of the Later Renaissance 1660–1830*, which he worked on in collaboration with the American writer Harold Donaldson Eberlein, again it was sprinkled with his own drawings. The houses dealt with were all from that group of medium-sized homes, manors and town-houses which had escaped the net and the notice of other authors, through being too small or too little-known. This like its predecessor covered much new ground because my grandfather was indefatigable in worrying-out information about a house or an architect, the date or origin becoming an excuse for a new flight of fancy!

It was always an experience to go with him on an expedition to a 'new' house, he was by no means always an expected guest, thinking little of demanding admission to any place he admired and even asking himself to tea if the architecture warranted it! 'My dear sir, I am one of the Royal Commissioners on Historic Monuments', was often the opening phrase, the prelude to a very literal foot in the door and a complete search of the house from cellars to attics before the astonished gaze of the owners. He would flash those hooded eyes round the interior, give a general synopsis of the house's history, the pattern-books the architect or builder had used, the office he might have been trained in, the type of wall-paper originally hanging in the main room 'Put it back dear lady!' and the colour scheme the possessor should adopt throughout! These off the cuff remarks were often spiced with Richardsonisms 'Good God – the desolation of tesselation' of one unfortunate addition to a Regency house or 'I see you're living under the Reign of Terracotta' of another house built in the 1880s!

Owners usually succumbed to his charm and the currant cake was brought out while he talked and attributed, re-attributed and post-attributed their house to a string of architects between gulps of tea. Those who suspected his powers of dating and accepted them with a wink, were often compelled to eat their words, for his accuracy was uncanny. One country house he visited in Rutland had a late eighteenth-century addition including a shallow bay window. My grandfather surveyed this for some time from the lawn and remarked 'Very good of 1787'. The comment was taken at its face value, 1790 perhaps, possibly 1780 at a pinch, but why 1787? Some months after the visit, the owner and his wife were cutting back the old wisteria which circled that side of their house and there on a chiselled stone, plain to anyone on a ladder, though not from below, was the date the Professor had given, 1787!

When my grandfather was called in to advise Beverley Nicholls about his attractive old house on the Green at Ham, he went over and spent an afternoon with the writer examining everything in detail. Every cornice, every chimney-piece or door handle gave him clues as to the house's history and Beverley Nicholls followed him around fascinated. 'You know, professor', he commented after an hour of surreptitious unravellings piece by piece, 'I shall have to write a book about a detective and make him an architect like you, uncovering the story on the barest shreds of evidence!'

The Duchy of Cornwall owned a considerable amount of land in Dorset and much of it in the little village of Fordington on the very outskirts of Dorchester itself. My grandfather had designed an attractive terrace of cottages on a sloping site in the village, grey brick, with sash windows, the Prince of Wales feathers delicately incised on a stone inset, denoting their ownership. It was a sensitive little composition in a sprawling village, as classically correct as any of the sashed houses in Dorchester's main street, yet very unobtrusive and regional. This was as it should be, for further along the road in the same village was Max Gate, the home of Thomas Hardy, who was still living there in old age with his second wife.

In August 1924 my grandfather and grandmother were making a tour of the West Country before settling down to a busy winter at Ampthill. *Regional Architecture* had been published that year, *The Smaller English House* was with the publishers, B. T. Batsford, and he was now putting his finishing touches to a third book *The English Inn Past and Present* due in 1925. Although my grandfather was by no means a great imbiber of public houses, I never recall him entering any of the Ampthill ones, he *was* a great patron of British roads and the great hostelries they sustained; the outcome of this interest was this book, the quest for information brought him to Dorset. After visiting the most important inns in Dorchester, the *Antelope*, the *King's Arms* and the *White Hart*, the grandparents drove on to Fordington to inspect the Duchy cottages, but first they called on Thomas Hardy at Max Gate.

It was not a totally unpremeditated call. My grandfather had asked Sir Walter Peacock whether he thought it was a good idea and Peacock had agreed that it was, grandfather's profession and connection with Fordington being a good introduction. Sir Walter had informed him that when he had taken the young Prince of Wales to Max Gate the previous summer 'Hardy was very pleased and felt it was quite a compliment' but being a retiring man he did not like being lionised.

Grandfather's admiration for Hardy's works was unbounded, his feelings about his poetry more reticent. The novelist's first career as an architect which came over so strongly in stories like *A Laodicean*, and *Desperate Remedies* was naturally of interest to him for he saw in it an accurate reflection of his own experiences in the profession during Victoria's reign. The relationships of architect to client, traditionalist to speculative builder, manufacturer to craftsman were tensions that he felt deeply and which were echoed in the Wessex novels. He had turned to Hardy wholeheartedly after the First War and continued to read the works yearly for the rest of his life, it was a passion that he and my grandmother equally shared. The visit, however fleeting, proved to be of considerable significance, it was the only recorded occasion that an architect talked to Hardy about his first career.

'I left my wife in the car', my grandfather recalled in later years, 'I did not want to embarrass Hardy with her presence as well – and went up to the door. Mrs Hardy opened it and asked who I was. I told her that I called at the suggestion of Sir Walter Peacock'.

Mrs Hardy explained to him that Hardy was at that moment sitting to a sculptor, the Russian artist Prince Yourievitch, for his portrait; if my grandfather did not mind waiting a little, Mr Hardy would come down and see him. He was then shown by her into a small downstairs room where Mrs Hardy indicated the writer's huge dog Wessex asleep by the hearth. She motioned him to a seat and then added of the dog, now regarding my grandfather with a cold eye. 'If you sit quietly Mr Richardson, he won't try to floor you!'

Sitting in the room waiting, he looked about him, noticing in particular that there were few pictures. When asked about this many years afterwards, he smiled brightly and said 'You see the pictures were all in his mind.'

'A little later I heard footsteps coming downstairs. Soon Hardy was in the room, the dog disappeared and we were able to talk quietly and naturally. He had a countrified voice, and enormous head, especially for such a small man, 5 feet 2 inches or so. He certainly seemed to sum me up correctly. I had not come out of mere inquisitiveness but to learn his views on architecture.'

'I began as an architect,' he said, 'I was with an architect at

Weymouth and we did various repairs to churches and we went from one church to another and eventually I left him and went off to London, and there I became an assistant to Arthur Blomfield. At the time he was designing a Bank in Fleet Street. I got tired of that and I started to write in the evening and got talked about'.

My grandfather was 'staggered at Hardy's knowledge of local architecture and lore'. Having just visited the three great inns of Dorchester, he discussed these with Hardy as well as local customs such as 'skimmingtons, tranters, etc'.

Hardy told him of a notice built into the side of Grays Bridge in the town, threatening any damager of the bridge with transportation for life. My grandfather jotted this down in his notebook and had the notice photographed for the forthcoming work.

Hardy had gone on to talk with him about the place of architecture in his own work as a writer. 'It taught me to place one thing on the other – it taught me taste – and I began to select views and ideas and localities – it made a great impression on me.' My grandfather explaining this said 'Architecture taught him to put one thing correctly, accurately and squarely upon another . . . he could build a human soul with human material in the same way'.

Grandfather told Hardy that he had read *Far From The Madding Crowd* at the age of seven.

'Wherever did you read that?' Hardy had asked.

'I spelt it out in *The Graphic*', he replied. 'when it was in serial form!'

He mentioned to Hardy that he was going on to inspect the Duchy cottages that he had designed in the village a few years before. Hardy at once suggested that while he was still at Fordington he should 'look around the ruins of a cottage there as he might find something interesting'. He had taken the novelist's advice and on going over to the derelict cottage had found a seventeenth-century barred bacon grill, which he valued very much for its connection with Hardy and which he took home to Ampthill to decorate his kitchen.

Of Max Gate itself, that strange villa that the writer had designed for himself in 1885, my grandfather's comments were brief, but not unenthusiastic – 'Simple, spacious and un-assuming – typical of the man. It was built to the traditional Dorset plan with a central stairway.' Or again 'Yes Hardy certainly showed his good taste in designing Max Gate. It was traditional and austere – like houses in Jane Austen.'

Before he had finally left Max Gate and shaken hands with Hardy on the threshold, he had asked for a photograph of the writer. A studio portrait was hurriedly found and given to him. It was of Hardy in the academic dress of some university that had recently bestowed a doctorate on him, the hood and gown seemed to swathe itself round the frail figure and the Tudo-bethan cap almost crushed that wistful observant face. Hardy did not sign it, simply writing on the back 'Not to be reproduced without permission,' but it was the bacon grill rather than the photograph that he liked to recall the afternoon by.

Returning from Dorset my grandparents had made a cir-cuitous route to take in Snowshill Manor near Broadway; this was the home of Charles Wade and few tours failed to include at least one night with the mysterious owner of this Cotswold house. There was an evening of gossip, talking about Hardy and Dorset in front of Wade's crackling fire before the last seventy miles to Ampthill.

Charles Wade was a long-standing friend of my grandfather's, they had entered architecture at about the same time, and their passionate interest in craftsmanship and the past had drawn them together. Wade was a very striking figure indeed and even in old age when I saw the two friends together, a rather frightening one! He was not tall and rather slight in build, but his angular features and sharp nose were surrounded by long straight grey hair worn shoulder length. The effect was rather like that of a wig or of the loose hair shown in the more infor-mal portraits of Charles II's time. Added to this, both he and his sisters had rather waxy complexions and looked like the ala-baster images of fifteenth-century tomb chests, by some strange twist of fate they seemed to have re-emerged into twentieth-century Gloucestershire. Although my grandfather hankered after eighteenth-century costume, he conditioned himself to wearing the conventional jacket and trousers of the businessman. Not so Wade, he was never to be seen in anything but breeches, stockings and buckled shoes with a loose shirt above them, an apparition likely to bring a chill into any heart not expecting it!

Similar in outlook and aims, Wade and my grandfather had completely different backgrounds. While grandfather's early career had been a struggle against family finances, Wade had been a wealthy man whose architectural schemes were a hobby rather than a headache. Wade's father had been a sugar planter in St Kitts on lands that the family had owned since the eighteenth century. His family has actually been involved in legal actions with the great William Beckford, an historical connection that my grandfather much appreciated. Wade had toyed with his architecture, designed a few buildings, but on inheriting the family estates had concentrated solely on restoration at the manor and his own ability as a craftsman.

At about the same time that my grandfather discovered Avenue House, Charles Wade had discovered Snowshill Manor, tucked away in a remote village above Broadway. The whole place shimmered with that golden-brown stone of the Cotswolds, and richer in colour, more architectural than its neighbours, was the derelict manor house, once the dowry of Queen Catherine Parr and the home of the Warners, Walls and Sanbachs. This building was close to the little church and literally dug into the hillside with the remains of terrace gardens stretching below it until they became orchards and fields. The handsome seventeenth-century entrance front shaded by trees had struck Wade's imagination before he had found unspoilt interiors of Tudor and early Georgian date, all decaying, neglected and ravaged by years of farm tenants. He had at once seen its possibilities and after purchasing spent a lifetime restoring it to its former glory, finally giving it to the National Trust.

Painstaking and methodical, Wade opened up his own workshop in the basement and patiently standing at the bench year in and year out, the wood shavings covering his buckled shoes, he repaired the manor timber by timber, panel by panel. There was little that he could not do, he carved, gilded and turned everything himself and almost totally restored the Brandreth family chaise single handed. And yet there was something rather mischievous about Wade and the old inscriptions on chests, grinning faces from beams and convincing sunbursts on ceilings did not always have the antiquity one at first supposed! The income from the sugar plantations provided for this devoted and leisurely existence; it was fortunate that they did for the antiques, tapestries, armour and costume continued to flow in from east and west the whole time that he lived there.

The keynote at Snowshill was smoke and murk, the first belching out in puffs or more thought-provoking wisps from the open fires, the second hanging round the heavily panelled rooms like a ghostly presence. There was always the smell of wood smoke at Snowshill, burning oak or apple in the hot ash, pervading the whole house even in summertime and mixing with the odours of drying pomanders and old faded stuffs. Lavender or orange-blossom scents might seep through an open door for an instant but were soon overcome by the all-embracing smells of age. Several of the fireplaces were large enough to contain ingle-nooks and deep recesses and Wade (and later his wife) made great play of these with his slightly sinister sense of humour. Either he would sit as still as a waxwork till one suddenly saw him or to my terror as a child, leap out from the parted flames of the fire with grey hair streaming. I somehow preferred my grandfather's less menacing japes!

Brilliant joiner and cabinet-maker that he was, Wade was well able to make these trades serve his sense of mystery. Whether the original owners of Snowshill had had priests' holes and secret passages is uncertain, but they certainly proliferated after Wade's arrival. Guests would all of a sudden find that their host had materialised through solid panels, making himself known by nothing more than a slight intake of breath. Sometimes he would disappear leaning against a tapestry or appear to vanish as he stood by an inlaid star on the floor! For anyone to accomplish such tricks it would have been disconcerting, but Wade's noiseless and cat-like actions made it doubly so, it was not surprising that the villagers were suspicious. Nor were the rooms in which his friends slept much more re-assuring, for Wade's tastes were catholic and very bizarre. Each chamber was given a mellifluous but cryptic name which related either to their contents or their position in the house, among them Turquoise Hall, Meridian, Zenith, Admiral, Seraphim, Top

Royal, Top Gallant, Mizzen and Mermaid. A bewildered visitor might find himself lodged for a weekend among suits of *samurai* armour or walls full of hideous native weaponry, prospects not improved by Wade as he handed out the bedtime candles – 'Don't touch the Spanish chest in your room, its designed to cut intruders' hands off!'

Charles Wade was not an intellectual or even very bookish, his dictum was 'Think a lot, say a little and write less' but he did entertain generously at Snowshill. My grandfather stayed there with Francis Brett Young and many other writers and artists who came out of curiosity to see the Manor's weird owner. Lovett Gill stayed sometimes, Hanslip Fletcher and Kenneth Hobson were frequent visitors and my grandfather brought with him cars full of students to 'savour the atmosphere'. His genius, as my grandfather realised, was in piecing together the house and mixing so many strange objects in such a satisfactorily visual way that they became timeless. There were sombre rooms bright with oriental lacquer or glaring Italian cabinets, deceptively small rooms heaped with musical instruments, keys, telescopes, Tibetan scrolls and scientific instruments. The barn-like garret at the top of the house called 'A Thousand Wheels' was crowded with every type of wooden-wheeled vehicle, hobby horses, velocipedes, childs' go-carts and the models of farm wagons and stage coaches, many made by Wade himself.

The only help he ever received at Snowshill was in the decoration and mural work from the poster artist Helen Cosomarti. Much of this was in the greens and faded golds of Pre-Raphaelitism, for Wade both in appearance and attitudes hailed from that movement or at least from the Morrisite end of it.

Snowshill had a strange effect on my grandfather. Whether it was the stone-built manor or the sudden injection of Cotswold air, his vivacity and outrageousness seemed to quadruple the moment the car nosed its way into Wade's courtyard. Ebullient and effervescent at Ampthill, he became overpoweringly so at Snowshill, continually talking, examining Wade's latest acquisitions and hardly able to contain his delight. He would usually arrive with a jar of expensive Grecian honey for Wade, because he knew Wade liked it. Wade always complained that he never saw the honey at all because my grandfather himself consumed it so quickly, what was left that is, from the frequent spillages on Wade's oaken table top. Meals indeed were haphazard affairs, for the manor contained no cooking facilities whatever, some dishes were prepared on the open fires but most had to be prepared by village women in the gardener's cottage. When Wade felt it was time to eat, he would clap his hands at the doorway and a solemn little procession of Gloucestershire wenches, all different shapes and sizes, would proceed from cottage to manor, each with a soup, a fish or a vegetable under silver covers. Often a child would bring up the rear carrying a pie or a Stilton as big as itself. With the courses served and the wine circulating, my grandfather would begin his favourite trick of drawing things upside down for his fellow diners across the table while Wade watched fascinatedly. The big 'Black Beauty' pencil slid across the paper and architecture, capricci and crowds emerged, generally these because he was poor at caricature. In the afternoons there were visits to F. L. Griggs or Commander Fred Hart at Chipping Campden, to Mrs Clegg at Broadway or Sir Philip and Lady Stott at Stanton Court. Grandfather irrepressible and bubbly and impatient for the evening's entertainments to begin.

These entertainments were more in the nature of one man shows by my grandfather, unscripted, impromptu, given simply for his fellow guests enjoyment and his own amusement. Kate Murray, the authoress, who with her husband and daughter were frequent visitors, wrote enthusiastically about the entertainments before a weekend in July 1925 – 'We are looking forward to fresh scenes from 18th-century high and low life, and a repetition of all the old ones'. It had to be confessed that with my grandfather the low life ones were a speciality!

Fortunately there was a sort of natural stage at Snowshill. At one end of the Hall there was a screen dividing the room from the staircase and the turned ballusters across it made an ideal architectural feature which was brilliantly utilised as a gallery. Lanterns and candles were cleverly concealed and in the shadowy passage behind the grill, my grandfather slowly emerged in wig and cloak impersonating innumerable Georgian

characters himself and conjuring up many more with asides
and imaginary dialogue. Among the favourite sketches were
'The Last Night in the Condemned Hold' with horrifying
groans and oaths and the dragging of chains across the floor and
'The Wives of Wapping Welcoming Home Nelson's Sailors' for
which my grandfather turned female impersonator in falsetto
cockney. Probably the most spine-tingling of these masques was
the one about the 'Plague Year'. For this, the house was completely darkened and nothing could be heard but the distant
footfall of my grandfather as he paced the extremities of the
house with swinging lantern, knocking on doors, opening them
on creaky hinges and intoning menacingly 'Bring out your dead!
Bring out your dead!' A more attractive variant of this was
when my grandfather, who had a good singing voice, sang out
the cries of the various London streets, the melodies getting
nearer and nearer as he walked along the corridors of the manor
accompanied by my mother.

The scene which most of the Snowshill house parties remembered however was 'A Night at an Inn' a splendidly presented
description of eighteenth-century discomfort and grime with
all the right sounds of coaching horns, ostlers shouting and dogs
barking. The audience in the hall below were spared no details
of the sordid inn bedroom, the damp sheets, the soiled maidservant, the lice under the wigs, the fleas in the mattress and
even the unemptied chamber pot below the bedstead! The
action would often end in the crescendo of a sword fight, a
generous selection of weapons being available from Wade's
armoury, before my grandfather finally collapsed exhausted
into a chair. The Murrays recalled one evening when he hit his
head a most tremedous crack on a beam and came reeling out
into the audience clutching it. 'Felled like an ox,' he kept
repeating, 'Felled like an ox!' Then he added more concernedly
'Could it have damaged the brain dear boy, are you sure?' A
minute later, such was his enthusiasm, he was back in the
gallery and continuing the performance to a round of applause!

When the last hectic scramble was over and my grandmother
had signalled that enough was enough, the guests looked at the
dying embers of the fire and climbed the uneven stairs of the
house to their candlelit rooms. Charles Wade was not among

them, for the strangest thing about the strange owner of Snowshill was that he never lived in the manor at all! He let himself out of the house each night and crossed the yard to spend his sleeping hours in 'The Jolly Roger'. This was a very large dog-kennel, where Wade, who had never much fancied beds, simply curled up and went to sleep! It was something of a mystery in my family as to where Wade dressed and undressed for the night, for nobody ever saw him leave 'The Jolly Roger' again and yet he was always spruce in the morning! When I remember him he was married and living with Mrs Wade in the cottage where the cooking was done.

Neither my grandparents nor my mother cared for the nights spent at Snowshill, for there were rumours of hauntings and it was popularly believed that Wade slept elsewhere for that reason. One of the Tudor beds in the manor was set into the panelling of the room and had doors like a cupboard that could shut it in. My mother was occupying this room during one visit and awoke to find the doors shutting on her, motivated by invisible hands. She shrieked and screamed and beat her way out into the room where my grandparents came to the rescue. There was no explanation for what had happened although Wade was suspected. My mother refused to sleep at the manor from then onwards, preferring the *Lygon Arms* at Broadway; my grandparents continued to brave the old rooms and their host's nocturnal prowling.

'When you enter the Manor House at Snowshill', my grandfather wrote in 1930, 'your feelings of surprise give place to deep curiosity. The mental process of reconstructing the past becomes less irksome. The evidences of former luxury become distant, there is something of pathos in imagination. You begin to think less of the objects and wonder what became of the users, those destined in turn to hand on traditions of humanity? ... It is in this enlargement and inspiration that the circle of our sympathies grows; and who in the light of this reasoning will have the temerity to begrudge our bachelor collector his catholicity of taste.'

In 1954 when manor and contents were handed over to the National Trust, there was no more fitting person to perform the ceremony than my grandfather. This he did, in the same hall where he had presided over so many Georgian revels. Charles Wade was there too, still mischievous, waxy complexioned, a medieval face seen through the wood smoke.

CHAPTER FIVE

A Lifetime of Collecting

As my grandmother fully realised, the move to Ampthill had not dampened my grandfather's ardour for antique collecting, if anything it had increased it. She worried about maids, dusting, polishing and arranging the rooms, he simply regarded the spaces remaining as crucial areas to be filled and filled them with astonishing rapidity! It was certainly not that the formation of a collection was taking a more prominent part in his life, it had always been a source of enjoyment, but Avenue House and his books gave him fresh insights. From the first room of his own in his parent's house to his first married quarters in Hampstead, objects that delighted the eye and stirred the imagination had slowly been filtering in. At the turn of the century he had acquired old oak, old brass and earthenware with an innocent, almost naive casualness, not from dealers but from cottagers and barns. Fifty years later when cornering his Rolls at speed in Elstree, he pointed out an old pub to me and remarked gleefully 'Went in there for a beer in 1905 dear boy, came out with a gate-legged table!'

His tastes had changed a lot from those early days but not his methods, a love of the older period of joined furniture which went with his training as an Arts and Crafts architect gave way to more fastidious styles of mahogany and satinwood, he still sought them out in unusual places. There were the predatory raids on Mr Parmiter, but he was interesting himself in much more than old domestic utensils. Both the grandparents were broadening their horizons as collectors and they soon got to know most of the dealers in their adopted county, if not always as allies, at least generally as friends.

One of the earliest contacts that added to the collection at Avenue House was with Mr Davey who had an antique shop at St Peter's Street, Bedford. The shop had a double window on the corner of two streets and was set into a pleasant early nineteenth-century terrace row. The Daveys, there were three of them for Mr Davey had a father and a sister, provided a wide variety of antiques on my grandfather's various jaunts to the shop. The window was crowded with small items laid out on ledges, families of jugs, silver tableware, miniatures and a preponderance of brass. The glass door into the shop was warped and stuck as you opened it and the jarring effect set up the most tremendous rattling of the innumerable objects, cow-bells, horse-brasses, old musical instruments and hunting crops that were wired to it. Large pieces of furniture liberally sprinkled with bits and pieces jutted out from all angles with thin channels of communication between them, closed to all-comers smaller in shape than Miss Davey.

Mr Davey, the christian name was Alfred but was not an appellation indiscriminately used, then approached from behind a curtained recess to greet my grandfather. Mr Davey was a large, impressive, big-featured man, with a Roman nose and a sonorous voice like a bishop's. This gave an impression of faded grandeur which went with the old furniture and stained sun-blind and was a left over of his early ambitions to enter the church. Portly and deliberate, Mr Davey was never to be seen in his shop without a black homburg hat on his head, rising above that large forehead and those bushy eyebrows. As my grandfather was never without a black homburg hat either and was also blessed with bushy eyebrows, it was a somewhat astonishing sight to see them staring at each other across a pile of antiquities! Mr Davey was like the clerk of the weather, in the winter-time he had a grey working jacket and in the summer time a white linen jacket like an umpire's, the black homburg being interchangeable.

Miss Davey was small and vague and with an air of Mrs Gaskell if not of Mrs Micawber about her. Her manner was very much of one who had found themselves in antique dealing by mistake and if 'trade' was mentioned she seemed to hitch up invisible skirts while the unfortunate phrase passed. Miss Davey would have seemed quite small by the side of her stalwart brother but they were in fact rarely seen at the same time. For my grandfather this was always a source of mild irritation, for whatever antique was picked up, whether diminutive thimble, sugar twist wine glass or Georgian sampler, it had invariably been bought by the one who wasn't there.

'How much is this entrée dish Mr Davey?'

The eyebrows ruffled, the homburg hat tilted in obedience to the wrinkled forehead.

'I'm afraid, Professor, I could not say, this dish was bought by Miss Davey and I will have to ask her.'

The fun of collecting was a spontaneous fun for my grandfather and he could only sigh while the entrée dish was removed behind the curtain. When Miss Davey was there at the same time as her brother, things were happier but hardly more speedy.

'I must just go and ask Miss Davey, Professor', was the reply to grandfather's urgent enquiry about a prisoner-of-war model. Mr Davey disappeared and furtive whispering came from behind the curtain. This time they both emerged, Miss Davey first, clasping the model, Mr Davey second, beaming. They had a strange habit between them of pushing their spectacles up on to their foreheads to regard an object with professional close-ness, this they now did, looking like a pair of vintage motor-cyclists donning goggles for a speed track.

'Mr Davey feels with me that it is a very nice model and I should think it would be about five pounds,' said Miss Davey comprehending it with love.

'I am bound to agree with my sister, Professor,' smiled Mr Davey.

It was all amazingly formal, on another occasion it was a little French boat which had been priced differently on at least six visits.

'I nearly entered the little boat to you price seven pounds ten shillings', said Miss Davey gravely, 'when my brother offered it to Mr Wade he said to him "Seventeen" and being hard of hearing I only heard "ten" and have been asking ten pounds for this since in error, is that not so Mr Davey?'

Mr Davey bowed majestically from the back of the shop.

'So we put it aside for your approval,' went on Miss Davey
and then with a faraway expression added, 'May I again say
how much we all appreciate the kind patronage of yourself and
Mrs Richardson and would like to thank you for the pleasant
way in which you come round and look at our poor little show
of antiques'.

This time my grandfather bowed and said, 'My pleasure,
dear lady, my pleasure'. Money was then passed between my
grandfather and Mr Davey, Miss Davey having found something to occupy her in the window while the vulgarity of commerce was attended to. Some of the items purchased must have
been bargains even in their own day, for example, needlework
panel 10s, Chelsea dish £1 10s, ivory and brass quill cutter
3s 6d, mahogany glazed cabinet £3 10s, 4 Worcester pots 15s,
Satinwood tea-caddy 17s 6d. It was from the Davey brother
and sister that he bought one of his most unusual portrait groups
of 'Three Indian Princesses' attributed to Johann Zoffany. Mr
Davey had sent it to Sotheby's in January 1930 but it had failed
to reach the reserve and was bought in for £68. Subsequently
my grandfather bought it from them for £50 and it was despatched to Avenue House and hung by him in the hall where it
remained for the rest of his life. The painting which shows the
Indian girls in three-quarter length, has rich whites and golds
in the brushwork and displays beautifully the women's South
Indian jewellery. It was the latter, that eventually identified the
painting as being by the celebrated Irish painter, Thomas
Hickey, Zoffany himself never having visited South India.

Around the corner from the Daveys at No 1 Tavistock Street,
Bedford, was the antique shop of Frederick Jones, a dapper little
man with a very red face and a remarkable round nose in the
middle of it that exactly resembled a juicy apple. Jones dealt
mostly in furniture and in furniture of a very specialised kind,
Sheraton and Hepplewhite of the best periods, Dutch and
French marquetry, bronzes, English and Irish silver and prints.
The line of expensive cars drawn up outside his windows on a
Saturday morning, my grandfather's old Bentley among them,
showed exactly the kind of clientele that Jones both encouraged
and expected. Those Saturday mornings were very much like a

club for my grandfather, who settled down into one of Jones's comfortable Louis XVI fauteuils to converse with his collector friends. They generally included Samuel Howard Whitbread of Southill Park, Cecil Higgins who was later to found the Bedford Art Gallery and Major Sidney Tabor from Harlington Manor. Mr Whitbread had been his friend for a number of years and he had advised on the magnificent Holland interiors at Southill and was later to write a chapter on its architecture in a book on the house. Cecil Higgins, the wealthy porcelain collector had visited Avenue House many times and Major Tabor had called grandfather in to design additions to Harlington Manor.

In a haze of cigar smoke and talk, deliciously isolated from the busy county town outside, they would enjoy one another's company at Jones's premises, discuss the latest articles in *The Connoisseur* and silently evaluate 'the prize' of that particular morning as they did so. Sometimes it was a magnificent serpentine library table of the 1770s, golden satinwood with fine crossbanding, inlaid sprays of wheat on the frieze, or it could be a set of eight or ten George II salon chairs with the embroidered arms of their owners still on their seats or finely carved giltwood torchéres and *garnatures de cheminee* by Matthew Boulton. It was often a question of amicable agreement as to where 'the prize' of the morning ended up, in the panelled rooms of Harlington, the chaste interiors of Avenue House or at Higgins tall and thin Georgian house in Queen Anne Street!

The impeccable Jones had absolutely no sense of humour and my grandfather's quips and asides had to be kept for more broad-minded dealers. Poor Jones was very sorely tried by the impecunious gentry of Bedfordshire who were for ever 'popping' things at his shop and then wanting them back! The greatest culprit among these was Rowland Crewe Alston of Odell Castle whose family heirlooms, walnut chests on stands, cushion mirrors and immaculate needlework, were frequently to be seen 'on long loan' at No 1 Tavistock Street! The crisis came when a purchaser was found before Mr Alston had shot sufficient rabbits on his estate to buy the whole lot back again! An infuriated landowner would then drive into Bedford and demand of Jones the exact whereabouts of 'his' property. One or two remarkable lots came onto the market in this way, the club of connoisseurs being much amused as the unfortunate Jones was caught in the Morton's fork of avid collector and outraged squire! From Jones he was to buy an early Louis XVI commode for £36, a mantel clock of the same date for £22 and a pair of carved wall-lights for £9 15s. Also from Tavistock Street came the superb white lacquer tables designed by Henry Holland and the other furniture from Oakley House, sold after the death of Lord Ampthill in 1936.

A quite different sort of dealer was to be found at Wheathampstead, which village and North Hertfordshire my grandfather usually took in on his round trips.

'We can't go home without seeing Collins!' he would remark.

F. G. & C. Collins had a corner shop at the top of Wheathampstead High Street, not far from the church. Grandfather had dealt with F. G. Collins 'Old Collins' when he lived at St Albans but my memories are of him visiting 'Young Collins' who had taken on the title of 'Old Collins' when his father died.

Charlie Collins was stumpy, thick-set and a considerable character. He had a sort of ambling walk, a rather square jovial face and a shock of thick white hair which gave him the appearance of a welcoming Scottish terrier. Grandfather would pad round the showrooms, pausing now and again as something took his fancy – 'What's that Collins?'

'Well Professor its a funny old night commode.'

'And that?'

'Its a funny old Sheraton table.'

Most of 'Old' Collins's descriptions of his stock in trade were prefixed by 'funny' or 'old' or both. Collins other expression was 'it's murder!'

On one of our visits my grandfather spotted a nice Sheraton settee from Sir Ernest Cassell's collection.

'How much is that, Collins?' he enquired.

'Fifteen pounds if you dare buy it, but it's murder!' was the reply.

It was eventually acquired by my parents for he had an uncanny eye for spotting things for other people. 'That piece is exactly a Mrs Raikes piece', he would say or 'a friend in Kensington Square is looking for one of those.'

Collins also had an old barn on the edge of Wheathampstead by a corner of the Brockett Road, a long sagging structure with as many doors in it as the flaps of a German Christmas card.It was very like this for every fresh door that Mr Collins dragged back on rickety hinges revealed new heaps of furniture to view, piles of eighteenth-century dining-chairs, side-tables, wardrobes, potties, corner cupboards and wash-stands. Magnificent Chippendale elbow-chairs toothless with missing splats lent at drunken angles and vast Regency tables groaned, not under the barons of beef of former times but under the weight of neglect, decay and the odd jug and basin. My grandfather stood in the overgrown driveway peering into the gloom and pointing with his shooting stick.

'What's that my dear Collins?'

Collins dived into the heap like a wild thing, shoving his stock to left and right, worrying the desired object out of its resting place and finally staggering back into the sun with a grin on his face for it to be inspected.

'I think its a funny old spit thing that they used to use in Buckinghamsheere!' Collins rubbed his chin, which was not always noted for the accuracy with which it met a razor!

'I'll have that', said my grandfather, 'it'll be just the thing for the country cottage I'm creating for myself! Did you know I was creating a country cottage for myself Collins?'

'No sir, I can't say as I did!'

'Yes Collins, at the bottom of my garden, my secret and far-away cottage where I shall write, just like Marie Antoinette at Versailles, Collins, a *ferme ornée*, Collins, a *ferme ornée*!'

'Three pounds ten to you if you dare buy it but it'll kill me!'

Sometimes we penetrated into the old barn itself, a maze of cobwebs and murk with only a few chinks of light coming through crevices and skylights. Furniture was to be seen on all levels, the building had several floors on stages and even the hay loft was crammed with chests. When our eyes were accustomed to the light my grandfather excitedly pointed out the handsome carved end of a Regency sideboard or the carved claw foot of an 1815 breakfast table with a long low whistle. Ducking our heads beneath the beams we fished out a set of coaching prints by James Pollard, coloured by hand and dated 1836, 'Coach in a

Flood', 'York Mail in a Storm', 'Coach on Newmarket Heath', the sort of things of which he was inordinately fond. Grandfather surveyed them and then screwing up his mouth on one side when he thought Collins wasn't listening murmured 'Forty guineas in St James's, we'll have them!' in a sort of strangulated voice.

Mr Collins was tremendously kind to his wayward customer, saved up little things that he felt might be of interest and brought them out of his pockets or from his back room with a sort of shy smile. On one occasion he appeared with a diminutive leather boot about four inches high and a tiny embroidered waistcoat scarcely suitable for a baby hardly even for a doll. These were two items of clothing worn by General Tom Thumb, the American midget, who toured England in 1848. Some of his clothes had been auctioned when he was exhibited at Luton and these had come into Mr Collin's possession, eventually finding their way to Avenue House.

Visits to Wheathampstead were rarely unsuccessful and the return journey through Whitwell and Lilley or skirting the park wall of Luton Hoo were always accomplished in tremendously high spirits, the boot bursting with treasures and the back of the car filled with clinking and rattling boxes. One trip to Charlie Collins ended in more sombre mood as my grandfather had to make an inspection of a nearby country house.

Lamer House, just outside Wheathampstead had been the home of the Garrard family for many generations, but had been vacated by the last of the line about two years previously. This was Apsley Cherry-Garrard, the Antarctic explorer, who had been on Scott's ill-fated expedition and returned to Lamer to write his famous account of it *The Worst Journey in the World*. As a member of the Royal Commission on Historic Monuments and a committee member of the Georgian Group, my grandfather had to make many such surveys of country houses that were threatened with demolition. With the years the lists of such visits increased, throwing him into greater and greater despondency. This was a particularly dark day and we obtained the key of the mansion and drove up the drive to look at it. It was an exceptionally handsome house which had been attributed to Robert Adam and had certainly been altered by

Humphry Repton when he landscaped the park in the 1790s. But shorn of its contents and purchased by a developer its future was not very bright.

We went in through the main portico into the chill interior, my grandfather traversing every room with his tiny steps and shining the beams of a pocket torch on to details of the architecture, for every window was shuttered. We mounted the curving eighteenth-century staircase, looked at the empty bedrooms while he flashed his light and exclaimed 'Look at the detailing of the cornices – magnificent' or running his fingers over the iron balustrade muttered 'superb, superb' in that long-drawn-out way of his until it echoed throughout the house. For some strange reason the Garrards had never moved the great console tables from the drawing-room and there they stood between the windows with the dim Vauxhall looking glasses above them. For an instant I saw my grandfather caught in the light and looking straight into its shadowy reflections, there were tears in his eyes as he murmured 'What a waste! What a tragic waste!' His plea to save the house was rejected as he must have known it would be and it was flattened, the parkland ploughed up and estate obliterated. It was sad that for most of his life, the legislation was totally inadequate to protect the things that he loved so much.

He seldom attended the sales at country houses, probably because he felt their dispersals too painfully, but the objects from these great collections found their way to his Ampthill house. He recalled, but did not attend the Wrest Park sale of 1917, the Deepdene sale of the same year, the Stowe sale of four years later and those of Cassiobury, Beau Desert, Hornby Castle, Rufford Abbey, Hartwell, Sandridgebury and Kimbolton. From the Deepdene collections came gilt wall-lights that Thomas Hope had illustrated in his book of *Household Taste* in 1807, books from the ducal library at Stowe, torchéres from Hornby and paintings from Lord Savile's Rufford Abbey. Even the salvage from these sad losses was treated with a sort of romantic reverence, Clive of India's door knob was rescued from a London house in the hands of the demolition gangs and given a pride of place in his library, Fanny Burney's shutter knob was attached to a box and prominently displayed on his desk. A visitor, remarking on the incongruity of an old battered baluster propped against the fine furniture of the study was greeted by the sharp retort – 'It was the great Doctor Johnson's, I saw it one day about 1900 when they were tearing down his house at Bolt Court, I begged it off the men and they gave it to me, it has been with me ever since!'

These forages into the country antique shops and 'finds' in the salad days of the country house sale might give the impression of a rather haphazard style of collecting. This was not the case for he was developing in his own mind a cross-section of eighteenth-century design that could be ruminated, digested, and drawn from like a well in the production of his own schemes. 'My house is my yardstick!' he would often declare, 'it is my measuring scale by which I contemplate the past and assess the future!' The sense of a living tradition was in everything that he touched and he felt very much a part of this tradition which stretched back to the time when classical influences had first entered the heart of British craftsmen.

The store of knowledge resulting from all this informed acquisitiveness flowed out from him in various ways. He was not only lecturing on his chosen period up and down the country throughout the year, but gathering material for books and articles. Much of the ephemera of eighteenth-century life, that he gathered round him at Ampthill, proved invaluable when he published his most popular book *Georgian England* in 1930. In it he could range over the history, social life and arts of the time, illustrating it with favourite objects from his own collection. Enthusiasm from the critics was really crowned with laurels by *Punch* who offered up their review of the work in verse –

> 'Its rather refreshing to bring to view
> In these hurried days (which are Georgian too)
> The leisurely Georgian days (of yore),
> And that's what *Georgian England's* for.
>
> Professor RICHARDSON, FSA,
> He is the author, and I should say
> The period hasn't a cranny or chink
> That he's failed to probe with his pen (and ink).

He deals with buildings and art and trade,
The stage, the forces, the fire brigade,
Drink and medicine, dress and sport,
With illustrations of every sort.

Indeed the volume (which BATSFORD'S backed)
Is so attractive and richly packed
That there's almost more than you ought to get
At the paltry price of a guinea net.'

He was also contributing articles on antiques to *The Country-man* for his friend Robertson Scott from about 1932 until the outbreak of the war. These included invigoratingly fresh subjects often drawn from his own experiences, among the titles were 'Boxes Odd and Curious', 'Old Utensils', 'Knives and Forks' and 'Famous Victorians' an early return to Victoriana.

Quite early on in his life he had begun to assemble architectural drawings and plans that might serve him in his work as architect and historian. There was a folio of original designs by Robert Mylne, the celebrated architect and engineer, another one connected with the Victorian architect C. R. Cockerell, yet other finely executed designs by Sir William Chambers, James Wyatt, Soane, Vulliamy and Lancelot Brown. These were referred to professionally when a teasing problem had to be solved in one of his restorations or leafed through to provide inspiration for a small country cottage or a gazebo. The notion that an architect should have a great library of past-masters' work was endemic to classical art, Lord Burlington had used designs in this way, so had Sir John Soane, but my grandfather must surely have been the very last to do so.

Avenue House returned under his guidance to the Regency home the Morris's would have known. It was more lavish in its furnishings probably, more heavily pictured certainly, but the interiors became redolent with the satinwood, mahogany and rosewood of the years 1770 to 1820. My grandfather was able to perform a number of rescues. The long scrubbed kitchen table which had been made for the house in 1770 was retrieved from a builder's yard and placed once more in the servants' hall, the pier-glass which had graced the dining-room for one hundred and fifty years was found in a cake shop and re-installed and

Mr Morris's account book obtained from a townsman and displayed in the study. The 'three conversation seats' with japanned frames and cane seats which had furnished the gallery in the 1820s were located through the long memory of old Harry Rixson of Dunstable. He remembered that he had bought the three of them at the sale of 1906, had sold two to Sir Philip Sassoon and kept one for himself. Sir Philip was persuaded to part with his pair for a nominal sum and all three were returned to their original home, indeed the original placing they had occupied in 1828. My grandfather's friend Howard Spensley of Westoning Manor, a former MP, had been a successful bidder at the house sale and he returned original porcelain and books with as good a spirit as Sassoon. The best of these included a garnature of apple-green Coalport vases which had been on the drawing-room mantelpiece from the 1830s and some remaining custard cups from a blue and white service of the 1820s. The house began to have that continuity which he valued so highly as well as the unity of period and taste which came alone through his perceptive eye.

The drawing-room was certainly the *tour de force*; the restrained classical mouldings, chaste marble chimney-piece and grand proportions of the room that the Bedford architect John Wing had designed for the Morris's in 1819, were ideal backgrounds to the rich furniture. Robersons of London hung plain purple curtains with borders from the four windows from his own designs and console tables were placed between the windows, substitutes for the original ones sold at the sale. Sheraton sofas and a white and gold drawing-room armchair in the manner of George Smith completed the ensemble. A close friend of my grandmother's Mary George, preferred this spare formality to the crowded arrangement of later years as more and more furniture arrived. Describing the room as it was in about 1925 she recalled, 'The carpet was grey, the curtains a rich plum colour with gold braiding and the room quite bare except for some very choice pieces of Regency furniture; these were covered in golden silk and the whole room seemed to shimmer with the colour of it.'

It was the same Mary George who told me of her amusement as my grandfather's resolutions to my grandmother not to buy anything more, were broken weekly if not daily. On one occasion she was sitting with her when my grandfather returned late in the evening from the West Country where he had been inspecting his building work for the Duchy of Cornwall Estate. Devonshire and Cornwall were always a temptation, there were far too many small antique shops to be resisted, besides there was Reg Andrade's cluttered floors at the Old Sugar Refinery, Plymouth, and Bruford's at Exeter. My grandfather was evidently weary with his journey but undeniably exhilarated underneath. He burst into the little sitting-room, pecked my grandmother tenderly on the cheek and presented her from behind his back with several boxes of silk stockings!

My grandmother's pretty eyes twinkled as she stared at him unimpressed.

'Yes!' she said quite fiercely, 'but what have you bought for *yourself*?'

He had shame-facedly to admit that he had bought a painting that was too large to transport by car, it was even now on its way from the West by carrier. The picture in question turned out to be the largest he had ever bought, the ten feet high by six feet wide canvas of the 'Escape of Gil Blas' by John Opie, RA, 'the Cornish Raphael'. It fitted exactly into the gallery and became a great point of anecdote and interest with him, having been the very picture that the young Benjamin Robert Haydon admired on his first coming to London.

Arrivals of this kind meant a general re-arrangement and re-hanging, often a time consuming operation, The walls were absolutely thick with pictures and it often took all his ingenuity as a planner to fit in one more row like a series of postage stamps. Sometimes he did it alone, perched on a step-ladder with a maid at the foot of it. The maid was paid sixpence if he didn't fall off! Usually, however, the builders' men were summoned for this work.

Charlie King, brother of the Ampthill builder would arrive with two or three assistants, cap on his head, cigarette stuck to his lower lip, grimacing and coughing as what my grandfather called 'the grand operation' got under way. Charlie removed his cap and laid it reverently on the stairs and then each painting was handed up to 'the Professor' to consider.

'I think it might just go there, my dear King – a little to the left please, a little to the right again – magnificent!'

This juggling might last a whole morning, the retinue of arrangers increasing as casual visitors, charwomen and my grandmother were recruited to the ranks, my grandfather more and more excited at every moment. Work was never struck until the main rooms of Avenue House were ankle deep in pictures and my grandmother had begun to berate the labourers for having let 'the Professor get away with it again!' One day after some decorating, King and his men were replacing the miniatures round the fireplace and hung them with Lady Hamilton, Queen Hortense and Mrs Fitzherbert all in a row. My grandfather flew across the room 'Never put two women together my dear Charles, it's absolutely fatal!' and he slipped in a portly Charles Edward Stuart between them with an air of finality!

The arrangements were strictly in accord with Georgian practice or what he conceived that to be. The dining-room furniture was set against the walls, the drawing-room furniture with an inner and outer ring of chairs radiating from the fireplace. The few gas fittings that remained there were removed and the room hereafter was lit by the warm glow of lamplight or the waving flames of candles. Mantelpieces were arranged with clocks and cassolettes according to the illustrations in old books and he was zealous about the ornaments on the outside being taller than those in the middle 'Otherwise the mantelpiece mews at you' he commented, without saying exactly what 'mews' meant.

Like every collector he had strong likes and dislikes, a bias towards anything architectural was paramount but he reacted strongly against anything showy or pretentious including buhl and heavy marquetry. The things that most irritated him were the circular gilt mirrors with eagles on top which were part of the Regency but endlessly copied.

'What do you think of this Professor?' a lady collector asked him one day, pointing to one of the offending mirrors.

'All right for an assembly room,' came the reply, 'but not for a *gentleman's* house!'

He could be quite rude on occasion. At Turvey House, he

turned towards the hall clock as he left and looking at Colonel Hanbury said 'I think that that is the ugliest clock I have ever seen!' After I had bought a small Regency chaise-longue which I was very pleased with and which I asked him to look at, I was rebuffed with the remark '*very* middle class'.

The rivalry which is an endemic part of collecting was not absent from my grandfather's spirit. He preferred to hunt alone and except for a few journeys in company with Fred Hart or Charles Wade, my grandmother was his only companion. Chauvinism mixed with a certain antiquarian sadism was known to creep in from time to time. On one Saturday morning he had arrived rather late at one of his favourite haunts, Harry Rixson's spacious shop in Dunstable High Street. A wealthy American with attendant wife and waiting chauffeur had beaten him to it and were already occupying all the attention of Harry Rixson and his son Philip. The star attraction of the day was an exceptional tall Adam longcase clock in a balloon case by an Edinburgh maker. The price was one hundred pounds. The American shuffled round the shop from room to room but returned again and again to the clock, viewing it with interest but wishing to be assured on every detail.

'Would you say that this was a fine example of the peeriod?' he drawled.

'I would say one of the finest examples I have had', Rixson replied.

'Then I might like to make a purchase,' the other mused, 'after lunch, perhaps' he added.

'Shall I reserve it till then?' asked Rixson.

'No, no,' drawled the visitor, 'we'll discuss it over lunch at the *Sugar Loaf*'.

As soon as the couple had left, my grandfather, who disliked foreign competition, stepped from the shadows with a cheque made out for a hundred pounds.

'Now Rixson,' he said, 'the clock's mine, let me into the shop at five minutes to two so that I can see their faces when they know its sold!'

According to him the American's surprise was well worth waiting for. 'Perhaps he learnt his lesson,' grandfather commented to Rixson afterwards, 'collecting is love at first sight, hesitation doesn't enter into it!' It was pure romanticism but it typified his attitude and much of his success.

Another robust piece of strategy was brought into play when we were on a northern tour. There were a pair of faience figures in the drawing-room at Avenue House which had belonged to Pierpont Morgan and of which grandfather was passionately fond. Stopping at Berwick-upon-Tweed, we went to visit Mr Knox's antique shop, a regular calling place. From across the street we could see in the window another pair of faience figures from the same set as the ones at Ampthill. We all saw them *at exactly the same time*; my grandfather, my mother and I bolted across the street in a fairly disorderly stampede and threw ourselves at Mr Knox's little door. My grandfather was very stout and with the number of overcoats and waistcoats that he usually wore, very solid indeed. The door did not give way but we became wedged in the tiny entrance each shouting 'I saw them first!' knowing full well that Knox was good and cheap. My grandfather held up his gigantic umbrella to bar our entry while he wrenched open the door handle and pounced on the faience figures. It was quite good humoured, but it was bulk that had the prior claim, not seniority as he afterwards tried to tell us!

Once installed at Avenue House with their carefully chosen positions and stories, my grandfather endowed his things with a kind of extra dimension and became their mouthpiece. There were items that were historical in themselves, the red leather case containing Nelson's hair, Mrs Fitzherbert's chairs, Lady Jersey's table, George IV's table-napkin, they needed no explanation. His genius was in making even the simple things come alive as he talked about them with his friends.

Some months after his death I was clearing out his study and noticed an old box lying under his desk. It was dusty and quite shabby and when I succeeded in opening it I found nothing inside but a yellowing piece of paper. On it was written in his unmistakable flowing hand the following –

THE IDLE THOUGHTS OF AN OLD BOX

Precisely as the clock struck four on the afternoon of October the 12th 1749, I received in my wooden body the last brass-headed nail that still holds a fragment of goat skin. The next day I was turned over to the youngest apprentice who lined my interior with the blue paper, which is even now intact. My maker, a short stout man, with a rubicund face and if I remember rightly, wearing a loose wig, regarded me through his brass spectacles and after praising my attractive looks, called his assistants round, while he discoursed on the mysteries of trunk making.

I then took my place on the shelves of the shop, and stared down through the panes of the window at the passers-by. For some weeks nothing further happened until one day, when I had received a comfortable coating of dust, my thoughts were abruptly disturbed by the entry of a gentleman who came to enquire for a box suitable to contain the kerchiefs and trinkets of his daughter, who if my memory serves me right was to leave for a finishing school after Christmas. 'Here is a fair box', said my master, 'just the size, lined on the outside with shagreen and covered with goat skin, a strong box, suited for a young lady, not too heavy to handle and finished with a brass clasp and a Birmingham lock, the price is two guineas.' Without further ado the bargain closed, and the same evening I was sent to Lansdown Place to begin the many trials which I was destined to experience in the course of, I hope, a very useful and adventurous life.

My new owner, Miss Emma Hicks was delighted with me, as I was with her, I was packed and unpacked a score of times, opened, shut, locked and dusted on every occasion and brought out at every opportunity to be shewn to admiring friends. The fateful day of departure came at last, my mistress amid tears took leave of her father, who had already put me in through the door of the chaise, which was to carry my mistress and her aunt from Bath to Gloucester.

For three years we lived under the roof of the stern Madame Lepage, who made it her duty to inspect my contents after each visit to my mistress's home until I too became disquieted with the interference and resented the rough handling and disrespect with which I was treated.

Once when the key was not forthcoming, I heard the termagant declare that she would have me broken apart, and that, at a time when I held a love letter from a young naval officer. Fortunately the danger passed and the letter was extracted before prying eyes could discover the secret loyally held by me. As my thoughts wander I can recall my happy days at Lansdown Place. There was the day of my mistress's wedding, when the most precious of her jewels were confided to my care and when at the going away I travelled on the floor of the carriage, and watched the pair of them make eyes at each other as they travelled to London. The wonder is that I survived the journey, for I was nigh to being left on the road at Devizes and in danger of robbery at Hounslow.

The years passed almost as rapidly as the milestones I have seen on the roads of England, for my travels have been many. Mistress and my Master, for such is the term that I must use for the gentleman who changed her name (although I never really liked the braggart and never forgave him for pitching me at the head of a refractory post-boy), first lived in Bruton Street in London, then we moved to Winterbourne Stoke in Wiltshire where I was relegated to the attic in the cold roof of the Manor House. So passed fifty years of my life, I almost forgot to say that my mistress had three children, a boy and two girls. The boy, poor lad was killed in the war with the American rebels, the eldest girl married into the French nobility and lost her life in the course of the Revolution, but the youngest Miss Penelope, stayed at home, inherited the Manor and its contents and received from her mother's hands my humble person with many relics of early days, some of which had been entrusted to my care before. This was in 1776, for my mistress did not long survive the death of her son. Miss Penelope Dawson, as a young heiress was soon the centre of a circle of admirers, at seventeen her hand had been sought by a rich squire of fifty summers, an impecunious lord who had devoured one fortune and was ready for another, a sleek young minor canon of Salisbury Cathedral and a handsome ensign of Dragoons.

Again I officiated at the going away, but from my position in the boot I could not witness the philandering. I am an old box now, but I can remember the children of this marriage, two handsome boys and three girls, one of the boys followed his father's profession and entered the army. The other took to the sea and fought with Lord Nelson at Trafalgar and on his mother's death I was given to his care, and so became the property of his wife, a sweet young girl the daughter of a Cornish parson, whom he had met at an Assembly at Truro, a year before Trafalgar was fought. From 1805 until 1849, I lived at Durnford Street, Stonehouse, for although my new mistress became the wife of an Admiral, neither of them had any pretensions for grandeur.

Dear People of the Old School, what a great shock I experienced when you both died, the master within a few days of the mistress. How I resented the coarse handling when my interior was rummaged for the modest treasures I held, the medals, the ribbons, the orders, the miniatures of handsome men and beautiful women. I was sold at the auction, for those who came into the property had no use for an old box, a stout farmer's wife bought me to take home to her farm at Callington. My release came in 1875, this time I went to a lawyer's office and did duty as a sort of deed box. He was not a bad man that lawyer, as legal gentlemen go, but with all his erudition he did not read my secrets. I doubt whether he even discerned the name of my first owner, which had been written on my body in a fair round hand, so many years before. In 1900 the good lawyer went the way of all flesh and likewise *my* travels started again.

Back I went to Plymouth and then amidst the rubbish of a second-hand shop, where I remained for twenty-two years, until chance brought into the shop a man whom I knew I could trust to use me with care. 'How much is that old box?' he said, 'I have a fancy for it, by its shape and size it was made in 1750 for a young lady to take to Boarding School. Why here is the lady's name, her age and the date purchased! Ten shillings, thank you !'

The man pleased me, he lifted me with care, extolled my

beauty, gave me a load of sketch-books and maps to carry,
pushed an old knife and fork in with the other things and
had me carried to a great travelling carriage. I had just
time to notice that the horses were not yet in, when the
great carriage started of itself without perceptible effort.
Once again the roads of England opened before me. There
were many houses I remembered which I had seen in my
youth, and many new ones, but the scenery *was* strangely
familiar. As we flew along I sought to speak but my new
owner spoke for me –

'Old box', said he, 'I will alter my plans, you shall be
lifted up to see Exeter, I will take you to Salisbury, you
shall be taken to Bath and Gloucester!' And to my amazement he kept his word. I am now in his study at Ampthill
in Bedfordshire but where I am to go after that time alone
can tell.

I folded up the piece of paper and returned it to the box; how
very typical of my grandfather's sense of humour and how
delighted he would have been to know that the story had been
read as intended!

CHAPTER SIX

The Chimes of Eaton Socon

My grandfather's consuming love for the eighteenth century, never obscured the fact that he had been trained for several years under a church architect. That period of apprenticeship had given him a deep love and a great knowledge of medieval buildings and it was only natural that he should seize on opportunities to restore and repair parish churches round his new home. Strongly deprecating the sort of Victorian restorations that had won Sir Gilbert Scott and his followers such a bad name in the Home Counties, he approached each church in a sensitive spirit, fitting each solution to the individual church as if it was tailor made, never tampering with the past, attempting to make his presence there as anonymous as any Gothic mason. The unrivalled expertise had not simply been gained through books but through his drawings and measuring countless churches in the 1900s. The collar-beam, king-post and double hammer-beam roofs of the village churches were like old friends to him, so were the external stones and carvings which varied region by region. A restored Richardson church would usually show clean pointing on the exterior, a whitened interior with carefully repaired woodwork and judiciously placed hangings and lighting. Occasionally a lamp in bronze or brass, unmistakeably from his hand with eliptical hanging glass or octagonal frame might intrude, but generally the church was as he might like to have found it. John Betjeman later commended his restorations for: 'looking so much like the original, with even the old pews still sloping at odd angles'.

Although the war memorial controversy had left a nasty taste in my grandfather's mouth, he was architect at Ampthill Church for many years, eventually repairing Clophill, Maulden, Southill, Cardington, Tingrith, Streatley in the immediate vicinity and many more beyond. At the end of his life the responsibility had spread to Buckinghamshire, Suffolk, Norfolk and Lincoln, churches in Lancashire, Yorkshire and Durham as well as in the City of London, a grand total of nearly sixty buildings. The first church tackled in Bedfordshire was at Flitton, where the tower was repaired for the vicar the Rev A. E. Houfe, MA. The Rev Houfe's consultation about the fabric, led eventually to the questions about the future of his son who showed artistic promise. My grandfather suggested he should study architecture under him at the Bartlett School, resulting in the seventeen-year-old boy becoming his student, later his son-in-law and finally his partner for twenty years.

His proposals were not always popular and there were some stormy meetings in church halls! He always maintained that he had to keep a greater vigilance on parochial church councils, 'gaitered idiots – archdeacons and others of that tribe' than on the dry rot, the damp and that ardent pest among the timbers, the death-watch beetle! Referring to the last-named insect, my grandfather loved to tell a story of an encounter he had with a church cleaner. One day, passing a country church that he had successfully renovated, he decided to slip in unannounced and look at his work. The place was deserted except for a friendly charwoman who insisted upon taking him round.

'It's a lovely old church isn't it' she said proudly, 'but it wouldn't be here now if Professor Richardson hadn't come and saved us from the ravages of the Black Watch!'

One of the early churches was Millbrook, the delightful fifteenth-century structure perched on a hill, high above its tiny village where my grandfather attended divine service after the rift with Ampthill. He enjoyed immensely its unspoilt interior, original pew ends and candlelit evensongs, he himself always using the pew in front of Westmacott's marvellous white memorial to Lord and Lady Holland and their daughter. This little girl had died aged nine and her parents' faithful librarian at Holland House, John Allen, had founded the Georgina Fox

Bounty in her memory. Once a year nine little village girls aged nine were provided with petticoats in memory of the tragic Miss Fox. On these occasions a local person usually gave them away, for many years it was Miss Romola Russell, my grandfather succeeded her and added an address from the pulpit to the other ceremonies. For more than thirty years on a November Sunday afternoon, the little church echoed to his thundering discourses from the pulpit, architecture, theology, puns, psalms and elegant rhetoric, poured out on the nine little girls in front, waiting bewilderedly for their gifts!

A great bonus to him in the early years of restoration was his strong friendship with Bishop Furse of St Albans and Archdeacon Parnell of Bedford, both understood good architecture and good craftsmanship and he enjoyed working with them. Bishop Furse was a tall burly man known for his ready wit and timely puns. During the work at Millbrook, the Bishop came to inspect it and was conducted by my grandfather and the fussy vicar the Rev 'Happy Harry' Pollard up to the tower to see the stonework. When the Bishop emerged from the doorway on to the roof, the excited vicar began pointing out landmarks that could be seen in marvellous panorama before them. 'My lord there is Bedford'. 'My lord there is Sandy'.

After working himself to a crescendo of delight 'Happy Harry' touched the Bishop's arm. 'My lord on a clear day you can see the Wash!'

The Bishop looked archly round, 'Yes', he murmured to my grandfather 'on a Monday morning!'

The restoration of churches brought with it a realisation that the traditional arts and crafts were falling into decay. My grandfather had to work with groups of masons, carpenters and metalworkers who were often elderly and seemed to be dwindling year by year. He could always rely on the superb skill and expertise of J. P. White's Pyghtle works at Bedford for his joinery and the prowess of Knights of Wellingborough for his ironwork, but he was saddened by the loss of continuity as old methods were abandoned and the loss of oppportunity as modern architects confined themselves to concrete. Church architecture was certainly a channel for these men but the amount of restoration of old ones was limited and the new ones under construction were few and far between. In a whole life-time in architecture, only three new churches were built by my grandfather: St Christopher's, Round Green, Luton, the Chapel at St Mary's college, Twickenham, and Holy Cross, Greenford with its dramatic and much-praised timber interior.

Contacts with church craftsmen and inspiration following a visit to Sweden in 1932, convinced my grandfather that something must be done for the crafts. The form it should take, he decided, would be a revival of the Spirit of the Guilds and he immediately began to lay plans for a great resurgence of interest in fine and honest workmanship, so long crushed by the machine. The first step was the setting up of a body called The Honourable Company of Craftsmen to foster creative indivi-dualism in the traditional building trade. Grandfather worked like fury in the spring of 1933, busily writing to his friends and colleagues and earnestly enlisting their support. S. E. Dykes-Bower, the church architect was his lieutenant and others actively interested included Sir Edwin Lutyens, Lord Gerald Wellesley, Alistair Macdonald, Professor Gleadowe and Randolph Schwabe, the Slade Professor of Fine Art. Alan Lennox-Boyd, his MP in Bedfordshire and a close friend, spoke on the decay of the rural industries in the House of Commons and used much material in the debate which my grandfather had provided for him.

The Honourable Company was fast becoming a reality. It was to have a Court in London as its governing body and a craft hall for the display 'of approved specimens' of craftwork. Besides its primary function of introducing the public to all forms of good design, the Company was to fight against the commercial exploitation of artists and to 'assist in the destruc-tion of the mass mind' – all my grandfather's phraseology.

He was quite determined, however, to keep his Guild on an entirely non-commercial basis, it should advise and direct and act as a middle man but it should not become involved with shops and companies or with any political organisation as had been the case with William Morris. 'The Guild is forming very slowly,' he wrote to his friend the etcher F. L. Griggs that August, 'it is backed by Lutyens and will be a very sound thing because it aims at being non-commercial. I am convinced that unless something of the sort is done there will be very little left of rural life, but we have to be careful of "arty" movements. It is a great thing to have your good wishes.' The dynamism of the man was terrific, my father once recalled how he crossed London in a taxi-cab crammed with potential Guild members at this time while my grandfather lectured them.

'Do you realise,' he suddenly said, indicating the cheap goods in the shops, 'we are the most important men in England!'

The aims of the Guild were published in a London newspaper with a series of Richardsonian aphorisms, pithy, provocative and to the point –

'In all works of general utility (everyday things) pots, pans, kettles, knives, forks, jam jars and what not, avoid being arty.'

'In furniture design give prominence to simple form, avoid pseudo-cottage types, eschew "ye ancient", "ye bleached", "ye smoked" or "ye charred". Remember good wood should not be disfigured. Encourage people to be measured for their chairs and tables. In church furniture avoid travesties of Gothic or Classic, suppress absurd lecterns, screens, altars and reredoses, which disfigure old buildings and turn new churches into showrooms.'

'In draughtsmanship aim at careful analysis. If you attempt the figure show some regard for anatomy'.

My grandfather's standpoint was a traditionalist one but it was at least an open-minded one in the 1930s. One article on the formation of the Guild remarked 'Richardson holds a peculiar position among English architects. He and his work are admired by modern young architects who use glass and steel, and also by those architects who use Renaissance stone-work on steel structures'. He was also putting some of his theories into a very literal sort of practice. A couple of workmen labouring on the walls of a particularly hideous bungalow on some new by-pass of that day, were amazed to see a huge black car stop nearby and a hostile looking man with long hair bundle out of it. They were even more surprised when the figure, ignoring the mud and lime, clambered up the scaffolding in his best blue suit and stood menancingly beside them.

'You men – what are you?' fired my grandfather.

'Bricklayers' replied the stupefied pair in unison.

'Damn bad bricklayers' snorted my grandfather, 'look at this work, you're all fingers and thumbs man, I'll show you!' With this he grabbed the workman's trowel and began to lay a course properly, talking all the time 'Like this, man! Like that, man!'

After a minute's silence one workman looked at the other.

'Come on Bill, he's barmy' he commented and they descended the ladder leaving the Professor to it!

In October 1933 he sent out over his signature a printed letter to scores of craftsmen all over the country. In it he argued that not only the art but the quality of national life had been lowered by centralisation in the factories, he cited the great works produced in the fifteenth and sixteenth centuries and 'the scientific intellect of today . . . substituting high explosives, poison gases and the culture of death dealing germs'.

'Here then' he wrote 'we present to you, for acceptance, the invitation to attend a meeting of the Honourable Company of Craftsmen, to accept the constitution now prepared, and to determine by your vote and influence that the Honourable Company shall become a potent instrument for artists and craftsmen, to the good of our national life.'

A mass meeting was held in the Royal Society of Arts rooms, John Street, Adelphi on 23 October and my grandfather told the audience that they had been promised a Guild Hall in Westminster. A resolution was passed for the forming of the Guild and the election of a Court and the assembly was jubilant and enthusiastic. Afterwards the delegates returned to their workshops, my grandfather returned to Ampthill and the scheme quietly expired.

The climate of the early thirties was probably not a good one for such an idealistic scheme; financial problems aside, the notion of a Guild ruled by a small dictatorial body of academics was perhaps unfortunate in a decade when many artists were winning more freedom for themselves. Lastly, and my grandfather would have been the first to admit this, his was a talent for dreaming dreams, for capturing a vision and providing it with its first impetus, not for forcing it through. He could admirably champion a cause but he could not be bothered with the details or the administration of it, that had to be left to the less impetuous but equally dedicated. Some of the lessons learned were certainly useful to him; possibly as a result of this campaign he was later elected Master of the Art Workers Guild and nearly twenty years afterwards he was to help found the Guild of Surveyors, becoming their first President.

Perhaps the greatest challenge in church restoration that he ever faced outside London was the rebuilding of St Mary's, Eaton Socon: for this all the crafts were called upon and all his knowledge needed, but it also involved him in one of the most awkward and acrimonious little rows of his career.

In February 1930, my grandfather had Harry Batsford, his publisher, and Charles Fry, another director of the Batsford firm, staying for the weekend at Ampthill. He had taken them on a lightning tour of Cambridgeshire and Huntingdonshire, darting into forgotten churches, through junk shops, finally ending up for tea at Mr and Mrs Wade-Geary's at Bushmead Priory. There in that strange tree-ringed house, half Georgian mansion, half monastic dwelling, they had sipped tea on chairs made for the very room in 1740, looked at Canalettos and watched Mrs Wade-Geary's bright canaries flit about the enormous aviary. On the return home they had stopped to admire the fourteenth-century church of St Mary, Eaton, Socon, standing rather peacefully back from the village green considered one of the finest parish churches in the county.

Three days later, my grandfather opened his newspaper to read that a fire had started by accident in the boiler room and swept right through the building. Apart from the exterior walls it reported, the entire church had been destroyed.

A telephone message came soon afterwards and he was immediately called in to advise on the rebuilding. He drove over to Eaton Socon and spent the morning walking round the still smouldering ruins, feeling the blackened timbers and touching the flaking masonry. A great deal had been lost at St Mary's but skilful physician that he was, my grandfather was insistent that the rebuilding should take the form of a reconstruction of what remained and that no expense should be spared in getting the materials and the best craftsmen available to work them.

The rebuilding was progressing well by March 1931, the outer walls were protected and repaired, the roof was completed and he was enjoying himself on the designing of fine woodwork including screens, lecterns, choir stalls and organ case with a spiral staircase to it. The white and light interior was to be improved by hangings and he was looking out for rich Flemish tapestries to put there. My mother, aged twenty, sat for her portrait as one of the angels on the right of the altar reredos. So satisfactory was the progress that my grandfather felt able to suggest to the rebuilding committee at the end of the winter, that their church should be completed by a clock chime on a fine peal of eight bells, ready for the dedication service the following year.

There had originally been a peal of only five bells in the sixteenth century but when the fire destroyed the church there were six, the fourth bell cast by Robert Oldfield in 1706. The second bell was seventeenth century, the other four were cast in the eighteenth and early nineteenth centuries. All of the bells were badly ruined by the fire, three of them had collapsed with the belfry and consequently they were all sent away to the foundry and recast as a peal of eight.

My grandfather suggested that the new chimes for the clock should be composed by Sir Edward Elgar with whom he was acquainted in London. This was agreed to eagerly, everyone felt that 'the occasion ought to be marked by something of our own'.

41 Russell Square,
London WC
11 March 1931

Dear Sir Edward,

I am venturing to write to you to ask whether you can assist in the reconstruction of the Parish Church of St Mary's, Eaton Socon, Bedfordshire which was destroyed by fire a year ago.

The church prior to the fire was a fine example of English gothic of the 14th and 15th centuries. The tower formed the landmark in the famous village on the Great North Road.

For the past year I have been acting as Architect, and it has been found possible to save and reconstruct a good deal of the original building. When the works are completed there will be little to distinguish between the old and new.

The matter on which your kind help is solicited is that of a chime for the clock. I suggested to the Committee that if you would consent to compose a clock chime for Eaton Socon it would become as well known to travellers as the chimes of Westminster and Cambridge.

The chime is to be on eight bells, toned from F sharp to F natural, to include the quarters and the full chime of the hour.

I am sending this letter to Brooks's of which I am a member, to be forwarded to you in Worcestershire, and I hope you will pardon the liberty I have taken.

Yours faithfully
A. E. Richardson

At first it appears, Elgar was unwilling to help with the Eaton Socon project, for he wrote in his flowing hand across the top of the letter 'Answer No'. After some consideration, however, the idea seems to have attracted him for he changed his mind nearly a month later and replied.

Marl Bank,
Worcester,
30 April 1931

Dear Mr Richardson,
Thank you for your note of the 11th – I shall be interested to hear what your committee says: if they decide against Westminster I shall be delighted to help in the affair.

Believe me to be
Yours faithfully
Edward Elgar.

On the 16 May the Vicar, the Rev P. Higham, wrote rather desperately to Richardson – 'I am holding up the clock till we settle the chimes as they are ready now for the work on these and waiting'.

But no music was yet forthcoming from Elgar at Worcester.

41 Russell Sq.
London WC
19 May 1931.

Dear Sir Edward Elgar,

I am sending you a copy of a letter I have received from the Rev E. P. Higham of Eaton Socon.

It is most kind of you to offer to compose the chimes. The occasion does call for more than an ordinary effort. The church was almost completely destroyed by fire in February 1930, but it is being rebuilt by local craftsmen, and when finished will not differ from the previous building.

Eaton Socon has a long history, and its name has been immortalised by Charles Dickens in Nicholas Nickleby. The name suggested Eaton Swill to the great novelist.

Yours sincerely,
A. E. Richardson.

On the 10 July there was still no music from Elgar and Richardson felt prompted to write again.

Brooks's
St James's Street
SW1.

Dear Sir Edward Elgar,

I have been asked by the Vicar of Eaton Socon to write to you about the chimes which you so kindly offered to compose. The new peal of bells is now in the tower and we expect the clock to be fixed next week. Pray forgive me for troubling you.

I am
Yours sincerely
A. E. Richardson.

Elgar sent his music in manuscript to Richardson three days later with a covering letter.

Marl Bank,
Worcester,
13 July 1931

Dear Professor Richardson,

I am sorry for the delay but I have been quite laid up. Here are the chimes: I have marked the time signature only in the 1st & 2nd, but the actual measure, which is purposely vague, can be made out from time in the 3rd & 4th.

The time should be about (metronome) √ 78–89.

I heard (at Birbeck I think) some modification of tone – *piano* & *forte*: I do not know if modern mechanism allows of this but in case it should do so I have added expression marks.

I hope you still like the chimes which should sound simple and pleasant.

Believe me to be
Yours sincerely
Edward Elgar.

The manuscript was sent straight on to the vicar at Eaton Socon, but unfortunately difficulties were already crowding in on this valiant attempt to introduce distinctive chimes for the rebuilt church. After Elgar's music had arrived, the Council in one of those wild moments that provincials are capable of suddenly decided to make their chimes a matter of open competition and invited several musicians to submit compositions. Dr Sydney H. Nicholson and Mr S. G. Wilkinson of Eaton Socon submitted music and these compositions were considered along with Elgar's. My grandfather was horrified as he saw his generous ideas being mutilated, the difficulty of placating Elgar was also uppermost in his mind. A large number of Eaton villagers went over to St Neot's one afternoon to hear the various chimes played over the bells of the parish church. According to Mrs Higham, the vicar's wife, 'everyone preferred Elgar's chimes, but there was a lot of feeling in the village'. Mr Wilkinson the organist's chime was chosen and Elgar was

dismissed with the weak excuse that there was no suitable
apparatus for his work. My grandfather was furious and blurted
out after hearing the composition 'Yes its nothing more than
"Ding, dong, bell, Pussy's in the well!" Elgar was under-
standably incensed that his kindness should have been treated
in this way, a touchy man with a sense of insecurity, it was the
sort of treatment that he most disliked and feared as is evident
from his reply.

> The King's Hotel,
> Brighton
> 19 February 1932

Dear Professor Richardson,

Thank you for your letter. I fully anticipated the result
of your effort. I fear I shall not be at the club for some
time, for the moment my only concern is the fate of the
MS. I do not want it to be in the hands of – – – Esq the
Organist!

> I am yours ever
> Edward Elgar.

> 41 Russell Sq,
> London WC
> 23 February 1932

Dear Sir Edward,

I must thank you for your letter of the 19th instant. The
whole affair has been a worry to me and I cannot tell you
how disappointed I am that my work has been marred by
faulty chimes.

I have asked the Vicar to write to you. The manuscript
is quite safe, it is in the Vicar's hands, and we will do whatever you wish. Personally I should like to frame it and
have it kept as a record of what might have been done.

> I am,
> Yours sincerely
> A. E. Richardson.

Worcester

26 February 1932

Dear Professor Richardson,

Thank you for your letter of the 23rd. I have now heard from the Vicar and have asked him to send the MS to me; I will then decide if it is worthy of the honourable preservation so kindly suggested.

Believe me to be

Yours sincerely

Edward Elgar.

The fate of the manuscript is still a mystery. It is not among the composer's other papers at Worcester and he may have destroyed it as hinted in his last letter.

From my own correspondence with Mrs Carice Elgar-Blake, it appeared the composer was deeply nettled by the affair and tried to avoid my grandfather for the last two years of his life. My grandfather's opinion of the church's councils was not improved and he was bitterly sad not to enjoy Elgar's company at Brooks's Club.

The last comment on this unhappy episode did not come from either the Olympian Elgar or my disconcerted grandfather, but from Percy Bentham, the sculptor, whom he employed for so many of his buildings. Using the carvers traditional licence, Bentham had already carved the heads of the Rev Higham, the churchwardens, the workmen and the foremen handing the church to my grandfather; he added his own humour to the arcade and depicted 'Discord' or 'a satyr snatching the pipes from the mouth of the musician'. The face of Elgar was not exact but the likeness of the satyr was a surreptitious portrait quietly taken by Bentham. Some weeks later my grandfather visited the church unexpectedly and stumbled on the organist looking very hard at the corbel portrait from which horns protruded so effectively!

CHAPTER SEVEN

Royal Occasions

In about 1930, there was a re-shuffle of appointments within the Duchy of Cornwall and my grandfather lost his much-coveted job as its architect after twenty years. There was a strong element of sadness in this as he had particularly enjoyed designing the small domestic buildings, farms and cottages, barns and village halls which the Duchy Office required. The visits to Devon and Cornwall ceased, but almost at once other and more intimate work appeared, bringing him into much closer touch with the royal family. In 1933, Lord Stanmore had suggested to Lord Hamilton of Dalziel that my grandfather should be the architect of the new Jockey Club rooms at Newmarket and he was appointed shortly afterwards. This was a building in which King George V took a personal interest and grandfather met him many times in the course of its erection.

On the day of the Jockey Club's official opening my grandfather escorted King George V right round the Club rooms. The King looked at everything and made odd asides to him with an amused twinkle. When they were in the Stewards room he noticed my grandfather's scheme where the walls were lined with saddle leather.

'Quite right Richardson!' he chuckled, 'you've put them in a padded cell!'

Then the King noticed that the door-handles were in the shape of horses' heads.

'What are these Richardson?' he asked in that slight guttural accent of his.

'I designed them sir with a purpose,' replied grandfather mischievously, 'Now no steward can ever say that he has never pulled a horse!'

The King laughed uproariously at this and then asked the Professor to tell him about Newmarket and its buildings.

'Well sir,' answered my grandfather, 'King Charles II had a house here!'

'Did he?' said the King, 'tell me more about King Charles II.'

'Well sir, when Wren was building some rooms for Charles II at Hampton, the King happened to inspect the work in progress and being a very tall and willowy man, his head almost touched the ceiling.

' "I find this rather low Sir Christopher", said the King, "rather low!"

'Wren who was a little short man replied "May it please your Majesty I find it tall enough!"

'Whereupon the King bent himself almost double to Wren's height and said "May it please *you*, Sir Christopher, so do I!" '

George V roared with laughter at this story and when he had recovered himself he turned to my grandfather again.

'Professor,' he said, 'put on your hat!'

My grandfather did so and accompanied the King to the waiting car, covered!

A year later he was asked to design the new Royal Pavilion for their majesties on the Ascot Race Course and this again brought him into personal contact with both King George V and Queen Mary.

My grandfather's contacts with Queen Mary did not come only from the racing world. The Queen was a very ardent and compulsive collector of antiques and her magpie tastes had added all sorts of trifles to the royal collection and caused any number of London dealers to raise royal arms over their doors. The Queen craved the society of other collectors and gathered round herself at Buckingham Palace, connoisseurs who could help her with her own impulsive and rather unformed type of collecting. Her chief lieutenant in all these matters was H. Clifford Smith, a friend of my grandfather's who had won the Queen's confidence after publishing his monumental *Buckingham Palace, Its Furniture, Decoration and History* in 1931. Grandfather had contributed notes on the architecture of the building and the Queen had superintended them through a tall and critical gold lorgnette. Clifford Smith was a keeper at the Victoria and Albert Museum, but according to my grandfather was seldom to be found there as he was always in attendance at the Palace.

Meeting Clifford Smith in St James's one day my grandfather attempted to speak to him.

'Can't stop, can't stop! I'm going to a tea party at the Palace,' came the reply as he hurried on.

Two days later my grandfather met him on the identical spot in the same state of perturbation.

'Another time! Another time!' was his hasty comment, 'I've just *been* to a tea party at the Palace!'

The die was cast. From that moment onwards he was christened 'Tea Party' Smith by my grandfather and 'Tea Party' Smith he remained.

'Tea Party' Smith soon involved my grandfather in this charmed circle of royal advisors and he found himself very much at the beck and call of the Queen, not always to his advantage as a busy college professor and practising architect. The summons would come from the palace through the lady-in-waiting, a summons which admitted no denial, and the royal Daimler would be despatched to collect him at Brooks's Club in St James's Street. The immense black machine, without number plates, was built specially high to accommodate the Queen's piled-up curls and formidable hats and completely swallowed up my grandfather's far from insubstantial form. Its appearance anywhere would have been sensational, but as soon as the royal cyphers on the doors were spotted, a crowd collected in the street and he had to push his way through to where a footman held open the door. Once he was mobbed by Americans under the impression that he was a duke or Walter Monckton or both; after this he made the journeys sitting on the floor of the car!

The Queen's interests were extremely individual, anything connected with past members of the royal family aroused her enthusiasm at once and she was zealous in acquiring miniatures of long-dead princes and princesses, jewellery they had owned or gold plate which had been made for them. Antique dealers up and down the country had a habit of collecting such items together when they knew that she was coming and shaking them out on to a tray at the last moment, as one might shake out a mixture of corn and nuts for a favourite but tiresome canary. The Queen would then peck through this assortment and retrieve the monogrammed étui or the coroneted snuff-box with a suitable sense of discovery. Her visits to country houses were rather more momentous for they were less visits than 'raids'. Objects that had even a modicum of royal history attached to them were 'returned' to her collection even when the owners were not anxious to part with them, the royal presence and the royal insistence, spiriting treasures away from even the most tight-lipped subjects! The ladies-in-waiting, who were all friends of my grandfather's, were kept very busy remembering where the antiques came from and in surreptitiously restoring the more flagrant 'acquisitions' to their owners.

At the tea parties, in between china tea and sandwiches the size of farthings, my grandfather was shown the latest 'finds' from holidays at Sandringham, stays with the Princess Royal at Harewood and tours in the West of England. Many of the things were small, precious and bright, gold boxes, Fabergé and jades, but he was also shown furniture made for Queen Charlotte, lost from the royal collection, but discovered again by Queen Mary's sharp and penetrating eye. Among many subjects that she consulted him on were what to do with old water-mills on the Sandringham estate, which city churches she should visit and what she should do with a very handsome and embarrassing present she had received. The present was in fact a complete bound set of Piranesi's engravings, given to her by Benito Mussolini in the middle of the Abyssinian War, a gift which had it been known about would have caused considerable annoyance! My grandfather wisely suggested that the volumes should be given to him to dispose of and he left the palace with them in the royal car!! They were later lodged at University College and ironically destroyed in the war.

Queen Mary very readily sought advice but did not so readily receive it. The tea parties were intended to be informal, but though the Queen tittered quite merrily on occasions, my grandfather sometimes found it like eating cake with a state portrait. The *tête à têtes* were usually in the private sitting-room or the Chippendale room which Queen Mary had arranged herself, highly cluttered with lacquers, jades and carved ivories.

On one particular occasion my grandfather's attention became rivetted on two handsome neo-classical ornaments placed on either end of the mantelpiece. The more he looked at them, the more he was convinced that their position was wrong, his fingers itched as he searched for an opportunity to say something. At last he could bear it no longer and jumping up indicated the ornaments.

'They would be much better aesthetically, Ma'am,' he said, 'if they were placed *here* and *here*' he gently changed their placing on the mantelpiece.

The Queen looked at him severely.

'But the *King* prefers them where they *were*,' she pronounced acidly and rising abruptly, she moved to the mantelpiece and returned them to their original places at either end!

Queen Mary had a great curiosity to see over one of the famous London clubs, principally because they were very historic but partly because they were jealously guarded male preserves. She asked my grandfather if she might see over his own club, Brooks's, a request which put him in a very awkward situation. To refuse would be more like refusing a command than a request, but equally it was against the club's rules, no woman had set foot in it during its one hundred and fifty years of history. He consented to escort her round, but said the visit would have to be made in mid-afternoon when the club was free of members; an hour's stay was sufficient to see the main rooms and portraits. A grudging acceptance by the club secretary resulted in the offer of tea at Brooks's. The response came back immediately from the palace, 'No tea is required'.

The Queen arrived promptly at 3 o'clock and was guided round the main rooms on the lower floor by my grandfather. She closely questioned him on the work of Henry Holland, the architect of the Club, and asked many questions about the Foxites, Richard Brinsley Sheridan and the Whigs of Carlton House.

Somewhat to my grandfather's embarrassment, she insisted on seeing the private members' room on the ground floor,

Sir Albert Richardson at work in his painting room.
A photograph taken in about 1960.

▲ Albert Edward Richardson aged three,
a *carte de visite* photograph of 1883.

▼ Albert Edward Richardson
aged twenty-one, a pencil
portrait by Charles Gascoig[ne]

◄ Albert Edward Richards[on]
as a young man in Verit[y's]
office, about 1903.

▲ A decorated envelope containing a love letter, written to Elizabeth Byers, whom he married in 1903.

◄ Elizabeth Richardson 1882–1958. A pencil sketch by Hanslip Fletcher, about 1912.

► Richardson as an officer in the RFC. An ink study by Hanslip Fletcher, about 1918.

Plate 3

▲ Avenue House, Ampthill, as it appeared in 1919 when the Richardsons mo[ved]
there.
▼ The drawing-room of Cavendish House, St Albans, the Richardson's home fr[om]
1909 to 1919.

The drawing-room of Avenue House, Ampthill, as it appeared in about 1921.

The drawing-room of Avenue House as it appeared nearly forty years later, showing Richardson's passions as a collector.

Plate 5

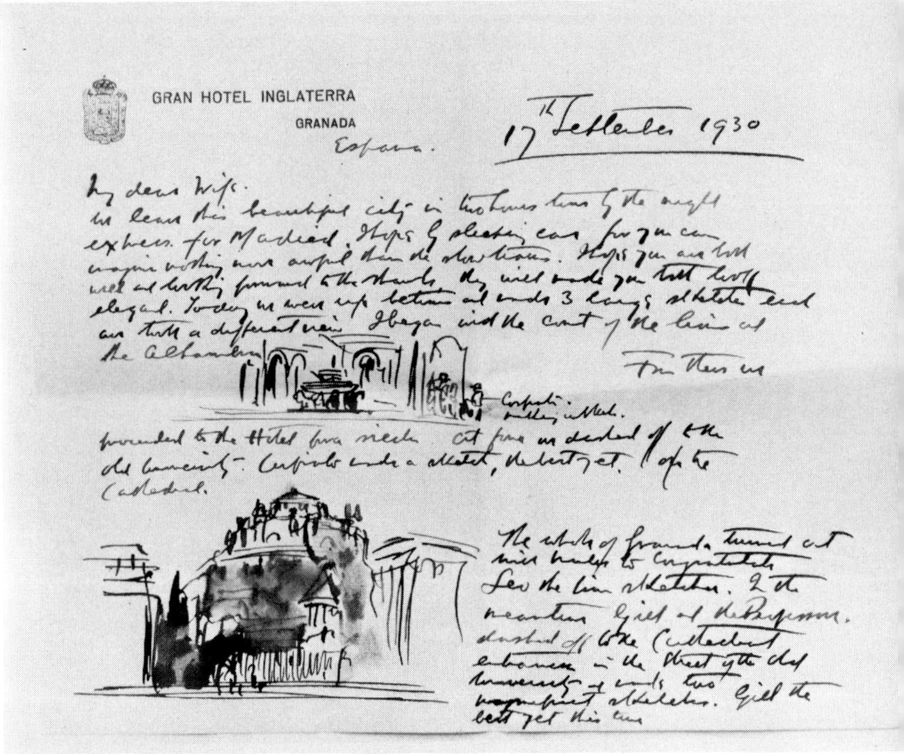
GRAN HOTEL INGLATERRA
GRANADA
España.

17th September 1930

My dear Wife.

▲ An illustrated letter from 'The Professor' to his wife, written from Spain and da
17 September 1930.

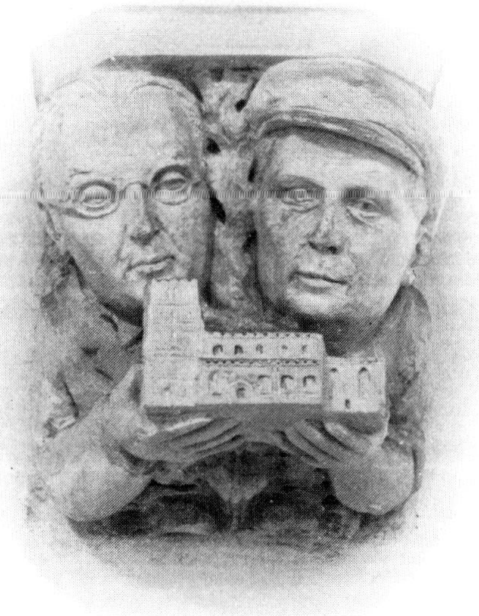

◄ A carved corbel in St Ma
church, Eaton Socon, show
Richardson and the maste
mason offering up the
completed structure 1932.

Caricature of Richardson
by Sir Edwin Lutyens
entitled 'The Professor
at a Bored Meeting'.

Houghton House, Ampthill in 1925. Richardson's efforts saved the mansion from demolition.

Plate 7

▲ Her Majesty Queen Mary leaving Avenue House with Richardson after her visit on 28 May 1934.

◄ Elizabeth Richardson in the grounds of Avenue House, about 1936.

▼ Richardson sketching with friends at Annecy 1936.

'The Professor' in costume playing the pianoforte at Avenue House.

In costume rehearsing a play.

▲ 'The Professor' at Southill Park, Bedfordshire, about 1938.

▼ Richardson's Rolls Royce *en vacances* with Sidney Powley at the wheel.

▲ Richardson at Avenue House with his greatest antique
'find' the missing bust of Lord Somers by Le Marchand

▼ Her Majesty The Queen at the Royal Academy with Richardson
and Sir Henry Rushbury in March 1955.

A characteristic watercolour by 'The Professor' of Dinan, France, exhibited at the Royal Academy in 1958.

'The Professor' and Elizabeth at the opening of an art exhibition in 1957.

'The Professor' relaxing at Hagbush Hall in about 1958.

▲ 'The Professor' sorting through his collection of drawings at Avenue House.

▼ Glimpsed at the opening of the *Courier Exhibition*, January 1956. His comment on the Barbican there made headlines.

The installation of 'the pregnant penguin' outside Avenue House in 1957. Its erection caused a running battle with the Council.

'The Professor' with his friend Ernest Marples, in the grounds of Avenue House about 1955

‘The Professor’ strolling into his garden with shooting stick and trilby hat.

‘The Professor’ with his favourite dog ‘Sherry’ in the grounds at Avenue Hou[se]
in 1962. A photograph taken by the author.

which he had not proposed to show. Inside, half a dozen elderly sleeping members, awoke at the sound of a woman's voice, turned round indignantly in their chairs and then rose dutifully to their feet. Perhaps a note of resentment showed through their expressions, because the Queen spent far longer in that room than in any other, examined every picture and piece of furniture minutely and kept them standing painfully on their feet for a full fifteen minutes! Then, still chattering animatedly to my grandfather she left them to their sanctuary without having addressed a single word to any of them.

After ascending the graceful Holland staircase and seeing the Subscription Room, where members played for high stakes in the eighteenth century, she began to express anxiety about returning to the palace. Despite the order that no tea was required, my grandfather had talked to Sir Walter Peacock and they had both remembered the Queen's partiality for chocolate cake. He had accordingly arranged for a small tea-table to be placed in the club's magnificent drawing-room, the cloth laid out with choice eighteenth-century silver, a rich chocolate cake decorating the centre of it. The doors were then opened into the drawing-room and the Queen was shown its furnishings and painted ceilings by Rebecca. When Her Majesty caught sight of the table and the chocolate cake, she hesitated, and all plans of returning to the palace vanished.

'I have changed my mind,' she said to the equerry, 'I have company at the palace, tell them they must wait!'

After tea and the signing of the visitor's book, my grandfather escorted her to the door and out into the car. Returning to the club entrance hall he was met by a flushed and angry-looking Lord Willingdon, peering ill-temperedly after the departing limousine.

'Has she gone?' he snapped, then added muttering, 'Damn it, Richardson, you've spoilt my afternoon!'

My grandparents were very friendly with two of Queen Mary's ladies-in-waiting, Lady (Margaret) Ampthill and the Hon Jean Bruce. Jean Bruce, the daughter of Lord Balfour of Burghley was a frequent visitor to Avenue House and knowing its collection well, had often talked about it with the Queen. It was only a matter of time before Queen Mary's curiosity was sufficiently aroused to express an interest in coming to Ampthill for herself. The date was set for the spring of 1934 but even so the exact day caught my grandparents somewhat unawares, my grandmother at once wrote to my mother who was away:

Avenue House
Ampthill,
May 20 1934

My dear Kathleen,

We are in a great state of excitement. The Queen is coming with Lady Ampthill at 12 noon on Monday 28th. This news is to be kept private, we are to keep our own counsel. I shall be awfully busy getting everything in order. Papa too will re-arrange things at the weekend. Don't let this leak out, not even the maids must know until the day. The police are being informed by Lady A. Her Majesty is lunching with the Ampthills. So hurry home and help. Pop says we must get beautiful flowers from Laxtons, for the house and something from the greenhouse. I shouldn't think there will be time to do the garden. I do hope Jean Bruce comes as it is entirely through her and not Lady A.

The Royal itinerary for 28 May was to begin with the visit to Avenue House, continue with lunch for Queen Mary at Lord Ampthill's house at Oakley and end in the afternoon with a tour of S. H. Whitbread's magnificent house at Southill Park. The Saturday and Sunday before the royal Monday were hectic. My grandfather arranging and re-arranging all the furniture, creating small dust-storms in each room he went through, my grandmother and the maids following hard on his heels to repair the damage to their pristine polishing. The dining-table was set out with Irish glass and a rose-bowl in the centre, filled with specimen blooms, the busts in the corridors were lightly cleaned with feather dusters and the silver sconces given a final rub.

Jean Bruce had warned my grandparents that it was advisable to remove from view any antiques with royal connections. Discretion she had suggested was the better part of valour where Queen Mary was concerned and long experience had shown her, that where temptation was offered, it was seldom resisted! The Queen's enthusiasm for royal objects extended not only to things associated with her predecessors, but more or less anything with the royal arms upon it! My grandparents began combing the house for offending items. A pair of chairs with the Prince of Wales' feathers on their backs were hastily hidden in a housemaid's closet, George IV's table napkin from Brighton Pavilion was secreted in a drawer with signed documents and favours from the Coronation of George III. My grandmother unceremoniously bundled the royal china with the same offending feathers on it into the servants' hall for the cook to take care of and my grandfather tucked away the gaudy and gorgeous carriage step of King William IV.

It was only when all these treasures were safely under lock and key that my grandfather remembered the carpet in the first floor sitting-room. 'Great heavens mamma, what are we going to do with that?' My grandparents gazed bewilderedly at the rich crimson Wilton carpet decorating the floor, rich not only by virtue of the royal colour but by the gigantic royal arms of George IV placed in its centre. The carpet was indeed one of my grandfather's prizes, he had discovered it in Bond Street in 1920 and authenticated it as the centre portion of carpet from the throne room at Carlton House. Across this piece of carpet all the major figures of the Regency had walked, Pitt, Fox, Sheridan. Nelson, Wellington, Byron and Lawrence, Brummell and Southey, to audiences with the Prince Regent. It was not likely that the royal eyes would miss such an historical square of ostentation!

The carpet was big and heavy, far more than a man would be able to manage himself and it was securely nailed down round the entire length of its border. My grandparents looked at the size of the task ahead of them, the quantity of furniture that would have to be removed, the number of tacks taken out, if the carpet was to be hidden. Grandfather remembered Jean Bruce's comment that nothing would stop the Queen if her spirits were roused. For a moment his mind was full of a fantastic scene in which the royal Consort, fumbled in the dangling reticule for pliers and began to tweak out the tacks one by one before rolling up the carpet and handing it to the lady-in-waiting!

'It'll have to stay,' my grandfather said resignedly, and my grandmother agreed.

On the Monday, all the maids except one were sent away for the day, a policeman was posted outside the front door and my grandparents and mother waited nervously inside. A little after twelve noon, the royal Daimler slipped over the hill and stopped at Avenue House, the visit lasting an hour and a half. The Queen had brought with her, not Jean Bruce as they had expected, but Lady Ampthill, another lady-in-waiting and Sir Gerald Chichester, her private secretary.

Once inside the house, the Queen's formidable cross-questioning began, nothing escaped her notice and she was hungry for dates, facts and previous histories in her rather gruff Germanic manner. My grandfather was hardly able to return replies before the Queen supplied her own or rushed on to the next question. She was engrossed in anything German, for example a beautiful neo-classic watercolour of Countess Catherine Tiesenhausen which she pronounced excellent, and anything unusual. In the dining-room she was intrigued by a large pottery casserole dish in the shape of a chicken, the head coiled round with a somewhat quizzical expression, she tittered over this and asked its age and date.

The drawing-room made the greatest impression on her, entering its atmosphere of 1810, which my grandfather had strenuously tried to preserve, she paused and looked round.

'Professor, this is a good room!' she uttered judicially, 'a good room!'

The Queen turned a beady eye on my mother who had been foolish enough to stand close to the handsome Merlin pianoforte of 1786.

'Do you play that?' came the question.

My mother had in fact learnt to play it, but any attempt to do so with Queen Mary as audience would have spelt disaster and like the china and the chairs, she wisely hid her talents and replied 'No Ma'am!'

The royal party was steered round the upper floor, my grandfather pointing out models, clocks, miniatures, marquetry, watercolours and porcelain to the Queen as they went. All the time they were getting nearer the royal carpet. The Queen was absolutely delighted with the 1848 barrel organ and particularly with the little automata that worked above it. The famous instrument of Ampthill Christmas Eves was now played, the tune thumped out and the little figures on the stage above it shook their heads and arms and rolled their eyes. The Queen giggled.

'Play it again! Professor,' was the order.

My grandfather whirred the wheel, the little figures resumed their gyrations and Her Majesty's parasol was seen to move ever so slightly in time to the 'Sailor's Hornpipe'.

'And again,' said the giggling Queen, and my grandfather turned the handle for her once more.

As soon as they entered the sitting-room, the Queen's eyes went straight to the carpet at her feet, its colour and royal insignia occupying all her attention. My grandparents froze.

'Tell me about this carpet, Professor!' She looked piercingly at him.

'This carpet is most interesting, Ma'am, it was the throne room carpet at Carlton House.'

'Indeed it was!' said the Queen, staring at the floor again. She raised her eyes with a certain indignation. 'And where did *you* get it?'

My grandfather played for time and chose his words carefully, the vision of it being packed into the royal Daimler was now very close.

'I found it in Bond Street, Ma'am, and exhibited it in the Regency room at the Wembley Exhibition, where it was seen by many people from the Empire!'

'And what then?' The Queen was playing impatiently with her parasol.

'I bought it for my own collection, Ma'am, to prevent it from going to America!'

'That was very well done,' said the Queen after considering for a moment. She then turned as if to leave the room but faced my grandfather again before she did so.

'I remember it well as a girl,' said the Queen, poking at the carpet with her parasol. Then she added with a triumphant treble in her voice, 'but a good deal was cut for the *back stairs*!'

With this she sailed out. My grandmother sighed with relief, the carpet remained on the floor.

My grandfather's troubles were not over, however, because the Queen had caught sight of a pair of busts of Hanoverians in the gallery.

'Who do the busts represent?' she fired at him.

'They are King George III and Queen Charlotte by Falconet,' he answered.

'They are not!' said the Queen immediately.

Grandfather was not used to being contradicted about his own collection in his own house, but he somehow stifled his wish to splutter out a protest and merely bowed.

'They are the Duke and Duchess of Gloucester', said the Queen.

My grandfather bowed again. Perhaps my grandfather's less than convincing assent was noticed; the Queen, despite her busy life continued to correspond with him on the identity of the two busts for the next twenty years!

In the hall the Queen signed the visitor's book with a fresh quill especially cut for the occasion. My grandfather noticed with admiration the way she used it, dipping her pen and writing with the reverse side in that large and flowing regal hand. She then said her farewells to my grandmother and my grandfather escorted her and her party into the car, where a small crowd had gathered to cheer.

The visit was followed by a rather bizarre little episode. It was understood that the Miss Russell's at Ampthill Park would be offended if a call at Avenue House did not also include a call on them. They also let it be known, however, that since their mother's death (some years before) they were not in a position to entertain the Queen at the Park, merely in a position to be acknowledged by her! Consequently the Daimler left Ampthill on the Woburn Road, turned off into the Park at the western entrance, traversed the west drive to the house and then the east drive away from it. At a given moment, as the car approached the north front of the mansion, Miss Constance and Miss Romola Russell came out on to the grand flight of steps and curtsied in unison as their Sovereign's wife passed! For their pains they had a fleeting glimpse of a bowing head in the car!

A month later, the following letter came from Jean Bruce.

Windsor Castle
26 June 1934

Dear Professor Richardson,

Please forgive my apparent rudeness in not having answered your kind letter sooner – I'm longing to see you and hear about the Queen's visit first hand, and shall hope to propose a day that will suit you both quite soon. I was in such a rush before I got here and life has been one long 'wait' since I got here and there has been no time for private letters. The Queen has twice told me how much she enjoyed seeing your treasures. I wonder if you did hide the royal china!

The war years intervened to end these royal rounds. The Queen lived entirely at Badminton and my grandfather was working throughout the war at Cambridge. After those five years many links were broken, the Queen was no longer so robust and so active as a collector, my grandfather was feverishly busy as one of the chief architects for reconstruction and restoration in London. Even before the war had ended, he was involved in re-building the Chancery Lane Safe Deposit, the bombed-out shell of University College, Wren's church of St James's, Piccadilly and Hawksmoor's church of St Alfege, Greenwich. Many of these projects brought him into contact with other members of the royal family and in particular with the Duke of Gloucester. He became a friend and advisor to 'Prince Henry' on architectural matters after the war, designed and personally superintended the alterations to his drawing-room at Barnwell Manor, Northamptonshire and made many visits there as architect and guest.

The new sights and sounds were now being recorded in daily journals, huge ledger books that were filled page after page with his scarcely decipherable hand, punctuated with designs and plans and sometimes running to a whole side a day. Through them he gave himself a record of the world as he saw it and the many listeners who heard him read aloud were entranced by their lively descriptions. A glimpse of the Queen, now Queen

Elizabeth the Queen Mother is provided by a typical entry of a garden party at Queens' College, Cambridge, on 2 June 1948, when he was architect there.

'We passed through the cloistered court where the undergraduates were rehearsing for *As You Like It*. And so to the President's Garden with the alumni. Met the Vice-Chancellor Dr Raven of Christ's, the Bishop of Ely, Master of Trinity, Provost of King's, Master of Downing, Master of Clare, Master of St John's and my friend Dr Deane the Master of Trinity Hall; also Master of Pembroke, the Master of Sydney Sussex, the Principal of Ridley Hall and his pleasant lady. Then to the reception in the President's Garden, the sun shone, the birds sang and the breezes were soft.

'The Queen came into the gardens by the President's lodging. We all stood. Then Her Majesty took tea seated in a pavilion in the E side of the garden. We continued talking and taking tea. Then HM rose and advanced to meet the students from all parts of the Empire. Then she turned into another tent pavilion to cut the cake, this had been modelled in semblance of a medieval subtlety.

'Then further conversation with the Master of Trinity Hall and Mrs Deane and so round in a circle to be presented to Her Majesty. The President presented me as the College Architect and also my dear wife who curtsied very prettily. Her Majesty asked me about the plans for the New Library. I explained that the perspective was only finished at 2 pm! Her Majesty was amused. Then the President said "I feared it would not be ready in time!" Then the Queen looked round at the old building and said "They had very good taste in those days!" "Yes Ma'am," was my reply, "they paid tribute to tradition".'

His rather urbane and courtly manner was popular but his irrepressible sense of humour and mischievous style of writing meant that some royal functions were not treated so seriously; an example in point was a visit to York.

'At 2.30 Her Royal Highness the Princess Royal arrived. There was a great excitement and not a little surprise for we were honoured by Her Royal Highness appearing in clothes out of fashion. Truly this is a democratic age! Her tam-o'-shanter was out of date and her cloak or coat was a Victorian style;

perhaps she was influenced by the date being November 5th?'

In the autumn of 1947, my grandfather received a telephone call at Ampthill which greatly surprised him. It was from the Duke of Windsor with whom he had had no contact since leaving the Duchy of Cornwall Office seventeen years before. When working for the Duchy he had completely altered and restored Tor Royal, the Tyrwitt mansion on Dartmoor, as a West Country residence for the Prince of Wales. He had taken great pains with the interior, introducing beautiful but severe ornaments and details like those in the houses of Sir John Soane. A fine marble chimney-piece had been installed along these lines and he had been well pleased with the result. The Prince, however, had shown very little interest in the house, only spending one night there, but my grandfather was noticeably nettled a few years later to learn that the marble surround had been taken from Tor Royal and set up in the Prince's favourite home, Fort Belvedere. The sourness engendered by this had never subsided.

So his astonishment was considerable when he found the Duke, on the telephone from London, seeking his advice about the design and building of a mausoleum for himself and the Duchess. The Duke favoured Windsor Great Park and it was agreed that they should meet there the following week, my grandfather having prepared some suggestions on paper. In the short time available, he made feverish preparations in ink and watercolour, consulting the enormous architectural tomes in his library and keeping the assistants and my grandmother up until the small hours fighting for fresh inspiration.

He made a number of designs, the most successful of which was in the form of a small pavilion in granite, standing on a podium, its central bronze door flanked by doric columns and surmounted by the royal arms. The sides of this mausoleum were steeply sloping and gave the building a decidedly Greek revival appearance, but its component parts were Louis XVI in style, a compliment to the Duke's love of France.

'October 11th 1947. Left at 8.50 for Windsor travelled by hired car via Bletchley, Tring, Berkhamsted, Rickmansworth, Slough, Datchet, etc. Left assistant at the Garter Hotel. Then to Fort Belvedere to meet HRH The Duke of Windsor. Arrived a₁ 11.10 am. Then to inspect the Fort in the company of HRH. Discussed project for building in the grounds. Visited several sites, made sketches on the spot and left them with HRH who is going to the Ritz Hotel, Paris on Monday and after that to New York. Discussed further details. Left HRH at 12.45.'

Ritz Hotel,
Paris.
16 October 1947

Dear Richardson,

I was very pleased to see you again last Saturday, and with the results of our discussion of a certain project at the Fort.

Since seeing you, I met Mr Eric Savill, the Deputy Ranger, Windsor Great Park, the official I suggest you should contact in connection with my business, who told me that the vandalism and desecration of monuments in the Great Park have already reached such proportions that, taking the long view, he was fearful of the security of anyone's 'resting place' that was vulnerable to the hooliganism which obtains today.

We accordingly drove on to Frogmore, within the precincts of Windsor Castle, where we explored the grounds and found a secluded site. I have told him to show it to you whenever you let him know you are going to Windsor. As the new site is in a glade, with banks on either side, it is equally suitable for our conception of the little monument to contain the Duchess's and my own ashes as the hill at the Fort.

I am staying here until the first week of November, after which my address will be the Waldorf Towers, Park Avenue and 50th Street, New York, NY.

Looking forward to hearing from you in due course, and with my best regards,

Believe me
Sincerely yours
Edward".

Two weeks later my grandfather sent off a further twenty-five drawings to the Duke and the following week spent the afternoon with Mr Savill at Windsor, inspecting various sites at Cumberland Lodge and Frogmore. The Duke soon afterwards developed 'cold feet' about the Windsor scheme and suggested a building in Baltimore, United States as an alternative. No more was heard after this and the idea without being totally abandoned was royally and quietly shelved.

CHAPTER EIGHT

Cambridge

The nineteen-thirties came to a very sudden end on 3 September 1939. Although they had been difficult years for my grandfather, they were also a period of solid achievement for him in both designing and writing as well as lecturing. Beginning with the Depression that had so greatly affected the building industry, they had led on to some notable works; the completion of the Sanderson Wallpaper Building in Margaret Street, London, the re-building of the Jockey Club at Newmarket and the construction of his first factory for John White's of Rushden. One of his most pleasurable small jobs was the restoration of St Dunstan's, Fleet Street, and the returning to it of its 1671 overhanging clock which Charles Lamb recalls in his essays. His successful book, *The English Inn* had been issued in a more popular version *The Old Inns of England* in 1934, prefaced by Sir Edwin Lutyens and subsequently running into five editions. This was followed in 1938 by his scholarly book *The Art of Architecture* which was written with Professor Hector Corfiato and he had also contributed to G. M. Young's famous history *Early Victorian England*. Those years had seen his first BBC broadcast in 1936 on 'Railway Stations', but more importantly the thirties saw his development as a fiery and forthright fighter for preservation, restoration and traditional values in building and design.

All of this was to change very rapidly for him after war was declared. His thriving office in London was swiftly emptied of all but the oldest staff, after urgent consultations he decided to end his long partnership with C. L. Gill and withdraw to the country. Everything around him seemed to be disintegrating as it had done before in 1914 and even life at tranquil Avenue House was rudely upset, the gentle rigmarole of writing, drawing and enjoying the garden was overturned by an invasion. My grandmother was valiantly trying to cope with the arrival of two evacuee families from the East End of London, wild and noisy children who had never been in the country before and mothers who wanted to drink beer all day in the kitchen. The small boys ran amok in the garden and dug up all the stones in the carefully laid courtyard until my grandfather was almost in a frenzy. My grandmother bathed and dressed the children and bought them underclothes which they had never possessed and they promptly got in the bath with them on! Plywood partitions were put up to prevent the boisterous guests from making a shambles of the best rooms and rampaging among the art collection. Poor Abbot, the elderly gardener, was in despair before his bushes and plants, and my grandmother's prized French cook gave notice. It was the end of an epoch as the grandparents fully realised, no more servants, no more leisure at Avenue House, nothing would run smoothly again.

Even so my grandfather managed to have the last word. One afternoon, incensed by the havoc the evacuee children were creating outside by digging up the cobbles and teasing the dog, he slipped upstairs and returned again wearing a hideous papier-mâché mask! Sporting this leering face he popped up at a window and stared out at the tiny miscreants. It had absolutely the reverse effect, they dropped everything they were doing and rushed to the window in wild delight! It was only when he snatched the mask off and showed his own and by this time fiercely belligerent features that they set up a tremendous howl and fled to the back quarters of the house. 'Want to go 'ome! Want to go 'ome!' were the cries that rang out from their room that night and by next morning their mothers were in agreement. Life in the East End under heavy bombardment was infinitely more pleasant than a day at Avenue House with its draughts and darkness 'funny old furniture' and 'odd folk'. The husbands drove down to Ampthill shortly afterwards and removed their families, the children still pointing at my grandfather's face with a mixture of fascination and awe! But the household was still in turmoil, officers replaced the evacuees, my parents on war work moved into the house and a pair of architects, foreign nationals, were adopted by my grandfather and employed by him there for the duration.

Just when my grandfather's patience was exhausted and his morale very low, the news came that the Bartlett School of Architecture, University College to be was evacuated to Cambridge. The announcement was like a blessed relief to him when he felt he could stand no more. Sixty years old, with no practice in London and no freedom at home, he felt at once that the only place to be was with his students at Cambridge. He heard that he and his colleagues were to have sanctuary at St Catherine's College and he needed no persuasion at all to go and live in rooms there and adopt the life style of a bachelor don. All the week and every week he was to stay in Cambridge, lecturing, talking, drawing, only between Friday night and Monday morning did he return to Avenue House with its beleaguered occupants, tiny rations of food by day and unpleasant accommodation in the cellars by night, if a raid was on. Devoted to my grandmother as he undoubtedly was, dependent on her for so many little things, there was a streak of insensitivity in the relationship that blinded him to her simple needs. She for her part, remained uncomplaining and loyal, but not only did she have to put up with his erratic behaviour and storms, she now had to break her back to keep the machinery of the house running smoothly. His weeks became filled with a welter of events, sprightly university conversation and excellent food and drink, while she lived a life of increasing drudgery, filling oil lamps, putting up black-outs, trying to cook and polishing the flagstones on her hands and knees. Years after the war when the introduction of electricity into the house would have made her life easier, my grandfather laughed the idea off and said that *he* had no use for modern conveniences. Delightful whim as it was, the purist pursuit of Georgian excellence scarcely touched him physically, but its full weight always fell on her though he was never able to see it.

Having been denied a place at Cambridge as a young man, my grandfather now entered the university with all the vigour of a freshman of sixty! His extravagance, generosity and eccentricity won him many friends and few enemies in the city, St Catherine's seemed to fit him like a glove and he had only a short walk to the evacuated Bartlett School at its Regency head-quarters in Scroope Terrace. The Fellows of St Catherine's had allotted him pleasant, panelled rooms in the seventeenth-century part of the college, the study in particular being a room of great character containing a fine eighteenth-century fireplace and a small casement window with views across the quad-rangle to Trumpington Street and King's Parade. He could hardly have found a more congenial nest in the whole of Cambridge and after the first week of the October term, he began to collect around him all the beautiful objects without which he found it impossible to exist. A van was despatched to London to remove favourite things from Russell Square and a selection of furniture was taken from Ampthill, all of it robust, mellow, and dignified, to suit the sombre appearance of the rooms. Paintings began to cluster on the walls, a seventeenth-century Vanitas, a putative Pannini, a clutch of Warwick Smith's watercolours 'picked up somewhere in the Midlands'. A Gothic architect's table served as his desk and a high-backed horsehair chair 'definitely Dean Swift's' was pushed against it. The mantelpiece was crammed with ornaments, figures, ships' models and candlesticks, while under the window, book-shelves began to bulge with the calf-bound folios picked up almost daily from David's market stall. When all was complete, Hanslip Fletcher came down to draw the refurnished room and enjoy his old friend's college life. Cambridge became more delightful week by week and my grandfather's frequent com-plaints about 'having to leave Ampthill' or 'having my life disrupted at my age' were gradually reduced to a bare mini-mum and only uttered then in my grandmother's hearing as part of his subtle diplomacy.

What did the Fellows of St Catherine's make of their new guest? The college was full of visitors because the building was accommodating members of the London School of Medicine as well as the Bartlett School, but it was generally agreed among the dons that Patrick Abercrombie and Albert Richardson were the outstanding additions to the High Table. The Fellows had instantly recognised that they had taken in a most unusual and entertaining man, lively and controversial in his talk, serious and scholarly when called to be, but without the scholar's irritating reticence.

My grandfather's nature had always been boyish and clubable. He retained the student's love of camaraderie, the Edwardians enjoyment of male society, that nineteenth-century mystique that made something rather secret of a man's world. Within the intimate circle of the High Table, spurred on by the historical surroundings, the good food and the equally vintage talk, he found relaxation for his omnivorous mind, not possible before either in London or in Ampthill. For once he had to be a conversationalist not a lecturer and for once he succeeded. He very soon established a warm but not a close relationship with the Master, Dr Chaytor, and made particular friends with the Chaplain, Canon Waddams and T. R. Henn, later the Senior Tutor. It is the late Tom Henn's accounts of this time that are the most spontaneous.

Tom Henn remembered that 'he had a quick and vivid insight into the characters of the High Table, including his own colleagues; witty, sometimes charmingly and confidentially malicious'.

The little mannerisms which had seen him through so many dull sermons and tedious banquets were used with agility in the convivial feasts at the college. 'He had an immense facility for rapid sketching,' Tom Henn recalled, 'and would often seize a menu card at dinner and draw on it to illustrate some point. He also had a tiny paint-box, perhaps two inches by four inches, which he carried with him always; with this and some dregs from a wine glass, he could produce the most astonishing little sketches.'

My grandfather was usually at his best on these occasions in Hall, where he entertained his companions with a whole succession of faintly scurrilous stories of eighteenth-century artists. He also 'had the habit at High Table of making incessant and execrable puns; for which (when they were particularly bad) we used to fine him a bottle of wine!' His humour was usually too topical, too immediate to bear scrutiny thirty minutes let alone thirty years later, but one St Catherine's pun has survived.

Someone had asked Dr Chaytor to give a Latin translation of 'Six Mile Bottom' near Cambridge. Before Chaytor could reply my grandfather had flashed back across the table 'Why my dear Doctor, ARSA LONGA, of course!'

Although he was completely at home in academic circles he disliked the preciosity and suspicion that they engendered, the continual searching for the Achilles' heel, the constant watch for a chink in the other man's armour. He was certainly not above the temptation of leading on an elderly and respected don into an elephant trap of his own making as this story of his Cambridge years shows. During his first term he was invited to dine at Jesus by the Master. During the meal he talked enthusiastically about the college buildings but confessed that *he had never been into the chapel*. The conversation flowed onwards and somebody mentioned Thomas Cranmer, who had held a fellowship at Jesus, and referred to the fine memorial erected in the chapel to him in about 1910.

'The memorial is inspired by the work of C. R. Cockerell,' my grandfather said gravely, knowing full well the sort of response this remark would bring.

The crusty Master alert to this flagrant inconsistency in his guest wheeled round and pounced at once.

'Professor Richardson,' he exclaimed, eyes blazing, 'I understood you to say that you had *never* entered our Chapel!'

'That is correct,' returned my grandfather amusedly.

'And yet you dare to attribute the design of the memorial!'

'Quite so,' continued grandfather quietly.

'Would you like to explain yourself,' the Master added triumphantly, looking round the table.

'That is easily done,' my grandfather announced, content that his quarry was completely in the bag, 'You see *I designed it in London!*'

His connection with St Catherine's was made more permanent and put on a more personal footing in 1940 when he was elected to an Honorary Fellowship. Soon afterwards he became an unofficial architectural advisor to the college,

advising on building work and ridding the old rooms of dampness by ordering a water table of stone slabs to be laid round the
outer walls. Tom Henn was amazed by his practicality and the
fact that he seemed to know and be on terms with all the
craftsmen of Cambridge. 'He had an almost sensual feeling for
textures, *patinas* of substances and craftsmanship. Very much a
conservative in all views and policies but in such a way that
this seemed integral with the whole man. It was the conserva-
tism of Burke and his age.'

Tom Henn also watched with admiration his new colleague's
ingenuity. Professor Corfiato was lecturing on pre-classical
architecture during the first months at Cambridge, while my
grandfather concentrated on his beloved Renaissance. Unfortunately, in the hurried move from University College, all his
architectural slides had either gone astray or been damaged so
that he found himself without his usual teaching material. His
celebrated blackboard sketches could be used but he needed his
slides too. He asked Henn the whereabouts of the nearest
photographic shop, went there directly and bought a large
number of $3\frac{1}{4} \times 3\frac{1}{4}$ inch slides. He had the whole lot developed
blank and then made his own slides of French and Italian
buildings, etching the emulsion with a needle point. He later
changed his technique and drew in black ink on glass slides,
covering the sketch with another protective glass and binding
them with passe-partout. These small drawings, thrown on to a
screen, had all the zest of his pen and ink work and he was
enormously proud of this piece of improvisation.

Almost as soon as he arrived in college my grandfather began
the Early Morning Tours. Five or six of the Fellows would meet
him by a tree in Walnut Tree Court, St Catherine's, at 7.30 am
and then set out on a high speed, fifteen minutes, architectural
tour of the Cambridge streets. Usually they followed him down
King's Parade and into the Senate House area, the Professor
tugging at the nearest arm, pointing out carving, pouring out
theories, until it was time to return to chapel and breakfast.
They were sometimes joined by the Master of Trinity, G. M.
Trevelyan. On one bright morning, my grandfather took
Trevelyan by the shoulder and led him to the Gate of Honour
at Caius.

146

'Do you realise my dear Master that the whole design is lifted from a 1553 French edition of Alberti! Look! They've even included a cypher of Diane de Poitiers!'

'Ah!' said Trevelyan archly, 'that *certainly* makes it jollier!'

When Tom Henn returned to St Catherine's after a longish wartime absence he was made aware of the more mischievous side of my grandfather's personality, which was even manifesting itself in these hallowed surroundings.

'The rooms that I was then in,' recalled Henn, 'were benevolently haunted; I had been aware of this since I moved in there in 1927 (*I* never saw the ghost; a number of other people had done so;) he was a figure of about 1680–90, I suppose an elderly don, who clearly wished me well. One night I was working late at my desk, perhaps one or two in the morning, with a single desk light. Very slowly the door creaked and opened, and a cloaked figure glided in, with a tricorn hat, buckle shoes, stockings and wearing a sword; and stood still near the fireplace. For a moment my heart seemed to stop. Then I saw it was Richardson! He had been to Littleport that day and bought what he declared was a complete outfit of late seventeenth-century formal dress. He said that it had belonged to *Grumbold* (the architect of Clare) and possibly implicated in the 1670 buildings at St Catherine's.'

A respite from the daily routine of the college and of lecturing was usually found at the homes of one or two friends nearby. He would often vanish for an afternoon to the Huntingdon Road for lunch and tea with his old acquaintance Sir Alfred Clapham, the medievalist. Clapham's huge book on the Romanesque had turned my grandfather back to the Middle Ages when he needed fresh material to fight modern trends. For longer stays he went over to Anglesey Abbey near Cambridge to spend weekends with Lord Fairhaven.

Huttleston Fairhaven was an immensely wealthy peer who had inherited a fortune from his father. My grandfather had altered a house for him at Englefield Green long before the war and struck up a friendship with him because of their mutual interest in art collecting. Fairhaven had moved to Anglesey Abbey, five miles from Cambridge in 1926 and transformed a modest manor house and park into a superb country home with extensive landscape gardens. With a nearly limitless purse and a desire to be continually improving the collection, he created in a space of forty years a notable array of paintings, furniture and statuary. The collector himself was tall, commanding and well built with a rather florid complexion and a very square chin. His great fortune, coupled with an inherent shyness made him seem stiff and unapproachable at times, life at Anglesey suited my grandfather, it ran like clockwork and nobody was ever late for anything. The only fault that my grandfather could find with Huttleston Fairhaven was that his life was *too* perfect, menservants moved noiselessly about, gardeners continually changed blooms from the hot-houses and it was reputed that guests had their shoe-laces ironed before breakfast. In the middle of this serenity Huttleston Fairhaven floated in un-reality, a fresh gardenia in his button-hole each morning, suiting rather too grand for the country. My grandfather recounted with glee the occasion when a tiny blob of candle grease had been found on his coat and the valet had been reprimanded. Any slight ripple such as this was apt to cause havoc in his world and the occasion when my grandfather's elderly car leaked oil over the gravel drive caused consternation from Fairhaven downwards!

Perhaps the retiring figure of Huttleston Fairhaven could have been my grandfather's greatest private patron, but there was no plan for building extensively at Anglesey and most of his energy was concentrated on the gardens. But despite differences in outlook, Fairhaven trusted him implicitly and called him in later to design the new picture gallery that housed his Windsor Castle collection and the Altieri Claudes. This trust extended into the area of collecting itself, my grandfather acting as *marchand mercier* when Fairhaven was considering a purchase. A number of pictures and also furniture and silver-ware were inspected by him in dealers' premises before they found their way to Anglesey.

At the beginning of the war, Lord Fairhaven had planned a chapel in memory of his mother, Cara, Lady Fairhaven at Bottisham Church and my grandfather was to design it. Despite wartime difficulties, this went ahead in a simplified form of memorial tablets, completed in 1941. Unable to attend the

dedication, he wrote to his friend setting out some of his own
feelings about his work.

Avenue House,
Ampthill,
Bedfordshire
26 August 1941

My Dear Lord Fairhaven,

It gives me great pleasure to hear that you are pleased
with the realisation of your ideas for the Memorial
Tablets. The idea originated with you and would not have
been realised without your close collaboration. My
thoughts will be with you when the unveiling takes place
next Sunday.

It is indeed most difficult to get craftsmen to carry out
work today. I suffer fearful pangs every time I undertake a
design. It has been brought home to me, through years of
experience that absolute perfection is nearly always
approximation to the ideal. Your own aims are towards
the perfect, and I must say you succeed. It gives me a
thrill to admire your furniture and works of art displayed
with taste and all in use. My own view is that the practice
of architecture or any of the arts is not possible without contact with fine things. In the old days, masters of art worked
in good studios, surrounded by things which they rever-
enced. Architects had good stocks of books and portfolios
of sketches. This I believe was still true of the best American
architects, McKim Meade and White and Charles
Goodhue led the field in this regard. At the beginning of
the 19th century, both Soane and Nash had private
museums.

The arts today suffer from lack of cultured taste and
judicious patronage.

My grandfather's own 'private museum' had been greatly
augmented during his stay at Cambridge. As already mentioned
books, and especially architectural folios were in plentiful
supply there in 1940, mainly due to the rash decisions of college

librarians to jettison old volumes in wartime. In the first few months at St Catherine's he had picked up armfuls of early Serlios, Vignolas and Palladios, all in original condition, many with seventeenth-century annotations. He snapped up the first edition of James Gibbs' *Architecture*, 1728 with the bookplate of Peterhouse in it, the very copy he maintained that Gibbs had presented to the college, and another day Sir Joshua Reynolds' own copy of *Les statues de Versailles*, 1724. All these bulky calf-bound books with their armorial bindings and marvellous crackling paper were delivered to his study at St Catherine's. There, with a sea of brown backs around him, he would ferret through their pages, burbling to his students and dropping a continual cascade of cigar ash into their interiors as he did so! To him they were old friends rather than venerated ancestors and he treated them with an easy intimacy; resting the huge spines on his knees, cursorily copying a vase or a plan on a strip of tracing paper, before letting the whole book slide to the floor with a crash. Then, selecting another great album of Italian *palazzi*, baroque altar-pieces or German fortifications, he would repeat the procedure with more puffing cigar smoke, more ash, amid the flying dust of centuries. This growing library may not have been waxed, dusted and catalogued in the way that it would have been at Anglesey, but at least it was being used as originally intended, the plates of Colen Campbell, John James and Sir William Chambers were being consulted as exemplars for new designs and new writings. From them the work of the smith and the joiner was flowing out into new pro-jects, his pattern books were literally used.

Cambridge also provided him with what was probably his greatest single 'find' of all his years as a collector. His chief resort among the dealers was Collins and Clarke's shop in Regent Street, a stone's throw from the Roman Catholic church, where he had bought porcelain and miniatures before the war. In January 1941 he dropped in at the shop because he had heard that a quantity of stuff had been acquired from Lord Clifden who had moved out of Wimpole Hall, the great Queen Anne mansion of the Harleys and the Hardwickes. Although the Clifdens were not lineally descended from the earlier families, they had bought much original furniture in 1890 and my grandfather was looking forward to some interesting pickings.

He had driven over from Ampthill that morning, having spent the weekend in his tiny wartime sitting-room at Avenue House, perusing Horace Walpole's copious *Anecdotes of Painting*. A few of Walpole's pithy descriptions remained fresh in his mind and in particular the accounts of the various sculptors working in the age of George I. Stopping the car outside Collins and Clarke's window, his eyes were immediately caught by a small white portrait bust of a gentleman in a periwig. Closer inspection revealed it to be of some statesman or other and unusual in being mounted on an ebony stand with an original early eighteenth-century glass dome to cover it. Concealing his suppressed excitement, my grandfather entered the shop and poked about for some time before showing a dawning interest in the diminutive bust.

The cover was removed and he was able to handle the little object for the first time, the smooth polished surface of ivory, the whole figure carved from one complete piece of tusk. Turning it to the light he could read the following inscription 'D. Le Marchand Sculp A.D. 1706'. My grandfather thrilled with excitment as the complete history of the sculpture fell into place as he saw those letters. The night before he had read in Walpole's *Anecdotes* an account of this very bust changing hands in the 1730s. Walpole's account was brief but illuminating. 'D. Le Marchand was a carver in ivory, born in Dieppe; was many years in England, and cut a great number of heads in bas-relief, and some whole figures in ivory. Mr West had his head carved by himself, oval. Lord Oxford had the bust of Lord Somers by him.'

Grandfather recognised instantly that it was this bust of Lord Somers that he was now looking at, modelled from the life, presented by Lord Somers to Lord Halifax, bought by Lord Oxford for Wimpole in 1739 and part of the mansion's furnishings until very recently.

'How much is this?' he asked, hardly daring to breathe.

'Fifteen pounds,' came the reply, 'Lord Clifden thought it was plaster and anyway he didn't like it!'

The little ivory was well within his grasp and yet he felt it ought to stay in Cambridgeshire. He was uncertain whether to buy it for himself or telephone to Louis Clarke at the Fitzwilliam Museum for them to buy it. In the evening he walked over to Louis Clarke's elegant home at Leckhampton House and told him about the discovery and the absurdly low price asked for it. Clarke, sympathetic and interested as he was, frankly admitted that the Fitzwilliam could not see its way to spending fifteen pounds in the face of wartime restrictions!

My grandfather returned to the antique shop in great excitement the next morning and asked to see Mr Collins.

'I want to take the bust,' he announced when the owner appeared, 'here is fifty pounds on account, I will send you another fifty next week'.

The dealer was astonished, 'but it's only fifteen pounds!' he protested.

Nonsense!' replied the jubilant Professor, 'I know its worth, it's the missing bust of Lord Somers, owned by Lord Oxford, mentioned by George Vertue and Horace Walpole, I wouldn't give you a penny less!'

There were two sequels to this story. Huttleston Fairhaven, who had passed the window several times and not noticed the bust, went straight to London and acquired a less virtuoso example for six times the cost! A fortnight after the ivory had been carefully displayed in my grandfather's rooms at St Catherine's, my grandmother, searching through an Edinburgh street-market found another Le Marchand, a plaque of Louis XIV's brother, which she bought for five pounds!

Not all of his activities had Cambridge as their centre however, he was involved in one noteworthy and patriotic piece of designing in late 1940 and in the following year manfully took up two far from popular causes. The first commission came as a complete surprise in a telephone call from 10 Downing Street. It was his old friend Brendan Bracken, now Parliamentary Private Secretary to Winston Churchill, asking him to come and see the Prime Minister as soon as possible. At their meeting, Bracken explained that on 18 August 1940, a young American pilot, William Fiske III, had been killed on active service while flying with the RAF, the first American citizen to die fighting for Britain.

Churchill had immediately seen the impact that this would have in the United States and discussed with Bracken and my grandfather the setting up of a suitable memorial to the young man. It was decided that a monument should be placed in the crypt of St Paul's Cathedral, next to Washington's and close to those of Wellington and Nelson, my grandfather was to design it, using only 'the best lettering, experts and carvers' so as to appeal to educated America.

Uncertain what form the tablet should take, though delighted with the challenge it presented, grandfather toyed with various ideas at Ampthill before eventually giving them up in despair. It was only when he wandered into the big drawing-room at Avenue House, unused for twelve months, and began to relight the candles in the sconces, that inspiration seemed to hit him. The tremulous light threw great shadows across the room and the fine classical proportions of the marble fireplace were thrown into relief, the restraint of its detail, the subtlety of its curved ends were perfect.

'Of course!' he exclaimed, 'the chimney-piece will be the basis of the memorial!'

Within hours a design was completed, a clear but simple alphabet was chosen and the drawings were despatched at once to Downing Street. Both Churchill and Bracken were delighted with the results which seemed to embody the classicality of colonial America. Richard Garbe, RA undertook the work at his home in the Lake District and its slow progress to completion was punctuated by terse notes from Churchill himself. Bracken explained that the Prime Minister considered it of incalculable importance that the psychological moment should not be missed.

The memorial was finished for Independance Day 1941 and was unveiled by the American Ambassador. To coincide with this, John Murray published a booklet about America's contribution to the war and distributed a million copies with the Fiske monument on the cover. After the ceremony my grandfather drove back with Bracken, now Minister of Information, to his ministry in Malet Street. There, over a celebratory glass of wine, these two unashamed Georgians danced a minuet round the wine bottle to the downfall of Goebbels and the death of Hitler!

The less popular causes which he felt compelled to campaign for were the retention of historic railings and the damage to great houses by troops. In the autumn of 1941, the Minister of Supply, Lord Beaverbrook, took the step of impounding privately owned railings throughout the country for scrap use in the war effort. The idea was seized on by local authorities with more haste than discrimination and before the year was out, the beautiful ironwork of Kensington Square, Spencer House and St James's Street had all been ripped up and carted off to government dumps. My grandfather began to act when the gates of Croom Court, Worcestershire were threatened and plans were afoot to denude the whole Circus at Bath of its original ironwork. He wrote to *The Times* in a quiet and rational way, explaining that the aesthetic importance of railings was a matter for experts and that they should not be removed indiscriminately. He added that as a rough guide, the year 1850 marked the borderline between craftsmanship and mass production, examples before this date should be examined with care.

One of his first successes was getting a reprieve for ornamental ironwork at Althorp and Lord Spencer wrote to thank him and express the view 'that the whole system is a scandal'. His hunch that most of the material gleaned in this vast salvage operation would be unusable proved correct; much of it lay corroding in heaps for years, but much *was* saved. At the end of 1941 an Appeal Panel, which he joined, was set up by the ministry and every deserving case was considered by experts. Ampthill town was one of many places that appealed for retention of its ironwork and he was pleased to ensure that it was all preserved. His action met with some hostility as he had expected it would. A local doctor's wife accused him of being unpatriotic!

When roused he could be extremely rude and this remark coupled with the effort he had put into the campaign infuriated him.

'Woman!' he bellowed at her, 'You have a common mind!

The doctor's wife returned home in tears and shortly afterwards a letter was received from the doctor demanding an apology. My grandfather replied that he was quite used to being 'railed against' and did not mind the doctor's 'railing' at all! This was unsatisfactory and so he composed a long letter in rhyming couplets which ended –

> 'Doctor since you vent your spite
> What is it you'd have me write?
> Can I be accused of conspiring ends
> When I try to educate my friends?
> Bid Madam wipe her streaming eyes
> And I'll say that I APOLOGISE!'

Although it was some time before the doctor's wife ventured to speak to him again, all criticism of the railing campaign was silenced, at least on his own doorstep!

Earlier the same year he had been disquieted while reading his newspaper at Cambridge to come across frequent reports of damage to historic houses by the troops billeted in them. As a former officer he appreciated that mishaps were inevitable but there were cases of whole mansions being burnt down, painted ceilings vandalised and staircase banisters used as firewood. This prompted another difficult letter to *The Times* –

'It seems to me perfectly monstrous that troops quartered in a requisitioned building should be at liberty to work their will on masterpieces of craftsmanship. At present, fine work must take its chance of being burnt or mutilated. Surely this is not in the National interest and no expense would be incurred in preventing such abuses.'

These words were written out of experience, he was already restoring one building seriously damaged, Chillingham Castle, and was shortly to be engaged on two others, Long Melford Hall and Wherwell Priory; Woburn too had to be extensively renovated after service use.

Chillingham, one of the finest fortified border houses in Northumberland presented a great challenge to him and one that he met with characteristic ingenuity. The sixteenth-century main block with Wyattville additions had been badly burned by the army and the Countess of Tankerville made a special journey to Cambridge to ask my grandfather to help.

He made a lightning visit to Chillingham and planned the restoration in confident mood despite the crippling wartime restrictions he assured the ministry that he would make the place 'wind and weather proof'. He managed to find two masons and a carpenter over military age and aided and abetted by Lady Tankerville, spirited up materials and thoroughly restored the castle. All the old lead was re-melted and re-worked on the spot. 'Exactly like going back to the Middle Ages!' he told a friend, and the timber for reconstruction was taken from old wardrobes and housemaids' cupboards.

The ministry inspectors visited Chillingham after work was complete and were both amazed and indignant at the thoroughness of the restoration; my grandfather was summoned before the Commissioners at Newcastle.

'I defy you to interfere!' he proclaimed in truculent mood, 'the thing's wind and weather proof as you wanted!'

'But we didn't want it like that!' said the Commissioners.

'Well I did!' the Professor retorted, 'and its done and that's the end of the matter!'

Shortly before the war, my grandfather had met at Anglesey Abbey, a Captain and Mrs George Bambridge, the new owners of Wimpole Hall. After Captain Bambridge's death he had designed the memorial stone for Wimpole churchyard and remained on very good terms with the formidable lady of the hall.

Elsie Bambridge was a smart widow in her fifties, the eldest daughter and only surviving child of Rudyard Kipling. It was her drive and energy that had brought a new lease of life to Wimpole and it was her money as sole Kipling heir and beneficiary that enabled her to go on living there in wartime. She was of middle height and on the plump side, with a well-featured face tending to sharpness around the nose and chin. She had grey-blue eyes which were an obvious asset to her, for the same colour formed the theme of her dress, mauves and greys of a scrupulous neatness and fashion, usually with similar tints in the grey of her hair. The eyes were the most sparklingly alive thing about her, they could twinkle with fun when she was in her most bouncy schoolgirlish mood, but they could also harden into something like spitefulness when one of her many adversaries was called to mind. Passionately jealous of her father's reputation she was always single-mindedly zealous over Wimpole and anything to do with it. She mounted verbal campaigns against villagers, trespassers, local farmers and in particular against the United States Air Force who occupied part of the park for many years.

She had of course made some mistakes. The Le Marchand bust had left the library at Wimpole if not with her connivance at least with her knowledge and she bitterly regretted its departure after my grandfather discovered what it was. She would not freely admit this, however, and laughed off the suggestion that it was 'really important'. A rather greater bone of contention were the portrait busts of Roman emperors which had stood in the entrance hall at Wimpole since the days of Harley. Mrs Bambridge had thrown out four of these because they were chipped, rather as one might dispose of an old Woolworth's tea-cup or a cracked jam-jar. These too arrived at Collins and Clarke's antique shop and found their way to Ampthill. When she discovered their destination she was slightly ruffled.

'I've got *your* Roman emperors,' Grandfather laughingly announced to her one day.

Elsie Bambridge pealed with laughter.

'Those *terrible* old things!' she exclaimed.

'They are very fine and look magnificent on my loggia,' he continued triumphantly.

This was too much for her and her eyes hardened into narrow slits.

'Terrible old things!' she insisted, 'and very battered!'

'Not at all battered dear lady,' added my grandfather, ignoring the fact that three out of the four noses were repaired with dental cement, 'on the contrary, magnificent!'

'Battered!' protested Mrs Bambridge with eyes blazing and there the conversation ended!

A serious row developed between them in late 1944 when my grandfather let slip a suggestion in the Cambridge press. Carried away with his usual enthusiasm he looked forward to a time when the University might expand its borders to take in the country houses of Cambridgeshire and especially Wimpole as extra colleges! This idea was widely reported and brought a very strong letter from Elsie Bambridge, blue ink on mauve paper, demanding a public apology. A disclaimer was published in the paper and their friendship continued to develop!

Mrs Bambridge reigned at Wimpole for thirty years after the war and I made many trips with my grandparents to see her, usually for impromptu tea parties, occasionally for dinner. She was a somewhat independent soul and kept herself aloof from her neighbours in Cambridgeshire, an isolation that increased as the years passed. She did not like visitors or tourists at Wimpole, was unapproachable about showing the place and only kept in touch with Huttleston Fairhaven who occasionally took her to the Arts Theatre, accommodating himself, her and my grandfather in one of the two boxes.

Despite her reputation for being a bit of a recluse, Mrs Bambridge seemed to tolerate and even enjoy the unexpected visits that we made on her. They generally followed an accepted pattern, my grandfather would turn the Rolls in at the gates on impulse and park on the deep gravel, gingerly ascending himself up the stone steps to the main door. A ring of the bell was followed by dead silence (portraits and busts seemed to be the only occupants); in fact besides Mrs Bambridge herself, there was only ever a lady companion, a butler and a cat in the entire place. A fumbling at the door was followed by the puffy red face of the butler, breathless, bothered, his spotted bow-tie awry, his black coat rumpled, evidence of recent sleep in the butler's pantry. This individual loathed my grandfather's visits because Elsie Bambridge never refused us admittance and he was always called upon to produce tea at short notice. My grandfather gave his name, the butler disappeared and returned again gruffly to open the door wide; we sailed in and Elsie Bambridge trotted briskly out into that rich columned entrance hall to greet us.

'Professor, what a surprise! How nice! How unexpected!' she was as beautifully turned out as ever, effervescently bright. She turned to the butler, 'We will have tea in the sitting-room!' The butler grunted, looked as if he could have killed all three of us and reluctantly left.

My grandfather was always entertained in the sitting-room

to the left of the entrance hall, a grandly gilt little room with views to the park. There was fine English and French furniture of the eighteenth century, fine hangings to the windows, but also silk-covered easy chairs and the signs of pastel feminine comfort. Grandfather sat on the sofa and talked, while Mrs Bambridge, a mischievous glint in her eye, egged him on to fresh excesses and exaggerations. The only interruptions came when she bounced up to show him a painting or two, the charming French portrait of a running footman or some landscapes. He was always particularly intrigued by a pair of Empire ornaments in the shape of pyramids of ormolu that she always had on her desk in this room. Each side of these skeleton pyramids had little hooks on them and from each of these dangled charms and seals and tiny objects of gold, collected with loving care.

'The little companions of Empress Josephine's long exile at Malmaison,' Mrs Bambridge explained, 'I think they are charming'.

There was a fresh interruption when tea arrived. The ill-tempered butler stalked into the room and in a last burst of annoyance, dropped the silver tea-tray on to the tea-table from a height of about two feet above it! The shattering sound of this was tremendous, the silver sugar basin and teapot lurched wildly, tea-spoons jumped and the china juddered, Elsie Bambridge remained unblinking. In turn, each of us received the same treatment, our cups, saucers, knives and plates were slammed down in front of us and the cake-stand slung at us with a menacing eye. We were relieved to see the door shut again. The Bambridges had been singularly unlucky with their butlers, an earlier member of the same breed had secretly drunk his way through the whole of Captain Bambridge's cellar during the war. When Elsie Bambridge's suspicions were at last aroused, she investigated, to find all the bottles carefully opened, consumed and re-corked on gallons and gallons of red ink!

It was always an effort for my grandfather to drag himself away from these congenial surroundings and he never left without a peep at the Thornhill chapel and Mrs Bambridge's begging off him some little sketch he had made there from the dregs of the teacup.

The war years ended for him as abruptly as they had begun. The pleasant conversations in the Combination Room at St Catherine's, where he had presented his colleagues with a Georgian bracket clock, ceased, so too the long evenings of silence in his panelled room, when the scratching pen was the only sound to accompany his longhand reminiscences of Victorian architects. Early in 1945 the Bartlett School returned to London and as he was over the retirement age he expected not to return with them. The treasures collected over the years were packed up and sent to Ampthill by road, the car was filled with books, and letters of thanks were written to Fairhaven and the Claphams as last calls were made and last buttery bills paid. In the event there was a stay of execution, for he was asked to remain until the end of the 1945 academic year in order to see the school safely re-settled, but it was the end of five happy Cambridge years.

This chapter of his life was concluded in a sudden and dramatic way on 30 June. My grandfather was driving my father back from Wherwell Priory in Hampshire, when their Morris car met with an accident. They had called on the artist Thomas Lowinsky at Oxford and were only a mile or two from home, when the steering failed and the car hit a telegraph pole, throwing both its occupants violently into a ditch. My father was seriously injured by the impact and my grandfather broke his right ankle in two places, resulting in a permanent limp.

They were taken to the Bedford Hospital and within a few hours of being admitted his proverbial high spirits were beginning to revive. Opening one eye and seeing my father lying opposite him, silent, unmoving and swathed in bandages, he chuckled inwardly and then shouted across to the recumbent figure.

'My dear boy, you look exactly like a Crusader effigy lying there!'

A fortnight later he was back at home and writing to Fairhaven of his experiences.

'I had a regal time in the Bedford Hospital,' he wrote cheerily. 'All my County friends appeared by magic, including the Chairman, Arnold Whitchurch. I am not mobile just now but I am not idle as you can imagine. The doctors say that I shall be in irons next week and therefore able to stroll through my rooms. I think with luck it will be possible to be about again in a month.

'As you can imagine I am surrounded by willing assistants, some carrying heavy tomes and others offering up sheets of translucent paper. All the details of the silversmith's work has been settled for the Chapel at Westminster. I think you will be pleased later on. We have tried to avoid the ordinary tricks. One can only design great things with exemplars equally great or better.

'Pray forgive this long epistle which gives me pleasure to write but which may bore you to decipher. Alas, all the good precepts about clear writing, learnt at Anglesey and set out so clearly in the visitor's book, vanishes when one faces reams of correspondence'. Despite discomfort at an age when most men are hoping for retirement, life for him was just beginning.

CHAPTER NINE

Travels with a Grandfather

The desire to be on the move, to be up and doing, was never far from my grandfather's heart, his diaries are peppered with expressions such as 'There is no time to be lost!' With increasing age there was no cessation of these hectic journeyings, in fact, they were speeded up as his public life became more intense. There were long car tours made all over the country to see the progress of his buildings and restorations, which could be as far apart as Kent and the Highlands of Scotland; there were lecture tours and permanent courses of lectures to be given at universities, as well as endless calls upon his time as an advisor and expert. The last were very time consuming, he was advisor to the dioceses of Ely, St Albans and Southwark and architect to the fabric of York Minster. He was still a long-standing member of the Royal Fine Arts Commission, council member of the Georgian Group and active participant in the Art-Workers Guild. Any one of these bodies and many more, might be instrumental in sending him off to remote corners of the country to inspect buildings and deliver his sage advice.

The preparations for such expeditions were colossal, the route and the timing was ably worked out between him and his two efficient secretaries, one in Ampthill and one in London. Somehow, miraculously, the calls that they mapped out for their unpredictable employer actually worked, the great arcs that he cut across England in his Rolls Royce more or less followed them, and isolated vicars had ten fleeting minutes with the oracle, before he swept on, cloak flying, to a lecture or a presentation. But for someone whose life was so busy, it was astonishing how much he made of his travelling, how much surplus energy could still be expended on the mere enjoyment of moving, seeing and thinking. The travels, through whatever part of the country, were anything but dull, however heavy the schedule or thick the appointments in his podgy black diary, there was always time to make a diversion, call on an old friend or discover a new inn with 'excellent cold beef'. He seldom travelled alone, how would such a compulsive talker have been able to bear it? He habitually took my grandmother or an architectural assistant as a companion on such jaunts. Increasingly, however, he had come to rely on Sidney Powley and this seems a good moment to introduce both Powley and the car he usually drove.

Sidney Powley had become my grandfather's chauffeur some years after the war although they had known each other before that. He was an amiable Londoner with a round, fresh face and thinning grey hair, only seen on those rare occasions when he was without his peaked cap. He was about fifteen years my grandfather's junior, as a young man he had fought through the battles of Mons and Loos and would often reminisce about them, but most of his life had been spent behind the steering-wheels of limousines. He was cheerful and willing and had a very lively sense of humour, an essential quality where my grandfather was concerned, as well as his own able wit which verged on the cockney.

Powley very soon became as much a part of our excursions with my grandfather as the bulging brief cases, shooting sticks and brandy flasks without which he found it impossible to travel. More important than this he became an integral part of the car, so much so that my grandfather's references to 'Powley' might be either chauffeur or black Rolls Royce. The Rolls which grandfather kept for London use and for long journeys was a 1934 *sedanca de ville* by the coach-builders Mulliners, it was quite high off the ground, had a long shining bonnet and a spare wheel on the back shielded by a gleaming cover. The general lines of the car were elegant and traditional, exactly like a road coach and Powley lovingly massaged the contours each morning with as much care as if it was a living creature.

Powley sat in front behind the wheel in his rather rubbed navy-blue suit and my grandfather lolled in the rear seat with the glazed compartment between them perpetually open. The back of the Rolls was quite lavishly appointed although not particularly large for the size of the car, the soft hide of the seats and door padding gave off a rich leathery aroma, the walnut finishings to the windows glistened and mirrors in the hood contained lights behind sunbursts with cigar lighters and vanity cases below. Immediately in front of my grandfather were two walnut cabinets which opened and shut with a satisfying well-fitted click and housed all the pens, pencils, chalks, paint-boxes, water-bottles and bulldog clips necessary for the journey. Also to be found there were the brandy flasks in Georgian silver, emergency rations of nuts, grapes and sardines and a large and powerful bottle of smelling-salts which my grandfather could resort to if all else failed. Then there was the box of cigars, the endless supplies of matches and the comforting black cough pastilles wedged together with a Regency travelling luncheon set of folding knives and forks. Somewhere in the mêlée were tiny sketch-books, barely big enough to take one pencil figure in frail outline. The larger sketch-books and the brown folder of David Cox paper rested on the floor, so did the library of books, editions of Hardy and Quiller Couch if he was going westward, Bronte, Scott and Stevenson if he were going northward, Dickens for Kent, Jane Austen for Hampshire.

'I believe in travelling on prongs!' he told an astonished Lilian Corfiato when she was surveying all this equipment.

'On prongs?' she queried.

'Absolutely on prongs,' he repeated, 'its the only way to travel.'

It was only some time afterwards when she was puzzling her mind about this extraordinary statement that she realised its true meaning. In his Georgian contempt for foreign languages and his atrocious way of delivering French she had actually been told that he liked to travel 'en prince'!

Over the years my grandfather and Powley developed a kind of team spirit as they traversed the country in this mobile studio. There was a very strong element of the Sancho Panza in Powley, complementing my grandfather's Don Quixote, but also of the nanny controlling the spoilt and refractory child. The relationship was one of mutual understanding of the others faults, the sort of unwritten code of unspoken looks which only the oldest batman or butler is allowed to perpetrate. It was not only my grandmother or I who saw Powley's raised eye-brows or shaking peaked cap, the signal that said 'The Professor's done it again!' Whatever 'it' might have been. So many miles of empty asphalt had been covered by Sidney Powley in my grandfather's company, such a barrage of verbal puns, esoteric information and professional reflections absorbed, that he had become a veritable Vitruvius among chauffeurs!

Even travelling alone with him, the faintest shadow of my grandfather seemed to be present in all his answers. One day passing a London church which I did not know, I remarked on it to Powley. He turned round to me in unbelieving contempt for my ignorance.

'Wren, you know,' he remarked condescendingly.

On another occasion he had driven us to Chelsea or Putney, some part of the metropolis that had a definite community atmosphere of its own. My grandfather was keen on the idea of London being a gigantic collection of villages, easily identifiable by their inhabitants, buildings and tempo. He had coined names for all of them, Marylebone Clinical, Islington Merry, Hampstead Delectable, spring to mind. My grandfather had asked Powley what he thought of the street scene.

'Very fine sir!' Powley replied gravely, 'one of the villages of London!'

On our travels Powley always dined with my grandfather at the various hotels en route, unless my grandmother was present, when he dined separately. When on duty at Ampthill, he lived at the *White Hart* and appeared at Avenue House after break-fast to receive orders, recognising instantly the particular bee that my grandfather had nurtured in his bonnet for that day and making a mental note of how best to humour him in it.

These breakfasts were crucial in the Richardson rounds, for not only did Powley find out what his day was to be like but the rest of the household did as well. A hot bath in a vast Edwardian tub made my grandfather peculiarly liverish from eight o'clock to nine o'clock in the morning. Breakfast itself was meant to soothe these humours but seldom did so. A great repast was spread in the under-heated dining-room, porridge, toast, bacon and eggs and a huge orange. The consumption of this fruit was a spectacle to behold for my grandfather did not eat it so much as rend it in pieces. At each gnawing ravishment of the orange, a shower of juicy spray shot all over the room, pips burst forth from it and peppered the floor, the occasional one bouncing off the old masters on the wall. The exercise was accompanied by the most tremendous groans and grimaces after which my grandfather searched for his napkin with saturated hands. Then there was porridge 'certain to stave off melancholy' and the main course, often completed by Georgian embellishments of kidney or kedgeree. The mountainous post was then torn open with savage gusto, no paper-knives here, and strewn across the floor over the orange pips, spilled porridge and sleeping retriever. Then and only then did the secretary, the gardener or Powley receive orders!

The main quarrels between driver and employer were over the manner of the driving and the direction. My grandfather was happy enough when Powley was driving the black Rolls Royce, but he had once let Powley loose on the grey fixed-head coupé which he kept at Ampthill. Powley had driven this car to York because the other had gone to Hythe Road for repairs, it was a solution that grandfather did not enjoy. On his return I asked him how they had got on.

'Powley drove it like a damn lorry!' he scowled.

One of the longest trips I made with grandfather was to Grantown-on-Spey where he was building a whisky distillery at Tormore. This journey caused one of the biggest disagreements between him and Powley which lasted for a whole day. Our route from the Midlands on the first day had taken us through Wakefield, where in Powley's hands we became hopelessly lost. My grandfather had become irritated, the conversation ceased to flow from the back of the car, the cigars were lit and re-lit a hundred times with stronger and stronger oaths and wherever we stopped the coffee was cold and the beef stringy.

By the time that we had reached the Border from York on the second day, the rolling hills and fast-flowing streams were beginning to lull my grandfather into a slightly more expansive mood, but worse was to follow. A little way beyond Hawick, we came to a T-junction without signposts. Realising that these valley roads were often circuitous and that a wrong turning could take us miles out of our way, Powley consulted his book. This was a huge blue volume which either dated from Powley's young days as a chauffeur or from the date of the Rolls, both events being well in the past. In the rear of the car, my grandfather turned to *his* books, all road books of the eighteenth-century, bound in matchless half-calf, among them *Ogilby Improv'd*, 1736, *Cary's Itinerary*, 1798, and *Paterson's Roads*, 1827, the most recent of all!

Powley reached for his spectacles and adjusted them on his nose, grandfather took out a glass to consult his early maps, both flicked obstinateley through the pages, determined that the other should not find the answer first. As was customary, Powley came up with a simple direction, grandfather floundered among turnpikes, toll houses and the distances calculated from Hicks Hall!

'We've got to turn to the right sir!' Powley said quietly, turning in his seat and addressing the smoke wreathed book bestrewn passenger behind.

My grandfather shut *Ogilby Improv'd* with a slam and bit hard at his cigar.

'I say it is to the left, Powley!' he snapped.

'According to my book, sir, it is to the right.' Powley persisted calmly.

'I say it is to the left,' shouted my grandfather, now sitting bolt upright in his seat 'To the left Powley!'

'And I still say, sir, it is to the right,' answered Powley, whose neck, a well-known lighthouse to his innermost feelings, had become flushed with excitement. Without another word, Powley let in the clutch, put the big gears into first and we moved off round the corner to the RIGHT. The effect in the back of the car was astonishing, grandfather brandished his cigar in one hand and holding the tasselled strap with the other, shouted out prevarications to Powley and blasted him out of Scotland, England and Wales. Powley took absolutely no notice, the peak cap looked dead ahead and nothing but that flushed and defiant neck was visible to my grandfather. As the miles passed and it became obvious even to the volcano in the back seat that we were on the correct road, the grumblings subsided though the tensions did not. The two of us in front became aware of a whirring noise, we didn't dare look round, but we realised that the glass partition was slowly being raised between chauffeur and employer. Powley waited for it to click into place and then several miles to elapse before he addressed me out of the corner of his mouth.

'If 'e can't keep his 'air on and wants to sulk in there, it suits me!' He said and then added, 'I think on consideration I prefer the company what I'm in!'

The glass partition remained sealed all the way to Edinburgh, but on the outskirts of the city we heard it creaking down again and the familiar chuckle was followed by a naughty couplet about the Adam Brothers. By the time that we were at the hotel the whole incident was forgotten.

The same tour was the occasion for another tussle between Powley and my grandfather. My grandfather was the possessor of a mackintosh which he preferred to call by its more Edwardian appelation of 'waterproof'. This garment had had a very chequered existence of about thirty years, it had served as improvised tent, picnic ground-sheet and had covered the inside and the outside of the Rolls engine in cold weather; it had acted in its time as rug, dish-cloth and towel and as an indispensible paint remover for the innumerable colour-boxes that we normally carried. Its increased diversity of use seemed to diminish at the same the original purpose for which it was made, it soaked in rain like a sponge through its grey and grimy autumn colours; Powley hated it, I hated it, the whole family hated it, in fact the only thing that was not repelled by it was the very rain for which it was created!

Powley had a very special reason to dislike it, its presence was an offence to his shining car and its appearance near to his well-brushed suit was unpleasant, to have to hand the portly bulk of the Professor into it from time to time was unbearable. Numerous tours with this unwelcome passenger aboard had hardened Powley's heart, he had watched its brown skin change to green like the iridescence of some greasy reptile and the light patches where buttons had been (the only spots where he could stand placing his fingers) gradually dimming to beige. Needless to say, my grandfather's attachment to this shabby covering had grown with the years, exactly as Powley's abhorrence of it increased; for the chauffeur it was a disgrace in which he was innocently implicated, for grandfather a battle-scarred companion of years! The patience of Powley in this matter had run out long before we started on our journey. He had determined that though he had to drive north with 'the Professor's waterproof' he had no intention of driving south with it again! Once Powley's mind was made up there was no stopping him!

One of Powley's duties was to make sure that our luggage was safely returned to the car after an overnight stop, no mean achievement considering the quantity of cases, rolls of drawings, books, lecture notes, pens and pencils that were carried in and out. At the *Station Hotel* at York, our first stop on our way to Scotland, the car was packed by the scrupulous Powley and all was set for the day's run. Powley had just closed the boot and his foot was on the running board, when there was a cry from inside.

'Powley, where's the waterproof?'

Powley retrieved his foot from the running-board and turned in slow motion to face the rear of the car.

'The waterproof, sir,' he repeated, looking as dull and dim as he dared.

'Yes, damn it, my waterproof – it's not here – must be in the room!'

'It must be in the room if it's not here.' said Powley, giving me a very odd look and then he turned back resignedly to the hotel. Minutes later he returned to the car-park, the bedraggled waterproof under his arm.

The stop at Edinburgh was highly successful, my grandfather had recovered his good humour, the classicism of the New Town had inspired him and his excellent rooms at the *Charlotte* had made him carefree. The next morning was bright, the prospects of viewing and drawing superb, so the baggage was packed, the porters were tipped and we were ready to roll. Powley's finger was actually on the silver button of the starter when a scurrying white figure came out of the hotel and tapped on the window; it was our tiny chambermaid holding aloft the same grey rag that had so nearly escaped us at York. Powley's expression was one of utter contempt as the waterproof was pushed through the door and the chambermaid received a shower of silver coins and a promise that she 'should have her portrait painted next time I'm in the Athens of the North'.

Powley recognised that his last chance was at the *Royal George* in Perth, after this a prolonged stay would make loss impossible. Our one night at the *Royal George* was followed by an early breakfast and early departure, the dining-room was deserted except for a couple who had arrived in a Rover the night before and had been installed in the room next to grandfather's. While he read the newspaper, Powley and I cleared his room and transferred the impedimenta to the garage. On our last visit to the room, Powley snatched up the waterproof and to my surprise darted along the corridor and into the empty room of the Rover couple who were settling their bill. He was back again in a flash having hung up the waterproof in their wardrobe! After collecting my grandfather we climbed into the car to be met with the same demand.

'Powley, my waterproof!'

Powley got down again, promised to search the room thoroughly, but returned without the waterproof. Three times he was ordered back to the room. 'The waterproof *must* be found!' But it could not be found!

Appointments were pressing and my grandfather's stubborness subsided into melancholy. Powley was told to get on and he climbed back into the driving seat. At that precise moment he looked in the mirror and saw reflected there a sight which sent a satisfied flicker across his face. Thirty yards behind, the couple in the Rover were staring in amazement as a most insistent porter persuaded them that a dung-coloured waterproof should be packed in *their* car! The Rolls slid out of Perth and Powley remained silent until the city was well behind us.

'I've got a feelin' that its going to be a wonderful day!' he remarked at last, leaning over to me and giving a very marked wink.

During the 1950s the growth of preservation and amenity

societies meant that my grandfather was constantly in demand as a speaker at their meetings. His flamboyance on the platform as well as his astonishing ability to draw at high speed on the blackboard, assured a full house wherever he appeared. He was booked by societies in Dulverton, Birmingham, Colchester, Cambridge, York, Oxford and Dublin, as well as by many organisations in his own home territory. Much of his success was in his apt turn of phrase, the outrageous statement or the suitable aphorism, his remarks usually hit the local headlines and societies relied on him to stir up local feelings. Sidney Powley faithfully delivered his passenger on time to nearly every meeting even when conditions seemed unpromising. The Professor had a way of riding over difficulties such as those when he delivered a lecture to the wrong group of people or arrived two days early. It simply did not matter, a few great gestures with the hands, a few asides, a few quick chalk drawings and the whole audience was ready to follow him to a man, preserving a green belt, a corn exchange or saving the character of a district.

His diary was crowded with hundreds of such engagements, in libraries, universities and grammar schools, but also in village halls, methodist chapels and even public houses. The subjects chosen could be anything from 'English Churches of the Nineteenth Century' or 'The Colour of English Market Towns' to 'Art and Religion' and 'Recollections of Travelling Before Motoring'. All of them were carefully written out and typed, but it was the unscripted parts that were most memorable, the unsolicited comments on politics, local government and fellow architects. But much of the lecturing was devoted to attacks on modern planning and design and defences of the old order, particularly the countryside and craftsmanship. After each meeting, Powley would be at the door holding the cloak, the homburg, and the oblong slide box of three by threes.

The Professor did of course propel himself sometimes, either in his 3½-litre 1927 Bentley, more like a locomotive than a car or in his grey Rolls. 'His driving is like that of Jehu, the son of Nimshi,' wrote Harry Batsford, his publisher, after a trip in the 1930s. 'He is never happy at less than fifty miles an hour, though this frequently rises to seventy when he finds himself on the long deserted roads of the open country towards Cambridge. To travel around with him is a liberal education; to see the churches he has tenderly repaired, the forgotten tiny hamlets and the remote country houses.'

Even in his seventieth year he was still driving himself huge distances and apparently suffering no ill effects from such an energetic life. The small branch office at the rear of Avenue House absorbed much of his time and if no chauffeur or member of the family was available he took an architectural assistant. A day in Norfolk in 1949 is not untypical of his busy schedules.

'Sept 5th. Left in my Bentley for Norwich. Reached Norwich at 1.45. A very fine run of 95 miles (lunched en route). Called on Mr Nightingale. Then to E Dereham, inspected the tower with the Revd Noel Boston, Sursham climbed to the top. Mr Pegg had repaired the flint very well indeed. After tea Mr Boston played various old English musical instruments. He also played a barrel organ. Left at 5.35 for Downham Market. Called on Major Andrew Wingfield at Lanes Farm, inspected Tithe barn of 15th century date. Then after a hasty supper of sandwiches, motored across the Fens by moonlight to Ely. I must say the effect of the lantern and the Western tower was awe inspiring. I have only seen one other Cathedral equally imposing by night, ie, Beauvais – Ely looked like this (sketch). Reached Ampthill at 11.15 very tired.'

My grandfather had several concurrent terms on the Royal Fine Arts Commission and many expeditions were made by him to look at buildings in company with the Commission's Secretary, the Hon Godfrey Samuel. He also acted as trouble shooter for the Georgian Group and as his diary shows for the same month, was prepared to alter all plans in order to save a building, in this case the doomed East Cowes Castle by Nash.

'Sept 14th 1949. A Hound Morning. Up betimes, caught the 8.23 to St Pancras and so direct to the Office. Worked on Trinity House revised designs for the new buildings. Then at 10.30 by cab to the RFAC Technical Meeting. Took Edward Maufe to lunch at Brooks's Club, discussed architecture with him. At 2.20 back to 22a Queen Anne's Gate. I was welcomed back to the RFAC by Lord Crawford. It is good to be on the

Commission again, in fact it is unique, being elected for the 3rd time.

'Left at 4.45 with Lord Crawford for Grosvenor Place to take the Chair at the Georgian Group. Discussed various cases including E Cowes Castle. Left at 6.50, then to St Pancras with Sisson, dined him. Discussed RA Schools with Sisson. Then caught the 8.10 to Luton.'

'Sept 15th 1949. A Hound Morning but in a different direction. Caught the 10 o'clock to London and Portsmouth . . . Isle of Wight. Arrived at Newport by 3.30, visited the Town Hall, met the Borough Engineer, the Town Clerk and the Contractors. Went over to E Cowes Castle to see John Nash's House. Arrived at E Cowes Castle through the original lodge and then drove through the park of 70 acres. Reached the Castle and found my way in. Alas – what a sight met my eyes, floors torn up, fireplaces smashed, windows broken, rain pouring in from the roofs which have been stripped of lead. A terrible act of *vandalism*. I reached the first floor by Nash's geometrical staircase (minus handrail) and found damage everywhere. Mr White of the UDC came with me. We examined Nash's famous gallery, removed here from the house in Lower Regent Street. On the floor I found one of the painted canvases for the lunette on the E side of the gallery. I had this packed up and took it off to the Office of the UDC at Newport. After noting everything including the staircase, we went on to Norris Castle and then to Royal Osborne which I have never seen. I was especially astonished with the Architecture which is plainly taken from Letarouilly's book. Then back to Newport after visiting St James's Church and inspecting the grave of John Nash who died in 1833 *aet* 83 years.'

The break-neck journeys up and down the country to save, protect and advise were often made with his fellow Commissioners on the Royal Fine Art such as Sir Edward Maufe and Louis de Soissons, but occasionally with John Betjeman. I remember vividly a trip made with him in the summer of 1952. Grandfather and the poet were supposed to meet my grandmother and the rest of the family at the *Mitre Hotel*, Oxford, after travelling back from Marlborough. The pair of them had been there to advise on street lighting and as the July day was beautiful and balmy, they had driven up on to the Downs to see the White Horse Hill and then returned to the Betjeman menage at Wantage for tea. 'He lives in semi-rural surroundings at Wantage,' my grandfather wrote in his diary, 'in a villa; his setting is curious, mostly reminiscent of Victorian and Edwardian, a sort of index to the last flicker of opulence.' After an uproarious tea-party at the villa, the two preservationists were very much behind schedule and set out for Oxford at least an hour late.

Sitting at the *Mitre Hotel*, my grandmother began to get a little impatient. It was very hot and close and although the Georgian windows of the hotel were pushed up, the general stuffiness made her uncomfortable. Six and seven o'clock went by without any sign of the Poet and the Professor. The head-waiter hovered around us with a menu and was continuously rebuffed, he approached again and again until we ran out of excuses and admitted that we did not know when our party of six would sit down. More procrastinations from the head-waiter, the kitchen would be closed at eight o'clock, did we want the cold fare? We didn't answer, simply craned our necks round at every new arrival.

At last we got an excited telephone call from John Betjeman in his characteristic staccato – 'Awfully sorry – bit late – couldn't be helped, order the muligatawny!' Our order was met with stoney stares from the staff, the hour of hot meals was passed it was cold soup and cold chicken or nothing.

Suddenly we heard a clamour from the street outside the hotel, some people were cheering and shouting and others clapping. My grandmother went over to the bay window and looked out, we following her. The sight that confronted us was astonishing. In an almost trafficless eight o'clock street, little knots of people, undergraduates and strollers, had stopped in their tracks to encourage a bizarre little procession. A hundred yards down the road, Betjeman's car, an elderly Vauxhall, was making snail's progress down the centre of the highway. Inside was the cloaked and homburg-hatted figure of my grandfather (never without these even in high summer) gingerly steering the vehicle. Behind the car was the puffing and blowing shape of John Betjeman, pushing my grandfather along, himself dressed in blazer whites and a college boater. The Vauxhall having spluttered over to Marlborough and wheezed up White Horse Hill had finally died on the edge of Oxford. The car came to a standstill opposite the *Mitre* amid a tumultous cry of applause!

Once inside my grandfather galvanised the staff into action in offering 'poor Betjeman' some refreshment.

'Freshly made barley-water if you please,' he ordered, 'laced with whisky, my own receipt – poor Betjeman needs it if anyone does!'

When Powley was off duty the task of steering my grandfather on his peregrinations fell to my mother, a responsibility that was never dull but could be very exhausting. His thirst for information and appetite for sight-seeing were insatiable and it was supported by a continuous burble of comment and reflection as the ash from interminable cigars tumbled down his waistcoat. We recorded some of these comments on a journey northwards about three years before his death, giving the flavour if not the exhilaration of such travel.

Our visit was to the North of England, the ultimate destination again being Edinburgh and we took our time slowly, travelling in leisurely fashion up Watling Street from Bedfordshire. My grandfather talked incessantly of the Watling Street, then of the Roman Empire, which he compared to the British Empire and the Golden Ages of Italy, Spain and Germany.

'Three hundred years generally sees a great country out!' he had remarked laconically as we left Lichfield behind us.

At about four o'clock we passed through Stafford and my grandfather began to get excited as we saw a mound from the roadside.

'Its Mow Cop, where Wesley preached!' he tapped exuberantly on the window and followed it by a long description of the rise of methodism in industrial England, reminded us of Dinah Morris preaching on the village green in George Eliot's *Adam Bede*, imagined her against a background of flaring industry like a painting by Joseph Wright. It was soon time though to stop and look over Little Moreton Hall which he had never previously visited and have tea while he sketched the interior. We worked round the main rooms, the chapel, the bedrooms and the long gallery at the top of the house which he appraised with a critical eye after recent National Trust restorations.

'They don't understand!' he said, shaking his shooting stick at the beams, 'the timbers were the silver colour of wood in the Middle Ages – not black! These fools have tarred them!'

He was equally unimpressed by the sloping appearance that makes Moreton one of the most picturesque of Cheshire houses.

'Not intended,' he commented wryly, 'the frame was built quite straight, the timbers have simply buckled and twisted with age!'

We drove on through the suburbs of Manchester, 'upper suburbia' as my grandfather termed it, where we passed rows of solid residences, memorials of Edwardian textile and cotton empires.

'Beasts,' shouted my grandfather, shaking his fists at each fresh outcrop of turret and gable, 'After making slaves of the population they build these palaces and show that they are no better than those they employ!'

From Manchester we skirted Rochdale and Hadlingfield before reaching Blackburn where the Professor's temper was cooled by coffee and tongue sandwiches at the *White Bull*, about half-past ten at night we reached the *Royal Arms* at Lancaster.

The following day my grandfather ate his customary large breakfast of porridge, toast and kippers and then met his friend and former student Mr Martindale in the hotel. They went at once to St John's Church, which grandfather was surprised and delighted to find a fine classical building of 1752. He met the vicar and Canon Collins of Lancaster on the stepway and swept them into the building with his enthusiasm – 'Magnificent my dear canon, look at the door! The nervous artistry of it!'

Inside he padded around with his tiny agitated steps, the vicar and the canon following dazedly behind. Touring every corner, he assessed the situation, darted his hooded eyes hither and thither and eventually walked back to the nave, hat in hand, sketch-book at the ready. Opening one of the doors of the high-sided box pews, he clambered in, shut it and sat down to consider. Retrieving a thick black pencil from an inner pocket he began to draw out the alterations necessary for St John's, handing out the pencilled ideas one after the other to the amazed clerics.

'I suggest that the treatment for the ceiling should be simple like this!' he began, handing over a wild sketch, 'The later fixtures in the church should be moved to give space like this!' He passed out another, 'the classical character emphasised like that!' A third sketch joined the other two.

When both vicar and canon were standing with fist-fulls of paper, my grandfather began fumbling in his waistcoat once again and brought out the tiny silver paint-box as thin as a pencil, that he carried everywhere. The silver brandy flask joined it on the pew seat and a slender paint-brush was dipped in the spirit to give enough moisture for colour to flow. There and then a complete perspective of the interior was drawn out, the colour scheme suggested, the improvements advised, all in brilliant line. After fifteen minutes the watercolour drawing, still wet, was handed over to the astonished vicar!

Even then he had not finished. Leaving the pew, he began to circle the nave restlessly like a bloodhound pointing a quarry. He stopped by a sort of recess which was curtained off by a purple cloth and peered behind it. A long low whistle was followed by exclamations of 'By George' and 'Great Scot'. He beckoned to the rest of the party.

When they were all round him, he drew back the curtain to reveal a magnificent mahogany table of grand proportions, carved at the knees and with feet of the highest quality.

'The Holy Table designed for this church by Gillows of Lancaster!' he announced dramatically, it was an unveiling worthy of any Inigo Jones masque. 'Vicar! I insist that this is returned to the East End!'

At York where we stayed for two days, my grandfather was in and out of the Deanery and the mason's yard in his capacity as architect to the Minster. The Dean, the Very Rev Eric Milner-White was a friend of Cambridge days and a scholar and connoisseur who much enjoyed these lively parleys. On this particular day there was a discussion about the placing of the Lord Mayor's arms, an eighteenth-century coat in carved wood, somewhere in the cathedral. The Professor went with the Dean into the Minster and tried the arms in various situations, until he suggested they should be shown as in an old print.

'But ought we simply to copy?' queried the Dean.

'Never be afraid to copy!' he returned instantly, 'for as Robert Louis Stevenson said "Unless you play the sedulous ape to a stylist you can never become a stylist!" '

The Dean nodded.

Such itineraries left very little freedom for holidays and in fact holidays in the accepted sense of the word were utterly alien to my grandfather's temperament. The wish to be constantly designing, creating, writing, lecturing or campaigning about something, meant that relaxation was only gained through work and even the most light-hearted visits were openings for research.

An exception were those weekends stolen away from Ampthill and from business at the homes of old friends. Latterly, his favourite among these was the house of Sir Eldred and Lady Hitchcock at Sodbury Manor near Bath. A grey-stoned retreat near the Severn which the Hitchcocks only used in summertime, it was an ideal spot for my grandparents to be together and yet be looked after. Sometimes the family were at home, more often my grandfather had the lovely gardens, panelled rooms and collection of Rowlandsons all to himself. Here he was really able to relax, set up his easel in the grounds, read aloud to my grandmother or her companion Mrs Lock in the evenings and take short runs into the countryside with Powley.

Sir Eldred was a short, somewhat abrupt man who had become the leading sisal baron in Tanganyika, like my grandfather he did not suffer fools gladly, he liked knowledge and he liked expertise, finding an overflowing of both in his guest. They had been brought together over schemes for Burford Church, the church that Sir Eldred had attended as a child.

Grandfather's profound mistrust and pessimism about the future of the arts in this country were not always shared by his friends, least of all Sir Eldred. It was he, who countered the Professor's gloom one evening in a charming and original way.

After dinner, my grandfather had bemoaned bitterly the failure of the public to buy quality goods and look for good design – 'The crafts are dying on their feet!' he pronounced,

'There is no new blood coming into them, they will all be dead in a generation!'

Sir Eldred quietly but firmly disagreed and there and then put a plan into operation. It was to be about six weeks before the Richardsons were again to be at Sodbury Manor and he notified his estate joiner of this. He asked him to complete a piece of furniture for the Professor in this time so that it would be ready and waiting when he was next in Gloucestershire.

The joiner was a very accomplished craftsman and a good cabinet-maker and he entered into the spirit of Sir Eldred's plan to prove to his friend that craftsmanship was not dead. When my grandfather arrived at Sodbury nearly two months later, he found awaiting him in his room a remarkable piece of woodwork. On the table before him stood a perfectly scaled down model in walnut veneer of a bureau bookcase of the year 1715. The finish was perfect, the details of brass mounted handles correct, the corinthian columns of the fitted interior and the alcoves all in order. Every drawer opened and behind the pigeon holes, hardly big enough to contain postage stamps, lay a complete set of secret drawers! When he had finished wondering over this he turned round to find an amused Sir Eldred beaming at him.

'Craftsmanship *does* live on!' he commented good-humouredly.

CHAPTER TEN

'Nylons, Pylons and Skylons'

The summer of 1946 saw my grandfather's active academic life come to an end. He retired from the Chair in the Bartlett School and was succeeded by his close friend and protegé Hector Corfiato. At a sad but not regretful ceremony, he recalled his twenty-six years in the Chair, years in which his lectures had become famous and students from other faculties had joined them simply to hear his exuberance. His old colleagues presented him with three handsome volumes of *Pyne's Royal Residences*, published in 1819, before he departed for his new London home, 31 Old Burlington Street.

This handsome house had been offered to him by Messrs Lenygon and Morant, the interior decorators, as a suitable headquarters for the new partnership with my father, Eric Houfe. Although the entire offices consisted of little more than three panelled rooms on the fourth floor, the *mise en scène* was Palladian if not palatial and suited him perfectly.

In a bombed and ravaged London, my grandfather found himself immersed and embroiled in the repair of more than a dozen of its most famous buildings. In the aftermath of the war, he discovered that a new generation of young architects had come on the scene, trained in social and functional building but knowing little or nothing of the great masters of the past. He realised as others realised too, that he was one of a diminishing number of architects who had grown up in the classical tradition, understood the disciplines imposed by classical art, respected craftsmanship and had long experience. He was called for on every side, to advise, to restore and repair the great holes that had been made in London's skyline during five years of blitz and holocaust.

For him it was an Indian Summer of classical architecture, a reprieve for traditionalism and a period of revived craftsmanship in an otherwise barbarous and alien age. All that he most revered in design was revived under his watchful eye, the baroque of Wren and Hawksmoor, the neo-classical subtlety of Wyatt and Chambers, the Greek revivalism of William Wilkins. Through all this welter of activity, he was able to live over his youth again, work with the City buildings that he loved so much and enjoy vicariously the life works of the great masters.

Masons, bricklayers, carpenters and turners, carvers and gilders, painters and glaziers were called back from semi-retirement or redundancy to work once again for their old friend 'The Professor'. Writing of his heroes, the eighteenth-century architects, in his book *Introduction to Georgian Architecture* which he was preparing at the time, he said they had 'to know all the mysteries of the crafts, to be sympathetic to the skilled workers, and in a position to determine detail and execution'. He might almost have been writing of himself, for he was immensely popular on the building site, easy of manner, sharing jokes or lunch with his workmen, but exacting good work from them and loudly condemning the shoddy.

Before the war had ended he was already at work on the reconstruction of his own University College buildings, badly damaged and shaken by enemy action. He produced eight separate schemes for this building before it finally began to rise from the rubble in 1946, a testing time for his patience and ingenuity. At about the same time he was asked to undertake the rebuilding of James Wyatt's masterpiece on Tower Hill, Trinity House, the headquarters of the lighthouse service throughout the country. It had been burnt out in December 1940 but the walls were still standing and he was able to work from some of Wyatts own drawings, brown and singed but saved from the fire. Other buildings followed swiftly, the rebuilding of the Chancery Lane Safe Deposit, a huge complex of offices with subterranean vaults and the total resurrection of the famous City Livery Hall of the Merchant Taylors Company.

Probably the most remarkable restorations were the two famous landmarks of St James's, Piccadilly and St Alfege, Greenwich, both great baroque town churches, the first by Wren and the second by Hawksmoor.

St James's, the only Wren church in the West End of London and well-known for its Grinling Gibbons' carvings, was seriously damaged by bombs in 1940. A high-explosive bomb had landed in the forecourt of the church and had completely destroyed the rectory and knocked the north wall of the church out of plumb. Nothing could be done until the war was over, but then he was able to rely on his own astonishing visual memory and the results of past work to guide him. He remembered the interiors of almost all these destroyed buildings from his student days and sent his assistants down to the Victoria and Albert Museum to work on the actual drawings that he had made of them forty or fifty years before. This was the case with St James's, although he called the saving of it one of the heaviest tasks of his career. He managed to keep the damaged north wall in position at the same time as retaining the supports holding the remains of Wren's compass roof. Slowly the whole roof was boarded and sheathed with copper in the manner of ship-building. Materials were incredibly difficult to get in post-war Britain and the restorations were slow and laborious. The restoration of Bath Assembly Rooms by him was protracted over a period of twenty years and the tower and spire of St James's was only completed by Eric Houfe eight years after my grandfather's death.

The fine church of St Alfege, Greenwich was in some ways an even more critical case. Less well-known than St James's and therefore less recorded, it had been completed in 1718 by Nicholas Hawksmoor, his only church south of the river. My grandfather had gone down to the site in 1947 and was appalled to see the baroque carvings for which the church had been renowned, smouldering on bonfires and being broken up by local children. He there and then gathered up armfulls of the woodwork and brought them home for study and safe-keeping.

Nearer at home there was the problem of Woburn Abbey which had been occupied by the services during the duration and left in an uninhabitable state. The Duke of Bedford, an elderly and difficult eccentric, who my grandfather had known for some years, decided to demolish the east side of the house in 1950 and did so hurriedly without consulting the experts. My grandfather was called in by the Ministry of Works to save what remained of the truncated ranges and give the eastern ends of the mansion something of their former dignity. This proved as difficult as the rest of his post-war work, materials were scarce and it was impossible to obtain adequate licences to use what timber and stone there was.

The arrival of the welfare state came to him as a mixed blessing, he had always been in favour of a planned programme for the re-building of London, in the classic manner naturally, but he strongly resented governmental interference. It was clear that he saw the new London as an artist rather than as a socio-economic planner! In an address he talked of his plan.

'I should have arranged for groups of artists, architects and thinkers, those interested in London, to have taken charge of London parish by parish and prepared various drawings showing silhouettes, sky-lines, historical buildings and so on. In fact all that machinery existed and could have been used, but no! the authorities preferred to take the advice of one or two individuals, with the disastrous results we know.'

Speaking in front of Clement Attlee at an RIBA dinner, he made his own position as an artist quite clear where state interference was concerned. 'I am sure that the Prime Minister will not mind another jibe,' he said, turning to the guest, 'I would say to him that architecture is not an art to be controlled by legislation, nor by pseudo-partnerships. Partnerships are very difficult in any case, but pseudo-partnerships are frightful, and pseudo-partnerships with the state are an impossibility. That is why we have enrolled *him* as an architect!'

Strangely enough, this life-long tory of the old school, found himself commended by the socialist government for at least one of his housing schemes. Immediately following the war, the Ampthill Rural District Council had asked him to prepare a model housing scheme for a site in a wooded glade on the south of the town.

He had declared that he wanted to erect '£1 a week mansions' for everyone and he saw to it that each house had the dignity of a panelled door and sashed windows. At his suggestion the houses, known as Chiltern Close, were placed round a village green and by the slight staggering of their positions, he gave them a pleasant feeling of natural growth. Each seven-roomed house cost £1,230 to build, and although the whole site was little more than three acres, there was a comfortable sense of space and seclusion for the twenty-five families who moved in. Aneurin Bevan, the then Minister of Health, said that he was much interested in Richardson's 'palaces for the people' and hoped to inspect them when he came to the area.

It was interesting that my grandfather showed so much concern for his council houses over the years although they were often on such modest and simple lines, he was also very concerned that the ordinary man in the street should enjoy his architecture. A friend recalled one visit to a council site at Croydon in Cambridgeshire, when a small boy, fascinated by my grandfather's long hair, flapping cloak and gyrating arms, attached himself to the party and followed him around the uncompleted houses. Noticing him, my grandfather took him by the hand and explained in a magical and absorbing way the real meaning of a house! He told the amazed boy that a house was really a human face, not a lifeless pile of bricks and mortar, that each house had a face and that every face was different. He then showed the child that the windows were the eyes and the soul of the house, the door was its mouth and the slate roof its head of hair. The boy had skipped away with a small drawing in which the rising council homes near his own house had become living beings!

So gentle and painstaking with ordinary people, he could none the less be very rough with petty officials, town clerks, jerry-builders, obstinate clergy and committees of almost any kind. For this reason, as the nineteen-fifties began, he developed a great reputation as a debater of lost causes and a powerful and fiery polemicist on any subjects involving the arts. Preservation of the heritage became a central issue, but so did the control of modern design, commercialism, functionalism and abstractions in modern painting and sculpture. His lectures were always making him headlines, rash statements and unguarded outbursts made him a welcome figure in the popular dailies. The headlines like his own speeches were pithy and to the point 'How to Get Rid of Ugliness', 'Professor Pleads For Preservation' 'Artists Don't Need Velvet Jackets But England Needs Artists', 'The Professor drops a street brick', 'Is There a Wren in the House?', 'Professor Richardson lashes out!' are just some of them. The intrusions of industry in rural areas were described as 'diabolical slave centres' and the manufacturing town of Luton, near his own home, was described as 'like hell – smokey and populous!'

Some of his definitions and aphorisms had an admirable freshness about them and have remained.

'Town planners – creatures never known to rise above the horizontal'.

'Functionalism – all bowels!'

'Tall buildings cast cold shadows!'

His opinion of concrete was absolutely unwavering – 'Concrete is an excellent material for foundations and structural supports. It is useful for shelters and esplanades, but it should be used wisely and remains a medium which should be clothed with superior material'.

Commerce came under the sting of his tongue too for the tawdry appearance of the shopping centres. 'Oxford Street is the worst in London . . . Its retail interests are nondescript, the architecture strange and the general effect chaotic. Regent Street with its megalithic buildings standing on pillared supports imparts an impression of gloom. The new blocks are out of scale with the width and length of this famous street.'

Of the goods inside he was equally critical, especially the furniture made of plywood and chromium, 'Shun these things!' he told one paper, 'I would rather sit on a banana box!'

At the end of 1948, my grandfather had heard with dismay that there were proposals being made for a World Fair on the South Bank of the Thames. It was to take place in 1951, exactly one hundred years after the most famous Victorian gathering The Great Exhibition of 1851. He registered this news with dismay because he was reminded of the fatuous designs of 1851, the vulgar commercialism of it and the effect it had produced on nineteenth-century art. He openly expressed himself horrified at the project and described it as 'a funeral service for the Great

Exhibition of 1851'. As the plans, under the superintendence of one of his own former pupils Sir Hugh Casson, began to emerge, he found his horror justified. The exhibition was made the excuse in his mind for a number of wildly experimental buildings that paid no lip service to tradition whatever.

After attending the private view of the South Bank Competition drawings he noted in his diary on 12 January 1950 'I must say they are the worst designs I have ever seen'.

He had already run the gauntlet in the press a week earlier by calling the Festival of Britain 'a fun fair' and adding that as a Royal Fine Art Commissioner he could let out the secret that it would never be finished in time! This brought a swift rebuke from the organiser Sir Gerald Barry; my grandfather only replied by dubbing the whole enterprise in the press 'The Festering of Britain' and adding in an atrocious pun that its chief building was merely 'The Dome of Dish-Covery'. When asked to comment on designs by the Editor of *Building* he remarked of the Festival restaurant 'Judging from the lightness of the construction – perhaps the lightness of the meals will provide a factor of safety!'

And of the much abhorred Skylon he wrote – 'Now the public will know the exact level of taste by which England will be judged in 1952. In the old days of decency a jet of water, an obelisk or a tall bronze mast would have been thought suitable. Present day theories incline to synthetic imitations of stratosphere rockets. Or what is even more unsatisfactory, a Heath Robinson erection which challenges the law of gravitation. Well, if the world laughs, gravity *will be* disturbed – that will be something.'

Somewhat surprisingly in view of all this, he was asked to design a small information pavilion for the Festival in a little garden on the south side of St Paul's Cathedral, only a stone's-throw from where his handsome *Financial Times* building was shortly to begin rising. Despite this concession he continued to vilify the Festival and developed a phrase of his own coining to describe the early fifties – 'The age of Nylons, Pylons and Skylons' adding with a wry wink 'all secretly suspended!'

The other great crucible of taste immediately following the war was the Coventry Cathedral Competition. This, like the

Festival was to be a barometer of the way taste was swinging and it was not one that he regarded with indifference. The reduction of the medieval cathedral to a shell after the Coventry raids made a new structure necessary and this was seen by the younger architects as the major challenge for a new type of architecture. My grandfather, an unsuccessful competitor in the Guildford Cathedral Competition twenty years before, decided to enter for this one in December 1950. His concepts for Guildford had been in a sort of free Gothic style, his ideas for Coventry were based on the brick mass of Albi in France. His design was one of the few that aimed to incorporate as much of the old church as possible, but especially the tower and spire.

When the results were announced in August 1951 my grandfather was absolutely horrified. 'We saw the winning design in *The Times*,' he confided to his diary, 'it gave us all a shock. Here is an Exhibition type of design, frightful to look upon and exactly like the Festival Buildings.'

His own scheme had been placed seventh and at the head of those of a more traditionalist character. All the designs were exhibited at Coventry, but only six in London, so that his scheme was never viewed by a wider public. The new Coventry, ironically the work of his former pupil Basil Spence, became another target for criticism and another bugbear which he had to live with. At the Royal Fine Art Commission meeting where it was discussed he refused to speak at all and was so truculent in the presence of Spence that he was asked not to attend a further meeting! But such an old lion could not stifle his roars for long and there were soon newspaper articles, attacks on the judges and grumblings from the sidelines. He kept one vow, however, his decision to have nothing to do with the new building; he never saw the cathedral or ever visited Coventry again.

There was a happier conclusion to another battle the same year, this time it was on a more domestic scale and the battle-field was his own doorstep in Old Burlington Street. One morning he had spied from his window, the figure of an old cockney lavender woman selling her sprigs on the corner of the street facing the Burlington Arcade. A number of street vendors had pitches in the area and he liked them all, but particularly this one because she was singing out the lavender-seller's traditional cry –

'Won't you buy my sweet blooming lavender,
It makes your room smell very nice,
Picked fresh at Mitcham this morning,
Only a penny for six bunches.'

My grandfather's sentimental heart was touched and he could hardly contain himself with excitement at encountering such a tangible piece of the eighteenth century in London. He rushed out time after time that morning and bought the old woman's entire stock, filling the offices with the fragrance of it and inducing his clients to wear her favours in their button-holes! The old woman herself, a stout and ungainly creature swathed in oddly matching coats and aprons scented a great deal more than the lavender that morning. She realised that she had a firm friend in the excitable and eccentric architect of 31 Old Burlington Street.

He insisted on having her into the house to learn all about her life and made her very red face even redder on glasses of cordial. She told him that she had learnt the cry from her mother forty years before and that it had been handed down for generations. Entranced by her basket, her history and even her ragged clothes, my grandfather escorted her to the door, assuring her of any help he could possibly give.

The next morning she was back again, seated on the door-step this time and my grandfather bought more lavender and encouraged more singing, the words bawled out in the most unmelodious manner. A policeman was seen to be observing her from a distance and in a fright she rushed into my grand-father's office and over more cordial informed him that she required sanctuary for her age-old trade. The police she con-fessed were not her friends and she told him that she and her fellows were shortly to be driven from the streets by law, could he help her she asked?

My grandfather at once became her ardent protector and wrote an article of protest at the change in the law for *The Sunday Times*. 'Machines,' he wrote, 'have already cut our roots and left us without the steady sustenance of living tradi-tion; but this particular lopping seems foolish and unnecessary.'

He personally approached Sir Harold Scott, the Commissioner of Police after this article, and the case against the lavender women was temporarily dropped. When the question was again raised, he offered his lady friends the protection of the courtyard at Burlington House. 'After all,' he remarked, 'they have inspired many English artists and the Royal Academy ought to make this gesture.'

The lavender woman continued to follow him about wherever he went and when he vacated Old Burlington Street in 1952 for a Georgian house in Queen Anne Street, she set up her pitch on the corner of Harley Street to be within his earshot! His new offices which contained a flat above them for himself, clearly showed the scale on which his practice was growing during the rebuilding of London. At this time his business had more than twenty assistants, a considerable number for a private architect and necessary as so many schemes were coming to fruition.

One of the earliest buildings to be completed was Trinity House on Tower Hill, a challenge of both restoration and rebuilding for as well as restoring the Wyatt work already mentioned, he had to create new offices for the Elder Brethren of Trinity House in Savage Gardens and add a new east wing to the main façade. This he did skilfully by the introduction of a segmental bay with a lead roof and flèche, a solution that in no way detracted from his Georgian predecessors admirable work. Some problems rose however on questions of finance, my grandfather was extravagant in his pursuit of beauty, and there was a disagreement on the minor finishings to the building. A meeting was called by the Elder Brethren to meet their architect and the venue was set as Richardson's own office in Queen Anne Street.

My grandfather was never very good at approaching a situation of this kind, he could become nervy and ill-tempered for hours beforehand although he was usually able to carry an interview through successfully. On this occasion he was more worried than was customary and regarded with alarm the half-dozen unsmiling faces that were ushered into his presence by the porter. He tried to be his genial self but failed miserably, the Brethren, made up of old sea-dogs and men of affairs, had come for explanations of expense and deviation from the plans and intended to get them!

Battle was about to begin and the spokesman was straightening his tie to speak, when my grandfather heard some sounds from the street below. It was the song of the lavender woman crying out her wares as she usually did when she knew he was in town.

'Gentlemen!' said my grandfather in a note of exultation, realising that in this lay his complete salvation, 'Gentlemen, may I have the honour of showing you a piece of Georgian London?'

Calling the porter he asked that the lavender woman should be shown straight up into his room where he was meeting with his friends.

A few minutes later the old party herself bundled into the room with her basket, dirty clothes and her own particular scent which was not of the lavender that she habitually carried. Dumping the basket down on my grandfather's Louis Seize writing table she looked around at the circle of elderly men and began to bawl out her song at the top of her voice. After the first rendition, my grandfather loudly applauded and asked for an encore, this was followed by several more each louder than the former till the room was reverberating with the lavender woman's toothless screaming.

The Brethren who had looked uncomfortable to begin with gradually became intensely embarrassed and even more so when my grandfather insisted on buying them all a sprig of lavender and despatching the good lady to pin it on them with such affectionate comments as 'all for you my lovely darlings!' After this he launched into a reverie about the glories of the street-sellers of the eighteenth-century and persuaded the lavender lady to try some other ballads not her own, while the admirals and aldermen got redder and redder faces. After half an hour the spokesman agreed to postpone the meeting as there was little left to say! My grandfather watched them meekly file out and then presented the lavender woman with a heavy tip, chuckling to himself on the stairs he murmured to a passing assistant 'I think *we* won!'

The opening of Trinity House by Her Majesty the Queen

was fixed for Trafalgar Day, 21 October 1953, the ceremony was to be a big one including the presence of Churchill and many leading political and city figures. The October day itself was foggy and murky and Tower Hill was shrouded for most of the morning in a heavy yellowish fog. My grandfather and grandmother travelled up from Ampthill for the occasion, the rest of the family being given a window in the Port of London Authority building next door. At 2.45 pm they went down to Trinity House and met some of those who had already gathered among them the Attlees, Sir David Eccles and Lady Churchill, who were inspecting the new library. My grandfather made a sketch of the crowd including Lady Churchill sitting on the dais at the end of the room, a dais that he had himself designed for the Queen's reception.

At 3.30 pm precisely, the Queen arrived with the Duke of Edinburgh, the Duke and Duchess of Gloucester, the First Sea Lord and Lord Alexander for the official opening. After the formalities, the royal party made a tour of the laboratories and the rear of the buildings before returning to the Court Room for tea. My grandfather had escorted the Queen round, explaining the plans and answering her questions. Tea was arranged at small tables at one end of the room, the Queen's table laid for three only, Her Majesty in the middle with Churchill on her right and my grandfather on her left.

'We had many laughs at the Queen's table,' my grandfather recorded in his diary, 'I told Her Majesty of the way horse racing started in France – Colbert and Charles II at Newmarket. She said she would not go racing but would let her horses race. We discussed the curtains in the rooms, the furniture and the decorations. I explained that we had yet to find an artist to paint the four river gods of England – Thames, Severn, Humber and Tyne. I suggested that Sir Winston might do this when he retires, we had a few quips about painting.'

Before the Queen left the table to sign the book, a curious little incident occurred. My grandfather noticed out of the corner of his eye that the Queen had dropped her black gloves on the floor, one on her right hand by Churchill and one on her left hand by him. He noticed that Churchill had seen the gloves too and looked to him for a lead. It was clearly impossible to grovel around on the floor under the Queen's legs and yet it was not very gallant to allow her to bend.

Churchill caught his eye and then cleared his throat.

'Ma'am,' he said, indicating the gloves by a glance, 'your companions are not very agile but their heads are alright!'

'Oh!' said the Queen laughingly and bending down she picked up the gloves, 'Here's one and here's the other!' she added smiling. My grandfather commented in his diary that night 'What an opportunity we both missed!'

CHAPTER ELEVEN

Presidential Honours

The Royal Academy and its members had always been in the background of my grandfather's career although he was well into his fifties before he had any part to play in it. In 1907, only a year after going into private practice, he had exhibited his first design at Burlington House. The drawing, within a gold mount, was a suggested 'Architectural Treatment for Waterloo Place', small in scale but alive with his flourishing penmanship a vision of the London he dreamed of, a Parisian London of great vistas, grand squares and *places*, arcaded streets. As is customary with exhibitors, he received a cream embossed invitation to the private view that May, and went along unknown and knowing nobody. At the head of the crowded main staircase, he had bumped into a young man in a grey frock coat, slightly older than himself. Their eyes met for a second in the mêlée before the young man hurried on and my grandfather proceeded into the galleries; the chance encounter had been with Winston Churchill.

He had first been nominated for the Academy by Sir Edwin Lutyens in 1923, Lutyens had added in a covering letter that it was an honour and a pleasure to propose him and that Giles Gilbert Scott would second him. This lapsed after several years although there were several later nominations of him by C. L. Hartwell, Malcolm Osborne and Walter Russell. All during this time his work was being hung regularly on the line and his buildings were becoming known. Lutyens again proposed him in 1932 and in 1935 came the final nomination which led to his election as Associate in 1936. The members putting their names to this successful nomination were, W. McMillan, H. Macbeth-Raeburn, T. Williams, W. Russell Flint, S. J. Lamorna Birch, Walter Russell, S. Lee, W. Curtis Green, Giles Gilbert Scott and Sir Reginald Blomfield. It was perhaps typical of the character of the man that his greatest support should come from painters or older architects, his outspokenness and traditionalism had not made him popular with contemporaries in his own profession. He remained an Associate for the next eight years, becoming a full Academician in 1944 after the death of the architect President Lutyens in that year.

Sir Alfred Munnings followed as President and it was a style of presidency and a quality of man that my grandfather found admirable. The jocular horse painter from Dedham with his breezy good sense, quips from the stable and distrust of 'modern art' and critics was bound to find favour in the Professor's ample Georgian heart. They had known each other since 1934, when Munnings had been commissioned to do a statuette of the champion mare 'Brown Jack' for the Ascot Pavilion and my grandfather had designed a base. Lord Hamilton of Dalzell had insisted that the statue should include the jockey Steve Donoghue up, but Munnings wanted the horse alone and my grandfather supported him. Munnings gave him a small sketch of the horse in return and a warm friendship resulted, thereafter they referred to each other as 'Alfred the Great' and 'Albert the Good'.

My grandfather was careful not to tread on any toes as a 'new boy' at the Academy but after a probationary period and with Alfred's help he began to bring out ideas. When the RA Schools of Painting and Sculpture reopened after the war, he was made Professor of Architecture, a post not filled since 1911. His duties were honorary but his fellow Academicians soon discovered that he had no intention that they should remain so. He threw himself at once into the task of canvassing for a new Architecture School, to run alongside the other schools and provide year long post-graduate courses. Supported by Munnings, it opened in 1947 with his former pupil Marshall Sisson as Master and a prospectus that concentrated on design and classic architecture, which official schools failed to stress.

His great hope was to attract Commonwealth students and some from the United States, but even discussions with the American ambassador failed to keep up numbers. The scheme lasted for only nine years, but during that time a number of bright young architects passed through it and enjoyed the contact with my grandfather even if they did not always agree with him.

Munnings' flamboyant leadership was exactly what he liked, a war against all 'isms' and pseudo movements and cant. The President felt that any art beyond the comprehension of ordinary men and women was not valid, he persuaded his Professor of Architecture to contribute fiery articles to a little magazine, *Art and Reason* which supported representational painting. But Munnings was sadly at the helm for only two more years and nothing became him like the leaving of it, this he did in a provocative speech at the Academy Banquet which my grandfather recorded in great detail and with great glee.

'28 April 1949. . . . to Burlington House. I found the Court-yard full of people, the Artists Rifles standing by. It is great fun arriving in state. We assembled below and then ascended the staircase to await the principle guests. Among them were HRH the Duke of Gloucester, the Duke of Athlone, the Archbishop of Canterbury and the Archbishop of York, Mr Winston Churchill, Mr Noel Baker, General Montgomery, the various Ambassadors, etc.

'The first part of the Banquet went off very well everybody merry – at my table I had Dr Chaytor, Wheatley, Worthington, Sir James Mann and others. We kept ourselves genially amused. After the toast had been drunk, His Royal Highness the Duke of Gloucester gave a fine sensible address very ably summing up the activities of the Academy during the years of war. This unfortunately was not broadcast. Then followed various other speakers. The gist of the Duke's speech was that the Royal Academy had kept the flag flying during the war years. Mr Noel Baker, Secretary of State for Commonwealth Relations referred to the recent meeting of the Commonwealth Prime Ministers, he referred to the changing conditions of the day. Lord Montgomery said that owing to the essence of his appointment he was now international. He said "In an age in which speed is the dominant factor, unless a nation is as ready for war as a fire brigade is ready to extinguish a conflagration, in no circumstances can it make good its peace time deficiencies." Like all the Field-Marshal's speeches it was dull and unimaginative. One could understand the limited knowledge of the humanities.

'Lord Goddard, the Lord Chief Justice of England said "the war had led to the destruction of many things we admired and loved. Reconstruction was slow, austerity was still the rule by day and night, but the fact that the Royal Academy had been able to restore that pleasant evening was a matter of sincere congratulation."

'The Archbishop of Canterbury, Chaplain to the Royal Academy referred to Mr Churchill as "a great commoner and a great amateur of painting".

'Then came the great tornado of words from the President, Sir Alfred Munnings, who attacked the critics and the high-brows – especially Sir Jasper Ridley, Anthony Blunt, Dr Rutherstone. Munnings said he was glad there were people who regarded Reynolds as greater than Picasso. He could not help being *blunt* and then he asked if Mr Blunt were present. He referred to the fact that when the King's pictures were on exhibition Mr Blunt had said Picasso puts Reynolds in the shade. (Such comparisons are vulgar and of no value). Some people said there must be something in this modern art and these young jugglers must be given a show. Personally he would regard their work as violent blows at nothing. He referred to recent exhibits of statuary at the LCC exhibition in Battersea Park as "foolish drollery" and said that some people were disgusted and angered by them. Similarly some people had been equally affected by the work of the Madonna and Child in a church at Northampton. There were certain interruptions from Dobson the eccentric sculptor, from Dunlop the painter and from Dugdale. The President's speech was enriched with such expletives as "By God", "by heaven", "I'm damned" and "kick him in the something". This referred to Picasso. Two of the interruptors, both Associates were escorted out by the RA Servants, they were obviously under the influence of drink.

'Then Mr Winston Churchill, Royal Academician Extraordinary, rose to speak (he was suffering from a relaxed throat). This was his speech as far as I can recollect.

'None could doubt that their President had strong views (laughter). It was fitting that a President of the Royal Academy should have a properly pronounced opinion. Everything should be done in this country to make sure that art should not lack the constant and steady support of an original and developing intellectual society.

'Art should be sustained by all the resources of the nation, we could not afford, he added (amid applause and cheers) to lower any flag at the present time. We must keep them all flying and he trusted we should succeed in maintaining our independence not only in the world of struggle and storm outside art but in the sphere of austerity we were now enduring at home and in those regions of art and philosophy without which no nation, however strong, could survive.

'I could not but admire the easy and graceful delivery of our honorary member who referred to his title honorary Royal Academician as an ambiguous title.

'Mr Churchill referred to the absent members of His Majesty's Government whose places at the table were so conspicuously vacant. He said that if these gentlemen were here they would become so enamoured of painting that they might begin painting one another.

'It was certainly a Bacchanalian performance, and one I would not have missed for worlds, because it was so purely 18th century. The speech by the President caused much misgiving in certain circles in fact the BBC was taken to task for not fading out the expletives.

'Eventually the long Banquet came to an end, the company broke into small groups and wandered through the galleries to inspect the exhibits. When in the Sculpture Gallery I saw HRH the Duke of Gloucester, he came over to me and for the next 30 minutes we went round the galleries, HRH pointing out the various pictures which he found agreeable to his taste.'

Afterwards the Duke and Richardson retired to the President's room where they found Munnings, Sir Walter Lamb, Sidney Hutchinson and the Duke's equerry, Major Michael Hawkins. There they sat down until 11.45 laughing over the evening's incidents and drinking 'moderate glasses of Scotch whisky'.

My grandfather quite often entertained Munnings to lunch at Brooks's as it was just across the road and was a break from the RA. His fellow members soon got used to their President's jocular conversation, brusque manners and noisy expressions 'in the saddle,' 'into the flat' and so on. 'Rather like dining with a horse coper' my grandfather commented dryly after one of these meals that had smacked more of the stable-yard than of St James's Street. Shortly before Munnings was to leave the Presidency, he suggested to my grandfather at one of their lunches that nobody could more fittingly 'take the reins' at Burlington House than himself. Grandfather was taken aback 'But my dear Alfred, I'm only two years younger than you are and with my position it's impossible!' Munnings was noticeably disappointed.

Sir Gerald Kelly succeeded Alfred the Great and during this time, my grandfather preferred to be solely Professor of Architecture, visiting the School two or three times a week, inspecting the students' work, giving an occasional lecture but avoiding the entanglements of the Academy's internal politics. Kelly was an accomplished publicist, put the Royal Academy on television and in the headlines of the press, but he badgered my grandfather about the School of Architecture which caused some friction. He had no further ambition within the Academy than to be a teacher, an advocate of moderation and tradition and to use it as a platform for promoting the greatest of the arts – architecture.

It was only in the early part of 1954 that there were the first rumblings of a discussion about who was to succeed Sir Gerald Kelly. Academicians of different colours and persuasions announced that they were backing various horses, most of these suggestions could be dismissed, but not those of Sir Henry Rushbury, the Keeper. In early May, my grandfather less than a week from his seventy-fourth birthday was given some strange news by Marshall Sisson.

'May 13th, Sisson told me of a scheme whereby it was thought that I should be PRA for one year to keep the place warm for Lord Methuen. I laughed this to scorn.'

He certainly did not regard the possibility at all seriously, for as well as not mentioning it again in his diary, he never referred to it once during the painting holiday he spent with his family that summer in the Loire Valley. There were châteaux to be visited, great monuments to be sketched, but even in his most vigorous moments, he must have felt that he was approching the autumn of his life.

At another meeting of the Academy in October, to attend the President's Prize distribution, he was told once more, this time by Sir William Russell Flint that many members, including Rushbury and Kelly himself, wanted him to be the next PRA. Rushbury, a short pink-faced man with white hair, was the 'Farington' of the Royal Academy; his opinions were much listened to and he had wide influence among the Academicians and Associates. He had been a friend of my grandfather's for years, he often visited the Rushbury's at Bourton on the Hill and he had some of the artist's soft watercolours of France on his own walls at Avenue House. Munnings too was lurking in the wings, regarding Albert the Good as the greatest fighter for traditional values, draughtsmanship, design and representational art, that the RA had. Alfred Munnings' canvassing proved the most effective, for he persuaded 'a party of reliable sculptors and painters to dine at the club' where they all agreed *en bloc* to vote for Richardson at the December election.

What had my grandfather got to offer the Academy at seventy-four years of age? There was no single answer to this for his chameleon-like personality embraced so much. His warmth, his enthusiasm and his unfaltering devotion to the arts in this country went a long way to explain it, but more so his youthful *joie de vivre* that he had somehow retained and carried through to three score years and ten like some architectural 'Peter Pan'. Disillusion with modern architecture, flats like tombstones that he called 'maggotries' and 'breeding boxes', office blocks that 'were filing cabinets for tea-drinkers' and city edges that changed from 'suburbia to submergia' did not dull his hopes for the future. That April he had written in his diary – 'At the age of 74 one still enjoys the thrill of living. The world is full of beauty both Natural and Conventional – I think the most exciting thing of all is the effect of light. It is always a source of wonder to me how commonplace things glow when rays of light strike them'.

Through his forthright attitudes and no-nonsense statements, he had won a great deal of support from the man in the street. His quips and puns about the Festival of Britain had gained wide publicity and so had his John Bullishness, his love of the eighteenth century and the popular belief that he went everywhere in a sedan chair. Among his own friends he was an important voice in defending the unpopularity of the Academy. 'Is the Royal Academy of Painting as good as the Slade?' Brendan Bracken had asked him in a letter, 'or is it a junior branch of those aldermen by nature who preen themselves on being painters merely because they are Royal Academicians? Apart from yourself and about half a dozen others, there are few artists among the bosses of Burlington House.'

For my grandfather, the Royal Academy was first of all a bulwark of tradition with its Georgian beginnings and secondly an independent art school in a sea of state control. His stature could win respect for it from men like Bracken as well as humanising the mystique and jargon of art for the ordinary person at the turnstiles.

Even as late as November he was still reluctant. He told Rushbury that month that he would stand but 'would not have a finger in it' and mentioned to Howard Robertson that he agreed to serve but had not asked for it and was very doubtful that he would get in.

As the election day 7 December approached, he took rather more interest in the part he had to play and was quite delighted when *The Times* telephoned a week beforehand and asked for his photograph. When *the* day arrived, he was extremely excited, not to say agitated, and began to appreciate the importance of being elected, an almost unheard of possibility six months before. His diary, which he wrote up by degrees as each hour passed, is full of nervous expectancy.

'Made up my mind not to be disappointed . . . thought things over and came to the conclusion that I should not stand an earthly chance in the ballot.

'To the RA, visited the Schools. Entered by the Schools' Door. Then at 4.25 to visit the exhibition (European Masters of the Eighteenth Century). Paused a long time before the Guardis and the Hubert Roberts. At 5 o'clock to the Reynolds Room. Signed the book, took my seat by the side of Sir Wm Russell Flint. Felt resigned to another candidate being elected. Preliminary business ensued'.

'Then the moment of decision arrived and I felt all my old fears. The first round found me with a substantial lead. The second round found me with an overwhelming majority, I choked with emotion when the President declared me PRA, my goodness I did not expect this.' (He had a majority of twenty-eight votes over his contenders James Fitton and Charles Wheeler.)

'Then came a pause while the news was conveyed by telephone to Her Majesty the Queen. Thirteen minutes later royal approval was given, then I found myself in the Presidential Chair speaking to my Brother Academicians, what a moment, what sensations. After this we adjourned to be photographed, then I found myself surrounded by Press men, answering questions and so on until 7.45. All excitement, everybody congratulating me. Made a vow to do things well!' A little earlier he had been able to break away for a few minutes to telephone the good news to my grandmother at Ampthill.

The twenty-first President of the Royal Academy in succession to Sir Joshua Reynolds was only the fourth architect to be elected in nearly two hundred years of history. He certainly intended to give architecture a better voice, but he had only twelve months to do it, the retiring age for a President being fixed at seventy-five. In those first stolen minutes with my grandmother, he had been able to collect together some of his thoughts and hopes for the Academy, these he now shared with the journalists. The next morning the Press showed itself to be universally approving of the choice 'Mr 18th Century takes over at the Academy' sang the *Daily Express*, 'Architect as New PRA' said the *Daily Telegraph* mildly, but went on to describe his Georgian eccentricities at Ampthill. 'Guests invited to dinner frequently find themselves expected to wear eighteenth-century costume' wrote their reporter, 'they are served with food of that period'. 'Everything Professor Richardson does has this emotional flourish' explained the *Sunday Times*, 'His eighteenth-century house at Ampthill is lit by candles (with oil lamps and gas here and there). His garden has paths and vistas and temples like a miniature design by Repton.' Some of his comments were like a newspaperman's dream – 'Ideas cannot be pigeon-holed' he commented 'they must be developed immediately' and of himself he added 'If you live at the rate of twenty-five hours a day you must squeeze in the odd sixty minutes somewhere!' His hopes for painting were short, sharp and to the point. 'Architecture is part of the same art as painting and sculpture. Buildings are crying for sculpture, interiors are crying for murals. The British public deserve real pictures on their walls, even if they are small ones.' Cassandra in the *Daily Mirror* questioning the new PRA's 'war record' in art controversies commented that his attacks on modernism had been far from dull. 'The Professor manages to make painting sound like a broken bottle fight in a brass foundry'.

The *Daily Telegraph* sought some other opinions for its columns. 'It is right that architects should be recognised as artists' wrote John Betjeman 'just as widely as painters are, since buildings are the permanent ever-open art gallery of our public streets.' Henry Rushbury was confident about the new President – 'The students will welcome his election' he said. 'He is a real father-confessor to them and takes them out in coaches for sausage and mash.'

Back at Ampthill the grandparents were smothered by a deluge of mail from well-wishers, friends from his schooldays, comrades from his wartime service and hundreds of letters from former Bartlett students now working as architects all over the world. 'You are one of the few who not only has the highest credentials' wrote A. K. Lawrence, RA 'but is also powerfully articulate, a rare combination in the RA's history'. A less solemn pronouncement came from his old dealer friend Charlie Collins at Wheathampstead 'Hope you are often hung but never hanged!' signed 'Murder' read his telegram. For several days the office assistants and his secretary were kept busy sorting this colossal post and the postmaster at Ampthill seemed to be ever on the doorstep announcing that he had more bundles of telegrams or another sack-full of correspondence. My grandmother, calm and self-effacing had her own share of the post,

no letters more charmingly expressed than this one from Lady
Munnings and her legendary dog Black Knight.

> From Black Knight, V.I.P.
> Castle House,
> Dedham,
> Nr Colchester.
> 31 Dec 1954

'Beloved Ladye. Your kind letter has filled me with en-
chantment. I am a curious dog with a power! I knew the
President's wish would come true. You could hardly
believe the people who for years have asked me for one
wish and it comes true.

No one *can* possibly tell you how delighted and thankful
we and everyone in the RA are your DEAR husband is its
President. We are very sad he would not stand at the
election when my husband refused to carry on any longer.
OH if only he had *then* become PRA *THINK* what he
could have done. His Exquisite building (Jockey Club,
Newmarket) the world would soon have been rid of the
mad, bad, insane stuff we are forced to suffer from. Hoping
to see you both some day and offer in person the congratu-
lations of us 3 and a Happy New Year.

> From
>
> A. J. Munnings, Violet Munnings
> and Black Knight.

From the moment of his election, his whole life was transformed. He was now continuously at the Academy's beck and
call, Humphrey Brook, the RA's tireless secretary was forever
on the telephone, lectures and openings were continually being
arranged and his diaries were crammed with engagements. It
proved almost impossible to undertake the heavy burden of
work from Ampthill and so he transferred himself almost
entirely to 24 Queen Anne Street, a convenient car ride from
Piccadilly. There, in the third-storey flat, he could spend a
quiet moment with my grandmother, doze in a comfortable
chair, pick up a favourite book, before being whisked away by

Powley to some city dinner, prize-giving or committee meeting, in which his reputation as a speaker, made it essential for him to take a leading part.

His family and close friends who knew his irritation and frustration where any form of committee was concerned, wondered how he would manage at the many Councils at Burlington House. He had not enjoyed Sir Gerald Kelly's paternalism at all, 'A sort of admonition to the children of the RA with a note of warning' he called them, but he had contained himself while they lasted. It was easier for him to be in the chair and somehow his good humour and sincerity won the day so that some academicians called his conduct of meetings exemplary. Sir James Gunn was one of these and recalled how on one occasion a member had held the floor for quite long enough and his fellow artists were becoming restive. 'Richardson jumped to his feet and curtailed him with gaiety and politeness' he said, 'the fact that the member had been interrupted was hardly noticed.' This was a tremendous contrast to some of the Art Commission meetings where he had been bombastic, sometimes rude and often sulkily uncommunicative.

My grandfather's tone during these years was politic and wise, but it was not muted. In the first major speech after becoming President, delivered at the London Master Carvers Association, he said he wanted to lead younger architects into a rebellion.

'There is talk of stream-lining elevations – all for notoriety. In fact nothing should be stream-lined except water-closets!'

'I will have an army at my back,' he declared, 'I have students who think the same way and are determined to rebel because I have incited them to rebel.'

'The idealists are far more important than the realists. They give me nothing but stark realism, whereas the idealists aim at beauty, which no writer has ever been able to define.'

'Art is anonymous' he went on, 'it does not belong to the individual. It is national and until we return to a national art we may as well go on blundering and not worry.'

'There should be fountains in the streets' he shouted with enthusiasm, 'with tritons throwing water at one another!'

Munnings rushed into support of this speech in the *Daily*

Telegraph as he was to do frequently in the next two years. 'Be he merely a peaceful Professor and not yet a Knight' wrote Alfred the Great, 'he certainly is leading a charge as a brave, gallant Knight should do. God bless him!'

The Professor's long association with the Royal Family probably encouraged their greater involvement during his short term of office. During his first interview with the Queen on 16 December to receive his badge of office, he asked her to visit and inspect the Royal Academy Schools.

This visit, the first in the history of the Schools, took place during the following March and my grandfather escorted the Queen through the three schools of Painting, Sculpture and Architecture. The tour began with a typically eighteenth-century flourish which he had specially devised for the occasion. As the Queen arrived, she was facing a plaster bust of George III, the Academy's founder, which my grandfather had had modelled in a day and placed in a convenient niche. As the Royal party passed, the President stretched up and detached a red rose from the right hand of the figure and handed it to Her Majesty. In the School of Sculpture she was shown Maurice Lambert's bronze statue of Margot Fonteyn and in the School of Architecture the large scheme for a piazza round St Paul's Cathedral that my grandfather was planning with Mr Duncan Sandys. In the library she looked at Queen Victoria's magnificent fitted paintbox and tried on Sir Joshua Reynolds' spectacles. The whole afternoon was agreed to have been a tremendous success, as one academician put it, the President had made the Queen feel that it was very much *Her* Academy and *Her* Schools.

A month before sending-in day for the Summer Exhibition, my grandfather travelled down to Chartwell to select the paintings to be shown by the Royal Academician Extraordinary. Churchill let him ramble around his studio while the grand old man lay in bed upstairs, then at luncheon he let him know what his choice should be. Typically, Churchill changed his mind before the exhibition and sent down 'Sunset at Roehampton' a work in the style of Monet, although he included 'Bottlescape' which as he put it 'you were rather struck by when you kindly came down and lunched with me.' Very soon after his election to the Presidency, Bracken had telephoned to tell him that Churchill had made him a member of his own exclusive dining-club 'The Other Club' which met at the *Savoy Hotel* from time to time. This was a great honour and he was genuinely surprised. 'I don't know whether I'm there as sage or court-jester' he commented delightedly.

The Summer Exhibition of 1955 is mainly remembered as the one where Pietro Annigoni's portrait of the Queen received its first public showing. Its powdery serenity enraged the critics and at the Private View it was the centre of interest although it had been placed in a side room. My grandfather was far more enthusiastic about this than about the Sutherland portrait the previous year. He defended Annigoni against the modernists of the Press. 'It is a fine portrait' he was quoted as saying, 'never mind what the critics say. Critics are owls, bats and fleas, owls because they hoot, bats because they see things upside down and fleas because they nip'.

Walking round the crowded galleries one day and listening to the comments of visitors, he returned to the President's Room chuckling to himself. Two ladies had been talking in front of an equestrian subject by John Skeeping.

'Who is the President now?' the first asked.

'Why Sir Gordon Richardson of course!' came the reply.

The Summer Exhibition with its Annigoni portrait produced outstanding attendances and he was able to report to the Queen that the number of visitors had been the highest for half a century. He was also able to tell her about two big loan exhibitions for the winter months, 'A Thousand Years of Portuguese Art' and 'English Taste in the Eighteenth Century'. The Portuguese exhibition was particularly attractive to him, he knew and loved the country, having spent a sketching holiday there and was impressed by its boast of being England's oldest ally. The exhibition which would take up the entire main floor of Burlington House, was to coincide with the state visit of the Portuguese President and needed months of careful planning. Six hundred exhibits were sent from Lisbon for the show, including paintings, scuplture and silverware, the celebrated Belem Monstrance by Gil Vincente and a complete sixteenth-century royal coach. President Lopes opened the exhibition in

October and in the Assembly Room at the Academy, invested my grandfather with the Order of San Tago de Espada. Television viewers were given a guided tour of the collection one evening by Thomas Bodkin and the President dressed in wig and ruffles like Sir Joshua Reynolds. The last scene of this entertainment showed the portly President clambering into the Portuguese State Coach, which lurched wildly and drunkenly on its springs at his unexpected weight.

The 'English Taste' exhibition was very close to my grandfather's heart and he was determined to stage it before his term of office expired. Under the expert eyes of Ralph Edwards and Clifford Musgrave, a magnificent array of furniture and pictures of the eighteenth century were selected. Many of the finest things were to come from the royal collection as the Queen reminded him on one of his official visits, recorded in his diary.

'You have had a good many examples of furniture from here' said the Queen, 'don't ask for the carpets!' I said that we could not hope to compare with the beauty of the royal apartments. Her Majesty looked very knowingly and said in reply 'Well I don't know!'

Before the exhibitions closed, a rumour reached his ear that Curtis Green was trying to get him re-elected as President for 1956. The paper being circulated was brief. 'Is it not in the interest of the Royal Academy that Richardson should be re-elected President for another year? He is a live wire and anxious to serve once more.' A special General Meeting was convened and after the Queen's assent had been obtained, my grandfather was unanimously elected for a further year, the first time that such a step had been taken.

In the July of that first year he had been able to take a week away from the Academy to visit Dublin. This was no ordinary holiday, but an excuse to meet all his Irish friends at the same time as being conferred with an Honorary DLitt of Trinity College. It was an exhilarating experience for him, strengthening the great bonds that he felt with that country, not only through my grandmother, but through the Georgian capital city, its architects and writers and his early memories of it as a youthful traveller.

He gave some of his thoughts to a Dublin newspaper. 'We

come here from England to see what London was. We like your tempo, we like your bookshops, we like the space and dignity of your streets, but we don't like to see Dublin turning into a cheaper London. O'Connell Street *was* dignified – it's a pity to see it degenerating into a display of cheap advertisements. The street needs cleansing of its aesthetic impurities. With trees planted along each side, you could hide the worst of the cheapness, and you might get something almost like a Canaletto!' He was invited to stay with the Provost in his superb grey stone residence in the centre of the city and walked across to the Degree Ceremony in Chambers' Theatre at the College. After the formalities he was asked to respond to the toast to the Honorary Graduates. In this he followed another recipient, a Professor from Harvard, who spoke drily and interminably for forty minutes, while the audience became restive and my grandfather began to search his waistcoat pockets for his smelling salts.

Rising to speak, he paused and grimly looked round the paintings in the hall. 'My lords and gentlemen' he began, 'as I stand here I see before me the portrait of Jonathan Swift, who taught us to belittle ourselves,' he pointed to a severe painting of the Dean. 'Over there on that wall is a portrait of Oliver Goldsmith who taught us to be charitable to one another and over there' he again pointed with more deliberation than before 'a portrait of Edmund Burke who advised us to get rid of America as quickly as possible!'

A burst of laughter and a ripple of relief went round the room for the lightness of his touch. After more comparisons between the two countries, he ended by criticising modern architecture in a way that would appeal to the country of the little people.

'If at birth the fairies are supposed to kiss infants on the hands for sensitivity of touch, or to salute them on the mouth for eloquence, or on the eyes for perception of beauty, the fairies rarely seem to kiss modern architects!'

Back at the Provost's House, my mother who accompanied her father on this arduous visit, received a strange telephone call in her room.

'Will you please ask Professor Richardson to meet Mr Bodkin

for lunch at the tea shop' said a mysterious heavily accented voice and then rang off.

My mother was somewhat bewildered by this message and went in search of the Provost's secretary.

'The Professor has been asked to lunch at the tea shop,' my mother told her, 'I suppose he knows which tea shop it is?'

A strange look spread over the secretary's face before she chuckled to herself and replied.

'I think you mean the Tao-siac not the tea shop' she said, 'your father is to lunch with our Prime Minister!'

This unofficial meeting between the Irish premier John Costello and Thomas Bodkin was to discuss the thorny problem of the Lane pictures. Sir Hugh Lane's collection of thirty-nine impressionist paintings had been a bone of contention since he died on the *Lusitania* in 1915. Legally they belonged to London but morally they belonged to Dublin, the wrangle had never been resolved. As a result of this meeting he promised to support Bodkin and discuss the matter with Sir Anthony Eden and Lord Salisbury. His efforts were eventually rewarded in part when the two countries arranged amicably to share the collection.

Despite the heavy work load at his office and at the Academy he was able still to advise on a hundred different little matters. He advised Margot Fonteyn on locating a new home for the Royal Academy of Dancing, designed a badge for the Newmarket Town Council, recommended a portrait painter to Lady Baden-Powell and suggested the type of carriages that should be displayed at Colonial Williamsburg. Somehow there was time as well to read and correct the proofs of his new book *Robert Mylne, Architect and Engineer* which was being published by Batsfords. There was enough time too in early 1956 to attend the opening by Princess Margaret of the astronomical clock that he had designed for York Minster.

His popularity as a lecturer never abated and he was up and down the country for most of the year, exploding into print with bombastic often outrageous statements about British complacency and vulgarity. The Barbican scheme which broke in January 1956 was grist to his unconquerable mill. Wearing a three-cornered hat, he attacked the whole thing mercilessly at a London preview. 'This Barbican will never be built. It is doomed and condemned because the British people will say "No we will never have a hideous thing like that" he proclaimed. 'It is a piece of exploitation by the millions of big business' he added. As an enquiry was pending the matter was *sub judice*, a fact that impressed him little. 'I am at liberty to express my views and shall continue to do so' he told *The Times*. 'Not only that – I shall increase my protests against the scheme.' The battles raged on, attacks on 'The Demon of Bureaucracy' 'Incubator Schools produced by the Ministry of Education' and 'The Curse of Office-Bound Planners'. He was particularly forthright about the future of the English village.

'Today' he pronounced at the Guildhall, 'the whole of England rises in indignation against the follies of indiscriminate development. Town planning, except as a protective agency, should never have been allowed to touch the once fair countenance of England. We still have the nymphs and fawns concealing themselves from the face of mortals, finding refuge in secret places. While there are still woods, spinneys and lush meadowlands, while rivers and streams remain unpolluted by detergents, while soft mists swathe the brooks and streamlets, those very nymphs and fawns will continue to inspire by their presence.'

At the Fanmakers Company banquet he took the Loving Cup next to Lord Justice Morris. 'You're supposed to face the other way to prevent anyone from stabbing me in the back while I'm drinking' the Lord Justice said. 'I'm sure a lot more people would like to stab *me* in the back!' was the reply.

When he appeared at Cheltenham in the spring of 1956 the *Echo* gave a full account of his performance in a speech 'as unreportable on paper as it was irresistable to the ear'. Dressed in a black morning-coat, wing collar and cravat and looking more like a figure from Dickens than a twentieth-century PRA, he poured scorn on the current abandonment of tradition.

'In the nineteenth-century, iron and steel became the materials for building. Today it is iron and glass, and they give us egg boxes and banana crates, not architecture. Can you imagine Buckingham Palace if it had been built looking like a glass factory?' 'When Wilkins was given £150,000 to build

London University he spent it all on a dome and the finest portico in Europe, with a few sheds at the back . . . and he was perfectly right.'

'It doesn't matter where you live if you have a decent front door and a decent elevation. It doesn't matter about drains. What we need is brains not drains!'

'All the time we are doing the wrong things, and then we invent the most brilliant ways of putting them right. That's part of the British genius!'

The proposed Berkeley nuclear power station also came under his lash. 'Is it conceivable' he spluttered, 'that some miserable contraption designed in an office remote from Gloucestershire should be planted *here* bringing in its train a mass of rubbish?'

These continual journeyings brought with them lapses of tiredness and exhaustion but usually the seventy-six-year-old's energy returned when he saw a full hall or a cause to fight for. The travelling itself landed him and his companions in all sorts of picaresque adventures, the unexpected always happened and he was always able to capitalise on it. The dim candles at Avenue House made packing difficult and many was the time that he turned up at functions in a dinner jacket and navy blue trousers or in white tie with a morning coat! There was little comment as his followers thought the garb was an intentional freak of individuality! Of all his journeying stories perhaps the most weird was on a visit to Lincolnshire in October 1955.

He had been asked by some friends of a few years standing, John and Bay Proctor, to stay with them for two days and speak at a meeting in Stamford. The Proctors lived about two miles from Stamford at Ryhall Manor, a small country house of various dates, set in a secluded garden near the village church. The L-shaped manor was of good Lincolnshire stone pierced by tall Georgian windows, a turret with a weathercock over it formed the central feature and the whole building was swathed with wisterias.

Powley had dropped my grandparents at Ryhall on their way south from York and gone on to London, my mother was to pick them up next day, so they had the afternoon and evening to enjoy the house and their host's fine collection. My grandfather puffed at a cigar in the drawing-room, ambled around the Regency hall looking at the furniture and glass, dated and re-dated the panelling in the dining-room and admired the portraits. After tea with the Proctors there was just time for them to rest in their elegant bedroom on the main front of the house before they dressed for dinner and the evening's engagement. My grandfather had the capacity to be able to doze at any time if a cigar, a brandy and a good book were handy, my grandmother sat in a chair giving her throat a gentle clear from time to time.

At about seven o'clock they decided to get ready for dinner, a knock on the door from their hosts reminding them that they had three-quarters of an hour. My grandfather roused himself for the bathroom, my grandmother moved to the dressing-table, both conscious that they could prepare themselves at leisure. Grandmother had brought two dresses with her, a long dress in case the evening was to be formal and a short dress if it was to be less so, their hostess had tipped the wink at tea that long dresses were to be worn. Taking the dress from the wardrobe she had prepared to slip into it and appear 'ready' before my grandfather emerged from the bathroom. To her utter surprise she found herself totally unable to get into it! Specially made for her and fitting like a glove, it none the less refused to go on, she could not even get it over her head let alone begin to wriggle into bodice or sleeves.

My grandfather emerged from the steamy bath, wrapped in towels, genial and eloquent, ready for the fray of the evening. To his astonishment he found my grandmother tussling in the middle of the room with her dress, twisting and turning in a mountain of cascading silk.

'Help me!' came a muffled voice 'I can't put my dress on!'

The PRA ran to assist her and together they joined combat with the dress. A casual observer would have been very surprised at the scene enacted before him. Here was the President of the senior art institution of the country whirling round a Lincolnshire bedroom, his wife half in and half out of her dress, the President himself in little more than a towel. The dress itself had now developed a sort of maniac ferocity, the arms not only tied themselves in knots but hit my grandfather in the face, the skirts of the dress were whipped up into a crazy dance and

performed such gyrations that my grandfather nearly missed
his footing. After five minutes of this strange blind man's bluff
in which all the futniture was bumped, the beds put in disarray,
the doors crashed against and the Proctors below wondered
what sort of people the Richardsons actually were, my grandparents subsided breathless and beaten on to their chairs.

'I'll have to put on the cocktail dress' grandmother submitted, even my grandfather's fighting spirit was broken.

'Yes' he added simply.

After a highly entertaining dinner party at which my grandfather held the table and an enthusiastic meeting at which he
roused his audience, the grandparents returned to Ryhall
suitably exhilarated. There, in the bedroom was the dress, still
draped over the sofa where they had left it, a challenge to them
both. My grandmother picked it up determinedly and lifting it
gently above her, slid into it at once!

Standing on the ground in front of the manor the next day,
my mother looked up at the long line of windows, the gnarled
forms of the wisteria and the eighteenth-century weathercock
above; something about the place seemed to stir her.

'Is your house haunted?' she suddenly asked.

Bay Proctor shifted from foot to foot while the luggage was
packed away into the car.

'Well not exactly' she replied, 'but of course we do have a
poltergeist!'

At the end of the year my grandfather heard that he was to
become a Knight Commander of the Royal Victorian Order.
The announcement was made in the New Years Honours for
1956 and hundreds of letters, if anything more than greeted his
election, arrived for him at Avenue House. The painter Henry
Lamb talked of his 'transformation' of the RA, and 'the sense of'
order, harmony and even happiness . . . you have brought us.
One letter that brought more than usual pleasure was from his
old friend and supporter John Betjeman:

43 Cloth Fair
London EC1

My dear Professor,
    All Bedfordshire will rejoice, all Ampthill will clap its

hands, the halls of the RIBA will reverberate, the saloons of the Royal Academy will resound, Vicars, Canons, Artists, Writers, Diocesan Advisory Committees, Central Councils, Groups Georgian and otherwise, Royal Commissioners of the Fine Art, musicians, sculptors, stone-masons, local antiquaries, will all join in the plaudits of the honour you have so deservedly received. Out of Heaven the shade of Henry Holland accompanied by that of Robert Mylne leans down to place a laurel wreath on your brow. Monumental classic architects of the 18th and 19th centuries sing louder in the Heavenly Choir, rejoicing to see justice done, to see the Champion of all that is beautiful left to us in this island made a Knight of the Royal Victorian Order. Even Leonard Stokes is pleased. Oh I am glad. God bless and prosper you.

Yours ever
John Betjeman.

Apart from a contretemps with Alfred the Great, the second term of office passed off smoothly. Munnings submitted a satirical painting for the Summer Exhibition of 1956 entitled 'Does the subject matter' showing the Director of the Tate Gallery, Sir John Rothenstein drooling over an abstract sculpture. My grandfather, however much he may have agreed with the ideas expressed, felt the subject was too sensitive and hung it inconspicuously at Burlington House. This brought down Alfred the Great's wrath on him and he said he wished he had included the President in the painting too!

My grandparents were not sorry to leave London in December after their hectic two years. It had been exhausting even for a man of his physical energy and for her it had marked a gradual decline in health. Avenue House was again awaiting them with its paintings, mellow interiors, trim garden walks and patiently attentive spaniel dog. 'I shall not be sorry when the term of office ends and I can get down to my normal way of living' he wrote to Lord Fairhaven, 'I have just completed ten watercolour drawings for Her Majesty the Queen. They will be kept at Windsor. Another watercolour made especially for HM the Queen Mother has also been completed. These works however will not preclude another work for Anglesey by Christmas! We have both survived the extraordinary activities of the past two years but it would be unwise to tempt providence by seeking a further term of office.'

On 11 December he took his place in Sir Joshua's chair for the last time and presided over the election of his successor. His last act was to place the chain of office round the neck of Sir Charles Wheeler.

CHAPTER TWELVE

Pregnant Penguins

It was with a great sense of relief that my grandfather returned to his own fireside in December 1956 and began to enjoy once more the simple pleasures of architect-squire within the borders of his own domain. The lecture engagements continued, so did the heavy responsibility of meeting clients and discussing repairs and restorations at countless different buildings, but there was much more time to devote to the garden and to his watercolours. An unrepentant Londoner, it had taken my grandfather years to adapt to his country environment and even now his interest in the garden was spasmodic. He had very little idea of flowers or shrubs, never bothered with painting them and in my recollection never looked a second time at a rose bush or a bank of carnations. His notion of the English garden was of fine trees, oaks, elms, limes and chestnuts, nothing exotic, bordered by green grass and decorated with statuary. The borders were left to the ubiquitous Shearwood, who cleaned shoes, stoked the boiler and occasionally put his long thin curved frame into a four-post bed when a night watchman was needed. Before going to London on an early train, my grandfather would pad round the edge of his walled garden, tiny and fussy steps followed by sudden halts and frantic pointings with the umbrella.

'The cotton-easter don't take under the wall' Shearwood would remark with traditional pessimism.

'Never mind, Shearwood!' grandfather would reply without having listened, 'black it in, black it in!'

In his estimation, borders were to be long lines of rich black earth which contrasted nicely with tree shapes and the white bodies of marble statuary, what went into them was of little importance though he had ordered lavender bushes in one and Edwardian roses still spread all over another. The key word for Shearwood was 'black it in!' and the luckless gardener spent much of his time turning over the topsoil to obtain the exact aesthetic effect to set off urns, busts, corinthian capitals and other forms of garden architecture. He had spent much of the previous year carving out little paths in a woodland bank on the west side of the garden, an area my grandfather mellifluously renamed 'the glens' and where he could stroll with my grand-mother on his arm. The only major gardening he ever under-took was to plant a semi-circle of flowering cherries, may and prunus round a white garden seat at the end of the tennis court, this made a bower for him to sit in while resting from his one garden sport – archery – which took place on the green expanse in front.

He had been much more successful with his statuary than with his plants during the ensuing forty years and attractive groups of eighteenth and nineteenth-century figures peered sightlessly from every corner, small fat Italian boys grinned at the stroller from the end of the avenue, sphinxes by Coade flanked the temple and Bacchus and Pan trod the woodland paths together. The finest acquisition was a large Italian baroque group on a plinth of Apollo flaying Marcyas, an un-pleasant subject, but large and grand and worthy of any Renaissance garden. This he placed directly below the big cedar and facing the avenue, so that a promenader on the raised walk could admire it from a good height. It was sub-sequently discovered that the group had come from Villa Martenengo in Northern Italy and had been mentioned by Lady Mary Wortley in the eighteenth century. Some other statues of bathers came from the sale of the Duke of Leeds collection at Hornby Castle and another pretty Apollo in marble, dating from about 1830 was acquired from Kimbolton. This he placed in a little grotto close to his verandah and con-cealing a musical box behind it, enjoyed the illusion of Arcadian music coming from its stone lyre! Some huge wooden figures of Negroes 'Charles Lamb must have seen them, dear boy!' were set up in a loggia and other poets, architects and statesmen skulked in bushes. Shearwood did not always remember where they were and at least one epic poet disappeared for a season inside a holly bush to emerge green and bird-stained after my grandfather's frantic protestations!

But the great passion of his life during these years had been the recreation of Hagbush Hall. Some time before he had acquired part of the neighbouring kitchen garden of Dynevor House and with it an old eighteenth-century cottage in poor state of repair. This was immediately christened Hagbush Hall and he set about reconstructing it as a garden retreat, half studio, half writing room, where he could laze away the week-ends or entertain parties of artists. The building lent itself ideally to such a scheme, consisting as it did of two rooms, one large and open to the timber roof, the other small and plastered. The first was formed into a Great Hall and a staircase and gallery from the Shambles at York were inserted at one end, the floor was laid with tiles bedded in sand and a copper hood was placed over the big corner fireplace. The effect was enchanting and the slants of light that filtered through the leaded windows into the dusty interior were a complete and intentional contrast to Avenue House itself.

With tremendous zeal my grandfather began to fill the Hall with rough-and-ready country furniture, gigantic oak settles, gnarled old tables, stout fireside chairs and the decorative bits of brass and copper without which a cottage hearth is never complete. A green and mottled tapestry which my grandfather claimed was of 'Somebody asking Henry VIII if he had a pain' was resurrected from somewhere, rush matting went down on the floor and candles were placed in the simple peasant chandelier like a penny wedding. A number of old farming contrivances which he had collected during the years were placed near the entrance to the Hall, yokes and flails and ancient digging utensils, giving the whole place an air of remote rural industry. Once King's men had completed the work, the last load of furniture had been delivered, my grandparents installed themselves in Hagbush Hall, she quietly reading or sleeping, he feverishly writing or occasionally making a sudden raid on the fig and fruit trees with which the cottage was surrounded.

Hagbush Hall was quite chill even in the height of summer and my grandfather seldom inhabited the place without having a roaring fire leaping up the chimney and sending showers of sparks on to the floor from the neat piles of logs in the hearth. He was oblivious to such niceties and went on with his reading while visitors jumped up and stamped on the smouldering edges of rush matting or rugs! Either through dampness or an inherent defect in the building, the smoke at the Hall rarely gave its undivided attention to the chimney but billowed out from it. My grandfather's guests, led through the meandering walks of the garden to call on the maestro, found him wreathed in smoke, some of it of his own making from the cigar at his side, much more from the wayward and recalcitrant log fire. If it was a watercolouring day he would rise to greet them through the wispy fog that clung round the floor and strayed to the rafters and point with his paintbrush in his hand over to my grandmother crowned by a conical Welsh hat or Venetian bonnet as she gazed distantly into the fire. The high-spot of the afternoon were the readings, when pushing his glasses up his nose and waggling his foot under the table he would deliver extracts from his journal while the logs crackled away behind him. Although his friends eyes very soon became accustomed to the gloom of the hall they did not adjust so readily to the atmosphere. First the smoke got into their nostrils and throats and began to tickle their larynxes, they dragged out their handkerchiefs and tried to stifle coughs by bottling them up. Then their coughs descended lower to their chests and their shoulders shook as painful asphyxias wracked their whole frame. Meanwhile my grandfather's rich voice went on unhesitatingly through the stately verses of Dryden or with passages of William Cowper's *The Task*, his total being absorbed by what he was saying and his monumental presence allowing no escape. Line succeeded line, his wig shook with the drama and grandeur of the words he was uttering, his captive audience for their part gasped and gulped and prayed that each rhyming couplet would be their last. Then the smoke began to attack their eyes, their eyeballs reddened and stung, their lids closed up and great streams of tears poured down their cheeks. My grandfather who had by this time progressed to Thomson's *Seasons*, looking up momentarily to see what effect the reading was having on his friends, found them so moved that he decided to continue for a further hour. But the illusion was short-lived; slowly and one by one, the chairs were hurriedly vacated and the guests hurled themselves like mad bulls at the stout wooden door and the blessed fresh air beyond. There, choking and coughing their hearts out on the grass, blowing their noses and wiping smarting eyes they compared notes about the shared agony. The beautiful and expressive voice continued inside, the flexible and sinewy hand repeatedly gestured above the open volume, but there was nobody there now to listen except the reader and my grandmother in her bonnet, placid and content and totally unaffected by the vaporous atmosphere.

The walled garden round the Hall, sloped gently south and was excellent for cultivation. Shearwood set to work at once growing giant dahlias and my grandfather organised beds of various ornamental heathers of which he was very fond. But his chief interest after the Hall itself was the rectangular pond in the south-east part of the property, a romantic enough spot with overhanging trees and a thick border of handsome bullrushes. For this he designed a Chinese bridge, mostly made from the wooden roof trusses of the old Morris brewery, the sort of ingenious improvisation which he greatly enjoyed. King's men were employed for some weeks after the hall was completed and the result was a trim little white bridge which pleasantly reflected itself in the murky waters below and which my grandfather at once began to paint. He also obtained a small dinghy which was moored on the bank and which he would occasionally paddle round the perimeter of the pond in his deerstalker and cloak! He later bought a pair of bronze Japanese herons which he placed as sentinels under the bridge and the garden seats round the pond were painted in chinese red, giving the whole place with its laburnums and cherries a very oriental appearance.

This rustic galliade was only possible in the moments snatched from the Ampthill office where half a dozen trainee assistants were always on hand with questions, away from the continual telephone calls and demands on his time from schools, societies and conservation groups. A good acreage of paper was covered by his flowing pen in the seclusion of Hagbush Hall, the sort of omnivorous subject matter that only a Victorian of his rotundity could have tackled. There were sallies against the tastelessness of bureaucracy, expletives at the rubbish in the shops and the apathy of the public in buying it. In January 1957 his privacy was opened up to a wider audience when the BBC television programme *At Home* visited Avenue House and spent half an hour subjecting the candle-lit rooms to its uncompromising scrutiny. Preparations went on for weeks, four television cameras were mounted in the house, their crews lounged about day after day and miles of cable ran through the grounds and in at the windows from an electricity sub-station. Produced by Humphrey Fisher and introduced by Hywel Davies, the programme was considered a grand success, my grandfather was relaxed and sparkling in the unfamiliar bright lights of the camera and in negotiating the even more congested furniture of his crowded rooms.

But a very different piece of publicity was shortly to hit the headlines and become an important battle quite literally on his own doorstep. This was his bitter tussle with the Ampthill Urban District Council on their choice and siting of lamp-standards in 1957. The controversy raged for many months and nothing before or since made him such a popular hero overnight, the newspapers devoted column inches to his comments and well-wishers sent him letters, telegrams and presents; the whole issue seemed like a storm in a teacup, but it was an issue of burning importance to the principals, my grandfather as an individual with strong ideas and the Council who were determined to go their own way.

He was of course arrogant and touchy about matters artistic and especially in anything concerning Avenue House and Ampthill town. But he was always generous with advice and encouragement, would go to any lengths to help a struggling local artist or a housewife who needed to buy a picture, and was popular with the man in the street. John Betjeman described as 'amazing' the way in which he could buttonhole an entire town council in a matter of minutes, taking them by the arm, leading them out into the streets, letting them sink their eyes into the landscape and showing them their home town from a new stand-point.

'To comprehend the character of a building' he wrote, 'is within the scope of all with seeing eyes. You judge an elevation as you study a face; if the features are comely, if the roof line is well defined, you can be assured that an artist has been at work. You should judge, therefore, from the standpoint of those who have the gift of creating buildings relating to human factors.'

It was his gift from the standpoint of 'creating buildings' that had prompted a number of towns to ask his opinion on their lighting schemes. He had travelled to Wiltshire with John Betjeman to advise on the lamp-standards at Marlborough and had succeeded in introducing well-integrated lighting to suit the texture and contours of the old town. Similarly he had advised on lamps at York, Cambridge, Wisbech, Stamford, Skipton, Morpeth and Peterborough to name only a few of the many historic centres.

It was therefore surprising that the Ampthill Urban District Council, when it decided in July 1956 to adopt new street lighting, made no attempt whatever to ask the advice of its most famous resident. A year later when the lamp-post controversy was at its height, it was asked why the Professor had not volunteered his advice directly the decision of the Council was published. But in July 1956, he was in the middle of his second term as President of the Royal Academy, much of his time was spent at Burlington House or at his London house, it was clearly impossible for him to keep in contact with every new development at Ampthill. As a public figure, he felt that any approach should have been made on the Council's side, but they in their turn were obstinate and independent.

Early in 1957, when my grandfather's term of office as President was completed and the rebuilding of Hagbush was at its end, there was leisure to reflect on the Ampthill street lighting. He was hurt and annoyed to think that he had not been consulted in a town which he had struggled so hard to preserve, and he began to say so publicly in no uncertain terms.

But it was only when the Council erected a single concrete stick in the town centre as a sample of their choice and invited comment, that my grandfather's blood really began to boil.

Thirty feet high, ungainly, bulbous and completely out of scale with the delicate architecture of the old streets, he recognised it at once as a brainchild of that same 'Festering of Britain' against which he had so vehemently campaigned. All the good manners gained in two years of Presidency disappeared overnight to be replaced by the old wrath and invective of a doubty septuagenarian warrior. The legendary explosiveness that had made the Mayor of Dover quake, customs officials shake in their shoes and bureaucrats reach for the door, was unleashed again on the elected representatives of his own home town. Filled with indignation he at once attacked the Council as 'ignorant little men' and had himself photographed glowering at the post! It was entertaining stuff and the press responded, but it introduced a bitterness into the campaign which was not an advantage.

On 18 March, the London papers began to carry big articles containing some of the Professor's views on why he had not been consulted, and what he thought of the posts.

'They are the ugliest in the catalogue' he told the *Daily Herald* reporter, 'just like attenuated concrete penguins'.

This gave rise to the watchword of 'pregnant penguins' which became his war cry throughout the battle.

'They will ruin this lovely town' he went on, 'Steel standards, fifteen feet high with traditional-type lanterns would give all the light needed. If these monstrosities are put up I'll stand for the Council myself to get them taken down again.'

In another newspaper he went a step further in criticising the Council.

'On the Council here, they're mainly young men. I was helping to make Ampthill lovely when they were playing with their hoops. Perhaps when they're older, they'll gain in wisdom.

'Perhaps then they'll realise that they haven't the right to introduce ugliness, casually and ruthlessly into this land of ours.'

The Council were still blinded by finance and obstinacy from the real aesthetic questions with which my grandfather was trying to involve them. Ampthill, they muttered, for reasons amounting to small town prestige *must* have modern-looking lamp-posts, but no extra money should be spent on making anything beautiful. For them, taste was simply not an issue, the fact that the town had fine Georgian streets and an attractive market square as a background for business, was simply ignored by them. When the Royal Fine Arts Commission, among whose members were some distinguished modern architects, gave the opinion that the chosen design was unsuitable, the Council ignored this too!

The meeting of the Urban District Council on the 21 March was to be the deciding issue; at the eleventh hour, my grandfather wrote to the Council offering his services for the first time and answering the remarks of a Council member who had met his opposition by saying 'Just think; what have these people done for Ampthill?'

'Gentlemen, I understand that the projected street lighting is to be discussed by the Council this evening and that members of the public are to be present. I should be grateful if the Council would allow this letter to be read.

'In company with many other responsible ratepayers I feel that the question of the form of lighting should be made public before any irrevocable decision is made. The issue is doubtless a delicate one, especially as it concerns taste. While there can be no opposition at all to the Council's wise decision for improved lighting, there is also the need to secure congruity between the lamp-standards and the characteristic architecture of the streets. This issue in the case of other towns has always been referred to other authority with excellent results.

'I am writing, therefore, to ask whether the Council is entirely satisfied on matters of aesthetic harmony.

'I have been a resident of Ampthill for many years and claim to have had a share in conserving and promoting the amenities which are famous throughout the nation. Here are a few of the amenities preserved by vision in the past: The Alameda and its gates, the House Beautiful, the preservation of buildings in the main streets, and lastly the securing of Ampthill Park during the late war by a Committee on which I had the honour of serving. When I was asked recently to design the cover of a proposed new Ampthill guide I undertook this in the same altruistic spirit.

'I feel sure that the Council in their wisdom will not embark on a scheme which must detract from the dignity of the finest little town in Bedfordshire.'

But the 'ignorant little men' were not to be persuaded by these soft words so late in the day. The letter was read, but the Professor's stalwart friends on the Council were defeated by four votes to eight and the war was on.

My grandfather received his greatest support from strangers and outsiders as Fleet Street unravelled each new episode. His post was full of letters from well-wishers who wanted the individual to be protected from ham-fisted bureaucracy. He was sent drawings of penguins, poems about penguins and a craftsman carved him a wooden pregnant penguin for his mantelpiece. The Glenny Twins, those two old ladies who attended every Pre-view of the Royal Academy in smocks and shepherds crooks, sent him a salt and pepper in the shape of Georgian lamp-posts!

Dear Sir Albert,

At a time when ideals are obscure, and convictions weak, we have been most stimulated by the sincerity of your approach towards Architecture, and forthrightness of your attitude to contemporary trends in design, and should feel greatly privileged if you would spare time to come and speak to us informally on a subject of your own choosing.

The Architectural Society of Students at
the Regent Street Polytechnic.

Balcarres,
Colinsburgh
Fife.
26 April 1957

My dear Professor,

I must send a line to say how unhappy I am to read that the Ampthill barbarians have got their way. I wonder if any other generation – or this generation in any other country – could have done this sort of thing. Is it merely utter ignorance on the part of those responsible? or is it something more than this? The next generation of course will have them down – but meanwhile these lamp-posts are over the country – the amazement of foreigners – all causing havoc. All one's battles these days seem to be losing battles – the only comfort is to think of all the battles you have won!

Yours,
Crawford.

24 Queen Anne Street,
London W1.
2 May 1957

'My dear Lord Crawford,

How very kind of you to send me your letter of support. I am very worried about the lamp-standards at Ampthill because I know they will ruin all the efforts I have made during the last 40 years to preserve the beauty of this historic place. I am afraid it is rather hopeless at the moment to dissuade them from their evil. Still, your letter gives me renewed courage.

With kind regards,
A. E. Richardson.

Immediately after the Council meeting, Richardson announced that he was going to stand for election in order to get the scheme rescinded, and that he was withdrawing his offer to design the cover for the town guide, which he had already begun work on. He also entered the lists in a traditional eighteenth-century manner by writing a broadsheet verse which was published in the newspaper:

> Artists when they strive for taste,
> Aim at checking needless waste;
> For Art responds to simple rules,
> Extravagance is but sop for fools.
>
> Should I, if my poor wit offends,
> Make enemies instead of friends,
> Excuse myself from qualms of duty;
> Or shelter in the realms of beauty.

Banish such things from all my thoughts,
For I have hopes as well as faults:
Art has taught us to be wise,
Beauty bids me shade my eyes.

Thus if my mind officious ventures
On fronts of urban representers,
'Tis but to state the case at large,
And pray that wisdom will take charge.

Would ye have me change my style,
Abandoning logic to win a smile,
Submitting to wrangling and contention,
Or beseeching reason and invention.

Councillors Ampthillian we may be your debtors
If you prove yourselves one better;
You too should *think* if you would gain us,
Then will good taste illuminate us.

On 23 April Richardson was in London where he met John Betjeman and discussed with him the next move in the effort to bring the Council to their senses.

43 Cloth Fair,
London EC1
24 April 1957

My dear Professor,

I could hardly sleep for thinking of the iniquity of the Ampthill Town Council. It is clearly a case of spite on the part of men with inferiority and I think it would be a very good idea to put a plaque up to commemorate the event on the wall of your house and have it very beautifully done and superb lettering so that it will look as though it will last much longer than the house. It should open, 'The hideous lamp-standards in this old and beautiful town were erected, despite the protests of local inhabitants and against the advice of the Royal Fine Arts Commission, by the Ampthill Town Council out of spite and ignorance.'

It should be made in a durable material and in large letters and out of reach of council officials and their employees. *If you will give me the inscription you decide to put up I will give it maximum publicity.* A paragraph in a newspaper such as 'At the moment when the Ampthill Town Council ordered concrete lamp-posts with which it intends to desecrate the town, Sir Albert Richardson has ordered, etc, etc.'

Yours ever
My dear Professor.
John B.

Ampthill,
25 April 1957

My dear John,

Your letter is splendid. I am afraid nothing can stop the erection of the posts, which will spoil this beautiful town, but until they are up I hesitate to order plaques because I am hoping, with the connivance of certain friends, to adjust the siting of the posts to avoid marring the superb elevation of my house. It would not do to inflame their minds until the worst has happened.

I cannot tell you how grateful I am to you for your suggestion.

With kind regards,
A. E. Richardson.

Support was still flowing in in letters and telephone calls. The veteran actor, A. E. Mathews offered his help and a chemist who was a fanatical follower of Richardson sent a present of his wares, but sent them to Munnings by mistake!

Castle House,
Dedham,
Essex.
8 May 1957

My dear dear Albert the good,

A B . . . . y great chemist's parcel that took me restive

minutes – hours to wrench open – contained the enclosed and I'm sure the man thought I was you? Lamp-posts, etc, etc, etc, hurrah!

No answer
Alfred the Great.

Richardson spent part of the summer sketching in Brittany (even the French press had headlines, 'Mr Pickwick déclare la guerre aux lanternes') and when he returned in early September found that the siting for the posts did not interfere with the façade of his house, but a post was to be placed right opposite to his bedroom window.

On 4 September Richardson sent another letter to the Council offering to site the lamp-posts. He received no answer.

'I have no animosity at all, but we are seeing England destroyed by those whose duty it is to protect it,' he remarked sadly. 'They are so confident of their own taste they ignore everybody. They have no taste and not even the taste to know they have no taste.'

The sign-board which Betjeman had suggested in the spring had been made in Bedford and was ready to be put up, immediately the last of the twenty-five 'pregnant penguins' had been erected. It was oval, with white classic lettering on a black ground and was surmounted by Richardson's arms and his motto 'Art is more certain than Nature' from the writings of the French seventeenth-century theorist Du Fresnoy. It read:

THESE INCONGRVOVS
LAMP POSTS WHICH DETRACT
FROM THE BEAVTY OF THIS
HISTORIC TOWN
WERE ERECTED BY
THE
VRBAN DISTRICT COVNCIL
AGAINST THE ADVICE
OF THE ROYAL FINE ART
COMMISSION

Originally when it arrived from the sign-writer, the board

had read 'WERE ERECTED OVT OF SPITE AND IGNOR-
ANCE BY THE VRBAN DISTRICT COVNCIL' but the
family lawyer had advised against this and it had been painted
out, though Richardson had impishly let it grin through the
overpainting!

On the day that the lamp-posts were finally installed,
Richardson watched from a window of his house in fighting
mood. The only incident however was when a council crowbar
was thrown inside the railings of Avenue House, a thing that
Richardson was particularly anxious should not be done and
he stormed out of the house followed by a member of his family
and a friend and removed it. The offending bar was carried
back inside Avenue House and only surrendered when a pair of
policemen came to retrieve it.

Richardson had lost his battle at home, but he believed that
because of his actions, sometimes tactless but always sincere, to
improve the standard of public taste, to shatter apathy and dull
acceptance of shoddy workmanship, other towns would be less
likely to indulge in doctrinaire attitudes, other men and women
would be encouraged to protest.

A few months later, Lord Esher introducing Richardson at a
dinner said of him: 'Albert is an old man in a hurricane, always
eagerly fighting for the great causes in which we all believe. No
doubt in the end he will be strung up on one of those lamp-
posts in his own town of Ampthill. But until his active and useful
life reaches that fitting close, he will continue to enchant us with
his vigour and charm.'

*   *   *

The vendetta with the Ampthill Council was the last imbrog-
lio to hit the headlines but it was certainly not his last tussle with
authority. In the next few years he was to take up the cudgels on
behalf of the Euston Arch 'It's a portico not an arch do you
hear!' he told one journalist, the Victorian Coal Exchange, the
Town Hall at Chesham and many other landmarks. He was
nearly seventy-eight, intensely proud of the fact and showed
remarkably little physical deterioration for a man of his years.
He had begun to lose his close friends during 1956 and 1957,

Charles Wade, Hanslip Fletcher and lastly Lord Stanmore, an early client of his. Rather than causing despondency these losses among the familiar faces of his circle only spurred him on to greater efforts in writing, lecturing and combating mediocrity and modernism.

If his hectic years in London had left him unchanged, ready to recharge his batteries and start afresh, the same could not be said for Elizabeth. The sudden removal to London at the age of seventy-two, the round of engagements, the continual publicity and the constant waiting for his return on late evenings, had taken its toll on her. Never very strong physically, the running of Avenue House after the war without staff and without energy, had broken her spirit and her ability to cope. The two years in London had taken her away from the country that she loved and Avenue House, which despite its hardships was the world that she had created for him. By 1957 she was extremely anaemic, weakly and getting very forgetful and confused, a burden that fell very heavily on my grandfather. Matters did not improve when he tried to get help in such an antiquated house, still no electricity, no refrigerator, no television, no aids to modern cleaning or convenience whatsoever. The eighteenth-century aura, which had been such a pleasure and such a joke while it lasted was beginning to backfire.

Fortunately my grandfather found an able and willing companion for my grandmother in Mrs Ethel Lock, a widow who felt sorry for them in their predicament and did not mind living a rather spartan life at Avenue House. In the summer of 1957 he had toured France with the family busily making water-colours, about fifty were the average for such trips and in the following year he had visited the North of Scotland to see the site of a distillery that he was to build for the Long John Whisky Company. All these holidays were an attempt to stir up my grandmother's mind and bring back to it a little of the sparkle and enjoyment of former times. All these efforts failed and by the summer of 1958 she was living a life of total absent-mindedness where sometimes she did not recognise her oldest friends or even her husband. The terrible sadness of this would have crushed someone of less resolve, but my grandfather applied himself more diligently to his work and showed her a compassion and consideration which nobody realised that he possessed. A last visit was made to the West Country in October 1958 to see Sir Eldred Hitchcock, Powley had to drive my grandfather down to Little Sodbury, my grandmother attended by this time with both Mrs Lock and a nurse. On the day of their return to Ampthill my grandmother suffered a stroke while sitting in her favourite chair in the morning-room. She was hurried upstairs, the doctor called, but there was a gradual decline for some weeks before she finally died on 17 December 1958, just passed her seventy-sixth birthday.

For some hours my grandfather lived in a sort of dream. He mechanically arranged for his wife's funeral and burial at Millbrook church, wandered around the rooms at Avenue House and dazedly faced the future. Immediately following the funeral service Kathleen drove him for a short holiday to Chester and in early January he went to stay at Anglesey Abbey with Fairhaven.

Although it was months before he could go anywhere that had associations with Elizabeth and he could not bring himself at all to traverse the hill to the graveside at Millbrook, it was not in him to remain idle for long. The pencil began to move across the paper once again, the watercolour box was re-opened and the battle for taste and dignity in the arts resumed.

In May 1959 he was busy once more in London giving two lectures at the Senate House, University of London on 'Excellence in Architecture'. These were well received and he had an enthusiastic letter on the subject from John Betjeman. 'While this marvellous power of seeing and sketching and conveying appreciation remains with you Professor (several people after the lecture told me they had never known you in better form) go on with the work! Publish some sketches of favourite buildings. Not finished, but those rapid things you do in ink. They could be reproduced in line block very cheaply or made to look like a sketch-book.'

Although he had given up a number of seats on commissions including the Royal Fine Arts and the Ancient Monuments, he was still the Chairman of one that he took great pride in. This was the HMS *Victory* Technical Advisory Committee at Portsmouth, where he enjoyed sitting in the place of honour in the admiral's cabin and being piped on board. He had been connected with the great ship since 1954 when the Committee was set up and enjoyed his contact with shipwrights and the craftsmen of the naval dockyard. His responses to the problems of labour and skill for the reconstruction of Victory were typical. A group of admirals and naval historians asked him at one of the early meetings where they could find the expertise for the work.

'Gentlemen!' he announced to a surprised committee, 'the Press Gang!'

'When you remove the plates from under the vessel', he told the Admiral Superintendant, 'look for the tarred brown paper!'

'Tarred brown paper, Professor', came the amazed reply.

'Yes, from the re-fitting of 1801. It will still be there!'

When the plates were removed the paper was found exactly as he had said.

In 1959 my grandfather made a Continental tour taking in Belgium, Germany, Switzerland and Italy and finishing with a week of sight-seeing in central France. He returned with the usual pile of bulging sketch-books and an assortment of antiques, books and carvings picked up along the route.

May 1960 saw a celebration that he had long talked about, his eightieth birthday. On the evening of 21 May, eighty of his closest friends were asked to a party on the Rose Garden lawn at Avenue House. Newman, the head porter of Brooks's Club and one of his London confidantes, took charge of the catering and there was a speech from Colonel Bill Dove. For once my grandfather seemed rather overwhelmed by it all and looked a rather elderly figure in his cloak with his stick by his side. He spent that summer quietly before fulfilling a lifelong ambition in the autumn, a visit to Greece, the islands and Turkey. This was at the instigation of his old student Merlin Minshall who arranged for him to lecture to the British Epicure Society on one of their cruises.

He left on 9 September for Paris, taking the boat train with Eric Houfe, Merlin Minshall and the rest of the party. After a brief few hours in the French capital they left the Gare de Lyon for Venice on one of the most modern continental trains. Within a few minutes of leaving the station the entire electric light system failed and remained out until they were in Italy! The party were in despair but my grandfather merely chuckled and removing the silver handle of his Georgian cane revealed a tiny candle perched in its nozzle! He was the only traveller that night to undress and read in peace!

At Venice they boarded ship and he spent several happy days in the Aegean, sketching feverishly, presenting his water-colours to fellow passengers and giving lectures in the main cabin. His first sight of Greece was an exciting moment and indeed he was thrilled by all the buildings that he had been lecturing about for years but had never before seen. Athens disappointed him 'a second-hand edition of Paris, but of course the Greek ruins make the difference'. Delphi he found superb.

After the mainland there were the islands and Istanbul. He travelled by steam yacht to Aegina and determined upon visiting the Temple of Athai, a small Doric temple of the fifth century BC which had always been one of his favourites. Against the advice of his friends he insisted on riding up the mountainside and ordered a donkey to be harnessed and saddled for him. It was primitive in the extreme, a wooden saddle, rope for harness and loops for stirrups, but he was tremendously pleased to have stormed the peak in this manner!

Arriving at Istanbul, he drove through the streets, sketched the bazaars and visited Santa Sophia and the Blue Mosque. They then returned to Venice by boat and spent a further three days in the lagoon enjoying the luxury of the Bauer Grunwald Hotel.

Only a week after his return to Ampthill his impetuous and ill-considered attempt at donkey-trekking led to a serious set-back in his health. As a result of the arduous ride he had a severe internal haemorrhage and was taken to Bedford Hospital where he remained for three days. His doctor, Sir Daniel Davies confirmed that he had a condition that was not operable in a person of his years, the condition though not necessarily malignant would be likely to weaken and debilitate him.

The following three years were difficult ones for him, he found himself slowing up in a way that he could not easily accept and his old spirit fought every inch of the way. He was in increasing discomfort, found sleep difficult and often read deep into the night to counteract this. More responsibility than ever fell on Kathleen to travel with him and Powley to drive him, for he was still determined to take up as many engagements as possible.

Perhaps his last major public appearance in something like his old strength was at a meeting in Dublin in January 1962.

This meeting was called urgently to try and save sixteen Georgian houses in Lower Fitzwilliam Street, threatened with demolition and to be replaced by electrical company offices. The Irish Georgian Society summoned him across the water as their last hope and he was privately received by President De Valera who gave him his unofficial support.

A large public meeting took place in the Mansion House and he made an impassioned speech about the country in which his own past and that of Elizabeth's seemed to be poignantly linked.

'Dublin is the Venice of the West,' he told his audience, 'in its colour, its arrangements, and its associations with the sea. The character of a nation is reflected in its public and other buildings. Buildings in this country have an endowment of charity and humility which the Irish possess more than any other nation. You are members of a soulful state. I would like to see Ireland a centre for the arts. Let the pursuit of beauty be your aim, but boycott everyone who comes here to make money out of you. In your resistance to the destruction of what you regard as beautiful lies the whole future of Ireland, this is your property, and nobody has a right to deprive you of it.'

He sat down to a great ovation. 'His enormous talent was for weaving architecture into the history of a country,' Lady Wicklow recollected of the speech. Although Fitzwilliam Street was not saved, it had been an extraordinary personal triumph for an ailing man of eighty-two.

My grandfather aged very quickly during the early part of 1963 although he summoned up enough strength in the spring to go up to Holyroodhouse and stay there as a private guest of the Duke and Duchess of Gloucester. In April he had the pleasure of seeing his lifetime's efforts as a watercolourist on show at Luton Art Gallery, followed shortly afterwards by a similar show at Bedford.

In October he travelled to Portsmouth for the last time to tender his resignation to the Victory Committee, he was no longer able to undertake the regular inspections or face the journeys involved. The drawing and designing went on but the increased weakness prevented him doing even that for any length of time. In December he suffered a slight stroke and from the end of the year he was totally confined to bed. He died in the early hours of Monday, 3 February 1964 three months short of his eighty-fourth birthday.

Perhaps the last word should go to Marshall Sisson, RA, his one time student and lifelong friend. Only a few months before his death, Sisson noticed my grandfather struggling up the steps of the Royal Academy looking pallid, frail but bright-eyed.

'What are you doing Professor?' he had asked considerately.

'I'm just beginning to study Gothic!' came the reply 'it's so exciting isn't it!'

Index

Abercrombie, Sir Patrick, 143
Ailesbury, Lord, 65
Alexander, Lord, 191
Allen, John, 112
Alston, Rowland Crewe, 95
Ampthill, 30, 35, 40
Ampthill cenotaph, 60
Ampthill church, 112
Ampthill House, 40, 47, 49–50
Ampthill House zoo, 47–8
Ampthill Park, 40, 43
Ampthill Rural District Council, 183–4
Ampthill Urban District Council, 221–30
Ampthill, Arthur, 2nd Lord, 96
Ampthill, Emily, Dowager Lady, 40, 44–5,
    46, 51, 54
Ampthill, Margaret, Lady, 129–30, 132
Ampthill, Odo, 1st Lord, 44
Andrade, Reg, 103
Anglesey Abbey, 147–9
Antique collecting, 91–106
Architects Journal, 30, 35
Architectural Review, 41, 44, 71
Art of Architecture, The, 140
Art Workers Guild, 71, 117, 162
Ascot, Royal Pavilion, 125
Aspen, Mr, 55
Athens, 234
Attlee, Clement, 183, 191
Avenue House, 36–8, 54, 70, 101–2, 130
Avenue House grounds, 39–40, 56

Baden-Powell, Lady, 209
Balfour, General Sir Alfred, 31
Bambridge, Mrs George, 156–9
Barbican scheme, 209–10
Barnwell Manor, 135
Barry, Sir Gerald, 186
Bartlett School of Architecture, 35, 61, 71,
    142, 180
Barton, The Misses, 51
Bates and Parmiter, 42
Bath, 26
Bath Assembly Rooms, 182
Batsford, Harry, 117, 171
Batsford, Herbert, 24, 27
Beatrice, HRH The Princess, 60
Beaverbrook, Lord, 154
Beckford, William, 26, 84
Bedford, 30, 236
Bedford Arts Club, 67–8
Bedford, Francis, Duke of, 65
Bedford, Hastings, Duke of, 182–3
Bedford, Herbrand, Duke of, 40, 75–6
Bedford, Mary, Duchess of, 75–6
Bentham, Percy, 123
Betjeman, Sir John, 71, 111, 173–5, 202,
    213–4, 221, 227–9, 232
Berwick-upon-Tweed, 106
Bevan, Aneurin, 184
Bidlake, Frederick, 15
Birkbeck College, 18, 22
Birmingham, 171
Blomfield, Sir Reginald, 194
Blunt, Anthony, 196
Bodkin, Professor Thomas, 208–9
Bolnhurst, 30

Bone, James, 24
Bossom, Sir Alfred, 68
Boston, Canon Noel, 172
Bracken, Lord (Brendan), 70, 152–3, 200
Broadstone station, Dublin, 25–6
Brook, Humphrey, 203
Brook's Club, 126, 128–9, 233
Brown, Lancelot 'Capability', 101
Bruce, The Hon Jean, 129–31, 135
Buckingham Palace, 21, 125, 210
Bunyan, John, 67–8
Bunyan's Country, 67
Bunyan exhibition, 68
Bushmead Priory, 117
Butler, Professor R. M., 000

Cambridge, 142–61; 171, 222
Cardington church, 112
Carlton House, 131, 133
Carpenters' Company, 27, 35
Cassells, Sir Ernest, 96
Casson, Sir Hugh, 186
Chambers, Sir William, 45, 101
Chancery Lane Safe Deposit, 135, 181
Chaytor, Dr, 144–5, 195
Cheltenham, 210
Cherry-Garrard, Apsley, 98
Chesham, 230
Chichester, Sir Gerald, 132
Chillingham Castle, 155–6
Churchill, Sir Winston, 9, 152–3, 191–3,
    195–7, 205–6
Churchill, Lady, 191
Civic Arts Association, 30, 58
Clapham, Sir Alfred, 147
Clarke, Louis, 152
Clarkson, J. Percy, 15, 20
Clegg, Mrs, 87
Clophill church, 112
Clutton, Henry, 76
Cockerell, C. R., 101
Colchester, 171
Collins, Canon, 176
Collins, Charlie, 96–8, 202
Collins and Clarke, 150–1
Compton, 43
Cooper, 48
Corfiato, Professor Hector, 140, 146, 180
Corfiato, Mrs Lilian, 164
Cosomarti, Helen, 86
Countryman, The, 101
Coventry cathedral, 186–7
Crawford, Lord, 172–3, 226
Curtis-Green, William, 194

Davey, Alfred, 92–4
Davey, Miss, 92–4
Davies, Hywel, 221
de Soissons, Louis, 173
Deepdene sale, 99
Devalera, President E., 235
Dorchester, 80
Dove, Colonel Bill, 233
Dublin, 25, 171, 207–9, 235
Duchy of Cornwall, 77, 80, 124, 137
Dulverton, 171
Dykes-Bower, S. E., 114

Eagles family, 44
East Cowes Castle, 172–3
East Dereham, 172
Eaton Socon church, 117–23
Eberlein, Harold Donaldson, 78
Eccles, Sir David, 191
Edinburgh, 169
Edward VII, HM King, 21
Edwards, Ralph, 207
Eggington House, Leighton Buzzard, 72
Elizabeth II, HM Queen, 190–2, 205, 207, 214
Elizabeth, HM Queen, the Queen Mother, 136, 214
Elgar, Sir Edward, 118–23
Elgar-Blake, Mrs Carice, 123
Ely, 162, 172
Emanuel, F. L., 24
English Inn Past and Present, The, 80, 140
English Taste exhibition, 206
Esher, Lord, 230
Euston arch, 00

Fairhaven, Huttleston, 1st Lord, 147–9, 152, 158, 214, 232
Fairhaven, Cara, Lady, 148
Farnborough, 30–1
Festival of Britain, 185–6, 200
Fisher, Humphrey, 221
Fiske, Pilot-Officer William, 152
Fitton, James, 201
Flanders, Denis, 48, 71
Fletcher, Hanslip, 18, 23, 29–30, 34, 45, 50, 61, 73, 86, 143, 231
Flitton church, 112
Flitwick Manor, 52, 78
Fonteyn, Dame Margot, 205, 209
Fordington, 80
Foster, Rev A. J. 67
Fox, Bounty, 113
Freeman, Herbert, 23
Fry, Charles, 117
Furse, Bishop, 113

Garbe, Richard, 153
Gascoigne, Charles, 18
Gayler, Mr, 53–5
George V, HM King, 124–5
George, Miss Mary, 102–3
Georgian England, 100
Georgian Group, 66, 98, 172–3
Gill, Charles Lovett, 22, 78, 86, 140
Gleadowe, Professor, 114
Glenny twins, The, 225
Gloucester, HRH The Duke of, 135, 191, 195, 197, 235
Goddard, Lord, 196
Goodhue, Bertram Grosvenor, 61
Goodridge, Henry, the Younger, 26–7
Gotch, Alfred, 68
Grantown-on-Spey, 166
Greenford, Holy Cross church, 114
Griggs, F. L., 87, 114
Grimmer, Albert, 40
Guild of Surveyors, 117
Gunn, Sir James, 204

Hagbush Hall, Ampthill, 218–20
Hamilton, of Dalziel, Lord, 124, 194
Hamilton, General Sir Bruce, 28–9, 78
Hanbury, Colonel H.C., 105
Handscomb, Francis, 53

Hardy, Thomas, 80–2
Hardy, Mrs Thomas, 80
Harlech, Lord, 67
Harlington Manor, 78, 95
Harpur Trust, 75
Hart, Commander Fred, 87, 105
Hartwell, C. L., 193
Hawkins, Major Sir Michael, 197
Helicar, Evelyn, 17
Henn, T. R., 144–7
Higgins, Cecil, 95
Higham, Rev P., 119–20, 123
Higham, Mrs, 121
Hitchcock, Sir Eldred and Lady, 178–9, 232
Hobson, Kenneth, 86
Hodgson, Joan, 72–4
Hodgson, John, 72–4
Holland, Henry, 128
Holland, Lord, 43, 112
Holland, Lady, 59, 112
Holyroodhouse, 235
Homelands Farm, Ampthill, 78
Honourable Company of Craftsmen, The, 114–6
Hornby Castle sale, 99, 217
Houfe, Rev A. E., 112
Houfe, Eric A. S., 112, 180, 182, 233
Houghton House, Ampthill, 41, 64–5, 66, 69
Hughtown, Isles of Scilly, 60
Hutchinson, Sidney, 197

Introduction to Georgian Architecture, 181
Irish Georgian Society, 235
Istanbul, 234

Jockey Club Rooms, 124, 140
Jones, Frederick, 94
Jones, Inigo, 65

Kelly, Sir Gerald, 198–9, 204
Kimbolton, 217
King, Charlie, 103–4
Kipling, Rudyard, 156
Knight's of Wellingborough, 113
Knox, Mr, 106

Lamb, Henry, 213
Lamb, Sir Walter, 197
Lambert, Maurice, 205
Lamer House, 98
Lamorna-Birch, S. J., 194
Lancaster, 176
Lane, Sir Hugh, 209
Lawrence, A. K., 202
Lee, S., 194
Le Marchand, David, 151–2
Lennox-Boyd, Alan, 114
Lenygon and Morant, 180
Limbrick Hall, Harpenden, 24
Little Moreton Hall, 175
Little Sodbury Manor, 178
Lock, Mrs E. M., 178, 231–2
Long Melford Hall, 155
Lopes, President, 207
Lowinsky, Thomas, 160
Luton Art Gallery, 236
Lutyens, Sir Edwin, 58, 70, 114, 140, 193–4
Lutyens, Robert, 70

Macbeth-Raeburn, H., 194
Macdonald, Professor Alastair, 114
Mahaffy, Dr, 25–6

Manchester Opera House, 29
Mann, Sir James, 195
Marlborough, 174, 222
Martenengo, Villa, 217
Martindale, Mr, 176
Mary, HM Queen, 125–34
Matthews, A. E., 228
Maufe, Sir Edward, 172–3
Maulden church, 112
Maulden Cottage, 52
Max Gate, 80, 82
McCorquodale, Mr, 63
McMillan, W., 194
Meakin, Annette, M. B., 67
Merchant Taylors' Hall, 181
Methuen, Lord, 198
Millbrook church, 112, 232
Milner-White, Very Rev Eric, 177–8
Milton Ernest, 78
Minshall, Merlin, 233
Montgomery, General, 195–6
Monumental Classic Architecture, 24
Moore, Miss Louisa, 52–3
Morpeth, 222
Morris family, 39, 46
Morris, John, 37–8, 102
Morris, Miss Maud, 38–40
Morris, Miss Sophie, 38–40
Morris, Lord Justice, 210
Mulvaney, John, 26
Munnings, Sir Alfred, 194–6, 199, 203, 214, 228–9
Munnings, Lady, 203
Murray, Kate, 87
Musgrave, Dr Clifford, 207
Mylne, Robert, 101

Nash, John, 172–3
National Trust, The, 66, 68, 84, 89
Newman, Mr, 233
Newman, Miss, 43
Newport, Isle of Wight, 173
Nicholls, Beverley, 79
Nicholson, A. P., 23
Nicholson, Dr Sidney H., 121
Noel-Baker, Mr P., 195
Norris Castle, 173
North London Cycling Club, 14
Norwich, 172

Oakley House, 96, 130
Odell Castle, 95
Office of Works, 69
Old Inns of England, The, 140
Opie, John, 103
Osborne, Malcolm, 193
Oxford, 171, 173–4

Page, Victor, 14, 17
Pankhurst, Richard, 74
Pankhurst, Sylvia, 73–5
Parmiter, William, 42–3, 91
Peacock, Sir Walter, 71, 77, 80–1, 129
Pears, Sir Charles, 69
Pembroke, Mary Countess of, 65
Perth, 170
Peterborough, 222
Pilgrim's Progress, The, 67
Pollard, Rev Harry, 113
Portuguese Art exhibition, 206
Powerscourt, Viscount, 46
Powley, Sidney, 163–70, 175, 232

Powys, A. C., 71
Princetown, 77
Proctor, Mr and Mrs John, 211
Pye-Smith family, 44, 51

Queens' College, Cambridge, 136

Reading School of Military Aeronautics, 29
Reeves, Herbert, 29
Regent Street Polytechnic, 22
Regional Architecture in the West of England, 78, 80
Repton, Humphry, 99
Richardson, Albert Edmund, 13–4, 23
Richardson, Sir Albert Edward, 13; enters architecture, 14; bicycling, 16; in Helicar's office, 17; at Birkbeck, 18; student pranks, 19; in Stokes' office, 19; marries Elizabeth, 20–1; starts practice, 22; moves to St Albans, 23; parties there, 23; research tours, 24; meets Goodridge, 26; joins RFC, 29; at Southampton, 31–3; goes to Bartlett, 35; Editor of *A.J.*, 35; buys Avenue House, 36; reactions to country, 41; neighbours, 44–8, 52–3; entertaining at AH, 49, 69, 70–1; designs cenotaph, 59; his water-colours, 60–2, 64; preservation societies, 66; Houghton campaign, 65–7; with Sylvia Pankhurst, 74; at Woburn, 75–6; as Duchy architect, 77; books written at Ampthill, 78, 100; meets Thomas Hardy, 80; at Snowshill, 83–8; collecting, 91; refurnishing AH, 101–4, 106; *Idle Thoughts*, 106–10; as church architect, 111; rebuilding Eaton Socon church, 117; letters to Elgar, 118–23; with Queen Mary, 125–34; with Duke of Windsor, 137–9; life at Cambridge, 142–61; protecting railings, 154–5; travelling, 162–79; retires from Bartlett, 180; and Festival of Britain, 185–6; Professor of Architecture at RA, 194; elected PRA, 201; with Queen at RA, 205; polemics, 209–11; created KCVO, 213; gardening at AH, 216–18; fight over lamposts, 221–30; death of Elizabeth R., 232; tour of Greece, 233–4; death, 236
Richardson, Elizabeth (*nee* Byers), 20, 31, 43, 49, 130, 211–2, 231–2
Richardson, Kathleen (Mrs Houfe), 23, 31, 56, 130, 232, 235
Richardson, Mary Augusta, 13
Richardson, Thomas, 13
Ridley, Sir Jasper, 196
Rixson, Harry, 102, 105
Rixson, Phillip, 105
Robert Mylne, Architect and Engineer, 209
Robertson, Sir Howard, 200
Royal, HRH The Princess, 127, 136
Royal Academy, 193–215
Royal Commission on Historical Monuments, 98
Royal Fine Arts Commission, 66, 162, 172, 187, 224
Rudkin, Mr, 53–4
Rufford Abbey sale, 99
Rushbury, Sir Henry, 198–9, 202
Russell, The Hon Constance, 45, 134
Russell, The Hon Romola, 45, 113, 134
Russell, Sir Walter, 193–4
Russell-Flint, Sir W., 194, 199, 201
Rutherstone, Dr, 196
Ryhall Manor, 211–12

St Albans, 23, 35, 162
St Alfege, Greenwich, 135, 182
St Catherine's College, Cambridge, 142
St Christopher's, Round Green, 114
St Dunstan's, 140
St James's, Piccadilly, 135, 182
St Mary's College, Twickenham, 114
Salisbury, Sir Edward, 24
Sanderson building, 140
Samuel, The Hon Godfrey, 172
Sassoon, Sir Philip, 102
Savill, Sir Eric, 138
Scala Theatre, 21
Schofield, Mr, 15
Schwabe, Professor Randolph, 114
Scott, Sir Gilbert, 111
Scott, Sir Giles, 194
Scott, Sir Harold, 189
Scott, Robertson, 101
Shearwood, Mr, 216
Shoreland, Frank, 15
Simpson, Professor F. M., 35
Sisson, Marshall, 173, 194, 196, 236
Sitwell, Sacheverell, 71
Skipton, 222
Smaller English House of the Later Renaissance,
    78, 80
Smith, H. Clifford, 125–6
Snowshill Manor, 83–90
Soane, Sir J., 101
Society For The Protection of Ancient Build-
    ings, 66
Southampton, 31–4
Southill church, 112
Southill Park, 95, 130
Southwark, 162
Spence, Sir Basil, 187
Spencer, Lord, 154
Spensley, Howard, 102
Stamford, 222
Stanmore, Lord, 71, 124, 231
Stanniforth, Mr, 41
St John, Ethel Lady, 44
Stoke Climsland, 77
Stokes, Leonard Aloysius, 19–21
Stott, Sir Philip and Lady, 87
Stowe sale, 99
Streatley church, 112
Sullivan, Bernard, 23
Syme, Ven Archdeacon, 58

Tabor, Major Sidney, 95
Tankerville, Countess of, 155–6
Thorpe, John, 65
Tingrith church, 112
Tormore distillery, 166, 231
Tor Royal, 137
Tree, Sir Herbert Beerbohm, 18
Trevelyan, G. M., 146
Trinity House, 172, 181, 189–90

Turvey House, 104

Ullswater, Lord, 67–8
University College, London, 135, 181
Urlin, Sir Simon, 39

Venice, 234
Verity, Frank, 20–2
Verpeilleux, Emile, 23
Victoria, HM Queen, 21
Victory, HMS, 232, 236
Vulliamy, L., 101

Waddams, Canon, 144
Wade, Charles, 83–90, 93, 105, 231
Wade, Mrs, 89
Wade-Geary, Mr and Mrs, 117
Wales, HRH The Prince of, 80
Walpole, Horace, 66
Wantage, 174
Watercolour painting, 61–2, 64
Watts, G. F., 43
Weaver, Sir Laurence, 68
Wendover, 78
Westoning Manor, 102
Wheeler, Sir Charles, 201, 215
Wherwell Priory, 160
Whipsnade Zoo, 48
Whitaker, Cedric, 23
Whitbread, S. H., 67, 95, 130
Whitchurch, Arnold, 161
White, John, 140
White, J. P., 113
Whiteford, 77
Wicklow, Countess of, 235
Wilkinson, S. G., 121
Williams, T., 144
Willingdon, Lord, 129
Wimpole Hall, 150, 156–9
Windsor, HRH The Duke of, 137–9
Wing, John, 102
Wingfield, Major Andrew, 172
Wingfield, Sir Anthony, 40, 44, 46–7, 49–50,
    54, 58–60, 67–8
Wingfield, Mrs George, 46
Wingfield, The Misses, 51–2
Winslow Hall, 63
Wisbech, 222
Woburn, 75–6, 182
Worboys, Edward Massingham, 14
Wrest Park sale, 99
Wyatt, James, 101

York, 169, 171, 222
York minster, 162, 177, 209
Young, Francis Brett, 86
Young, G. M., 140
Younghusband, Sir Francis, 67
Yourievitch, Prince, 81

The Old Brewery
The Temple
The Avenue
Rose Garden
The Conservatory
Avenue House
Church Street